Handbook of Corporate
Performance Management

PARIS
No 2378

Maille Bell

Wet sponge toss
Bubble Breathing
Therapeutic DIY

glitter food color

Teachers pay teachers
free worksheet

LAUGH

Handbook of Corporate Performance Management

MICHAEL BOURNE
PHILLIPPA BOURNE

WILEY

A John Wiley and Sons, Ltd, Publication

This edition first published 2011
© 2011 John Wiley & Sons, Ltd
Registered office
John Wiley & Sons Ltd, The Atrium, Southern Gate, Chichester, West Sussex, PO19 8SQ,
United Kingdom

For details of our global editorial offices, for customer services and for information about how to apply for
permission to reuse the copyright material in this book please see our website at www.wiley.com.

Library of Congress Cataloging-in-Publication Data

Bourne, Mike.
    Handbook of corporate performance management / Mike Bourne, Pippa Bourne.
        p.   cm.
    Includes index.
    ISBN 978-0-470-66936-5 (hardback)
        1. Performance—Management. 2. Performance—Measurement. 3. Organizational
    effectiveness—Measurement. I. Bourne, Pippa. II. Title.
    HF5549.5.P35B68   2011
    658.4'013—dc23

                                                                        2011028964

A catalogue record for this book is available from the British Library.

Typeset in 11/13 Times Roman

Printed and Bound in the United Kingdom by TJ International Ltd. Padstow, Cornwall.

Contents

Preface

Measuring and managing performance has been an enduring topic of debate for decades with various theories gaining favour according to the sensibilities of the time. These have ranged from the "scientific" methods such as those proposed by Taylor to the more recent laissez-faire style. Our view is that each of these approaches has its place. It is important to have underpinning processes and methods but these are all but useless without the exercise of good judgement and good leadership.

Since our initial implementation of a performance measurement system 15 years ago we have worked with and studied the process of performance measurement and management in a wide variety of organisations from businesses to public sector and charities. We are now convinced it is the combination of the tools and processes with the people management and leadership that makes a difference. The blending of these two perspectives forms the basis for this book.

Acknowledgements

Many individuals have helped shape our thinking around the area of performance measurement and management and so directly and indirectly contributed to the creation of this book.

Mike would like to thank his friends and colleagues at the Centre for Business Performance, Cranfield School of Management for their support and ideas that have helped to inform this work. In particular current members of CBP, Dr Monica Franco-Santos, Dr Dina Gray, Dr Veronica Martinez, Dr Pietro Micheli, Prof Andy Neely, Dr Andrey Pavlov, Dr Jutta Tobias; former colleagues, Dr Yasar Jarrar, Dr Michael Kennerley, Bernard Marr, Dr Steve Mason, Dr Giovanni Schiuma, Dr Bassil Yaghi, former and current doctoral students, including Dr Ingo Forstenlechner, Mark Baker, Mike Lauder, Gillian Pratt; our visitors, Richard Elliot, Patrick Hoverstadt, Dr Lorenzo Lucianetti, Dr Matteo Mura, Prof Goran Roos and Art Schneiderman and last, but certainly not least Lisa Hall for holding it all together whilst the book was being written.

Mike's early experience and academic career greatly benefited from friends and former colleagues from Cambridge University, in particular Dr Ken Platts, John Mills, Gerry Frizelle, Huw Richards and from undertaking projects and research with colleagues more widely, especially Prof Umit Bititci, Dr, Jill MacBryde, Prof Steve Melnyk.

We also need to acknowledge Dr Ruth Bender FCA, Reader in Corporate Financial Strategy at Cranfield School of Management, whose comments on the measuring financial performance chapter were invaluable and who also provided us with figures 16.2 and 16.3 from her lecture notes, Prof Malcolm McDonald for figure 10.1 and Nigel Atkinson who assisted us with his ideas on sustainability drawn from his Cambridge University dissertation.

We would like to thank people from the companies we have worked with over the years including Mark Bromley at EDF Energy, Andrew Brodie at Faccenda, Geoff Thomas at Shell, John Wilkes, and Sue Best at ICAEW and those who gave their time to be interviewed, namely Dr Andy Wood, Mike Ophield, Nigel Bond, PY Gerbeau, Paul Woodward, Mark Lever, Baroness Sally Greengross, Richard Boot, David Child and finally Charles Carter, who also provided introductions, support and encouragement for the writing of this book.

Introduction

At first sight the concept of measuring and managing business performance is straightforward – not necessarily easy to do – but a logical process that is easy to define and understand. On deeper inspection that is not the case. Performance management and measurement is complex, reaching every level of the business from the development of strategy to the management of individual employees. The performance management process often raises fundamental questions about the purpose and direction of the business, questions senior managers do not always want to ask. It brings to the fore many grey areas and problems for which there are no easy answers but which may have been lying, untouchable, within the organisation and causing trouble for years. It involves a wide range of activities and skills from strategic thinking to detailed analysis and from facilitating discussions to gaining commitment to actions and just making sure things are happening. It is ultimately about getting the right things done.

Many businesses fall into the trap of treating their performance management process almost as a 'tick box' exercise, something that can support and run alongside the implementation of their strategy. In fact, if it is to be successful, it needs to be an intrinsic part of strategy formulation as well as being integrated into everyday business. It should involve a broad range of people with different skills and it should touch every employee. However, too many businesses waste substantial amounts of money, time and employees' goodwill on half-hearted processes that do not work or cause more trouble because they lead the business in the wrong direction. The businesses that invest time and effort in getting their systems right can gain a considerable competitive advantage.

Although there are some golden rules, there is no single 'correct way' to manage and measure performance. You may already have processes and systems set up – most organisations have. The book is designed so you can dip into selected chapters and take from them what you feel is appropriate. In the interest of making the book readable, references have not been used in the body of the text in the academic tradition. Clearly all the ideas are not our own so we have included at the end of each chapter a set of further readings that capture both the original source of the ideas and more detail for people who want to investigate a particular subject further.

In the early chapters of this book (Chapters 1 to 7) we will look at what performance is, at the role of measurement within it and at what you can hope to achieve by setting up and implementing a corporate performance management system. We will look at the 'toolkit' – frameworks and processes you can use within your organisation as part of your performance system. Then we will explain how you can use the toolkit to build a generic performance system that will add value and help you develop your business.

In the next four chapters (Chapters 8 to 11) we will explain how you can use performance measurement in the management of your business. Here we present a set of tools and processes for monitoring and reviewing performance, before explaining how you can use measurement to test your strategy and how you need to keep your measurement system up to date.

The next six chapters (Chapters 12 to 17) examine how you measure specific perspectives of your organisation – from measuring customers to measuring people. Each perspective has its own characteristics, so we have presented here examples of customer satisfaction measures, the different frameworks for processes and resources as well as a view on key financial ratios.

The final part of the book (Chapters 18 to 20) is about how you bring together and put to good use the results of your processes. The dictionary definition of 'performance' refers to executing commands and carrying into effect tasks, promises or operations. It is about 'getting things done'. After all, even the best-crafted process is a waste of time if you do not make good use of it or if you cannot galvanise your employees to give their best. As the book is not specifically about management or leadership we are not going to cover those subjects in great detail, but the leadership and culture aspects should not be ignored. If you sow a seed on stony ground your yield will be less than if you plant it in fertile, well prepared soil. The same is true of your performance system. You have to create the right conditions for it to flourish. So the third section is about leadership and culture, the environment that you need to create to encourage high performance. We finish the book with a few vignettes and case studies of individuals from very different types of organisation who have all delivered amazing results.

1
Performance and the Role of Measurement

1.1 INTRODUCTION

In this chapter we will look at what good performance is and at the factors that combine to create good corporate performance. We will also set out what a good measurement process can do for your organisation, not only to help you track your progress but also to help you encourage and maintain better performance. You need to recognise that performance measurement is a tool to be used by management and we end this chapter by reflecting what good leaders need to do to ensure that the tool is used effectively in taking the organisation forward.

1.2 WHAT IS GOOD PERFORMANCE?

The answer to this question is simple – it is about achieving your objectives. Of course that is not the whole picture; it is far more complex than that. Objectives themselves do not remain constant; they usually change over time. The world moves on and if you do not keep reviewing what you are doing you will have a problem. How you achieve your objectives is also important – you may be successful in the short term at the expense of success in the longer term. Before launching into setting up a performance measurement system it is worth reflecting on the nature of good performance.

1.3 WHOSE PERSPECTIVE?

Any benchmark of business performance will depend on the definition of success for that business. In turn, the definition of success will depend on the view of particular groups of stakeholders.

Let us take an airline as an example. Someone going on holiday will be happy when there is plenty of room beside them because the next seat is empty, they are offered another portion of lunch because there is extra food on board and the cabin crew have plenty of time for individual attention. The airline's customer service manager may also be delighted with performance because there have been many emails praising the service. The airline's CEO, on the other hand, will probably be dissatisfied with performance because there are too many empty seats, money is being wasted on catering and the cabins are overstaffed, all of which contribute to unsatisfactory financial performance. Shareholders will be dissatisfied because they see a poor return on their investment.

Therefore, the definition of success and 'good' performance depends on perspective and that will vary within different sections of the organisation and according to the stakeholder group.

It is essential for employees, at the very least, to have a clear consensus, understanding of and commitment to the overall goals of the organisation. Once they understand the goals, they need to know what success looks like. When there is a clear sense of purpose at the top of the organisation, divisional, departmental and individual goals and measures can be fitted underneath the overall organisational goals so they contribute towards achieving them. There will, of course, always be conflicting requirements, as you can see from the example above, but a balance has to be struck and conflicts have to be resolved or at least acknowledged. Achieving clarity and commitment to overall goals of the organisation requires strong leadership.

1.4   MAKING COMPARISONS

Performance is not absolute; it can only be relative. Your company's profitability has to be judged against peers in your industry sector and against your previous years' results. So you need to consider performance relative to external comparisons and to internal benchmarks.

From an internal perspective, employees need to know what is expected of them. Quite simply: are they expected to process 10 claims an hour or 20? If the company receives 100 customer complaints in a year is that good or bad? It is also important to know whether progress is being made. Is your performance improving? (That applies both to the individual and to the overall company performance.) It is impossible to determine this if you do not have some form of consistent measurement process. Taking this a step further, it is important to know why you are not making progress because that could be the result of external factors such as a new competitor taking your market share rather than a failure of your employees to do their work.

A measure of performance is meaningless on its own. It makes sense only when viewed against either a standard, a previous measure or another comparable measure. Thus, a figure of, say, 6.5 for May means nothing, but when April's figure was 10.5 and March, February and January were 11.5, 13 and 14 you are beginning to establish a trend. If you also discover your biggest competitor is measuring the same activity and their figures are 20, 23, 24, 25 and 26 you may be able to deduce something about your business and/or your market.

From an external perspective investors need to know how well the company is doing and what the expectations are for the future. External reporting is a subject of its own and does not form part of this book. However, the way an organisation (business or not-for-profit) looks to the outside world is important for its success. Stakeholders of any type (investors, employees, customers) need to have confidence in the organisation with which they have dealings and external reporting of performance is the mechanism for doing this.

1.5 PRESENT SUCCESS AND FUTURE SUSTAINABILITY

Factors contributing to performance (such as customer service and financial outcome in the example above) can be linked both positively and negatively. In the airline example, passengers may be delighted with the service they receive as a result of the empty seats on the aircraft and that may encourage them to book again with the same airline. This will lead to a perception of success in the short term as passenger numbers increase, but over time passengers will probably see a decline in service as seats fill up and they will start to book elsewhere. If the airline is not charging enough to cover the additional costs of the 'deluxe' service or attempting to secure loyalty among its passengers, it will ultimately face financial disaster.

It is interesting to note that sustainability and durability may come from factors that are not always apparent in short term performance indicators. In their book *Built to Last: Successful Habits of Visionary Companies*, James Collins and Jerry Porras spent six years researching business success. They identified 18 'visionary' companies and examined what was special about them. What they found surprised even the authors. They deduced that success did not come from having great products and charismatic leaders but more from a dedicated devotion to a 'core ideology' or identity and a highly active indoctrination of employees into commitment to the company. These are not short term performance indicators.

No business is invincible. Names of once-successful businesses that are no more trip from the tongue – Rover, Enron, Arthur Anderson, Woolworths. Even if in their later stages they were flagging, at some point they were regarded as models of success. Success in present performance is important and is an indicator of future performance, but it may be fleeting unless the senior team is giving sufficient thought to the future. It is too easy to be motivated by current success and to do more of the same, spending all the time focusing on the needs of the present. Building indicators of future potential is an essential element in measuring and managing performance.

In establishing what good performance is, you must know what success looks like to different stakeholder groups, how your performance compares with other organisations and against internal benchmarks and whether today's performance is sustainable into the future.

We will turn now to how you create good performance.

1.6 HOW IS PERFORMANCE DELIVERED?

The performance of a business is delivered through a mixture of people doing their best to achieve the right 'things', supported by effective processes and sufficient resources.

Getting people to work harder does raise performance levels and we will look at how you measure people's performance in more detail in Chapter 12. But there is a limit to how much harder people can work and high levels of intensive work of any type are rarely sustainable over time. Therefore, in a labour intensive business, while it is obviously important to ensure people are working to their full potential, if you go over the threshold of what is sustainable, performance will inevitably decline after an initial period of improvement. The other perspective on this is whether people are being *forced* to work harder or *want* to work harder. When people are forced to work harder they naturally resist and find ways around the system. However, if people engage in their task or in the aspiration of the organisation, then you achieve a better outcome.

Working harder can be simply the exertion of more effort. However, even from the origins of scientific management in the late nineteenth and early twentieth century (the work of Frederick Taylor), it was conceded that emphasis should be put on doing things better. Taylor's idea was that there was one best way for a worker to do a job. Workers should be given the right tools and then trained in the right approach. Once this happened, a rate could be set for the work that an individual could achieve over a normal day at a rate that was sustainable in the longer term. There is much to be said for the basic concepts of Taylor's scientific management, but it does suggest a very mechanistic conceptualisation of the organisation, and very few jobs these days are that simple. Understanding how a job should be done, giving people the correct tools to do the job and appropriate standards to achieve is a good start.

Real performance improvements come from changing the process. Here is a very simple example. One council in the UK was struggling to make its six week deadline on assessing building applications. When the process was examined, the planners were shown to be efficient at their work. The biggest issue was the delay between the monthly meeting at which the planning application was assessed and the next monthly meeting where the minutes of the previous meeting were approved and the decision was ratified. The solution was simple. A coffee break was held at the end of the planning meeting following which attendees came back immediately afterwards to approve the minutes. The planning process was speeded up by 30 days.

Performance measurement should focus the thinking on the outcomes to be achieved rather than just on numbers. It should encourage people to look for alternative ways of doing the job better. It is important, then, to emphasise and measure the achievement of goals and play down the process measures. If, in our example, the council had purely focused on improving the efficiency of individual planners, the target of reducing time taken for planning applications to be passed would never have been achieved. We will return to this theme again in Chapter 14.

At times of economic hardship companies often take the decision not to resource fully the activities of the business. While this can make sense in some cases, it is very important to think through the consequences of the decision not only for current levels of performance but also for what may happen in the future. There are many good examples of companies taking seemingly sensible decisions only to find they had unforeseen results. An IT company employed staff with specialist skills for writing user manuals. To save money they decided to make these people redundant and give this task to their programmers. After a short while it became apparent that the user manuals were not user friendly any more as the programmers did not have the right skills for producing them. The company had to resort to using agency staff at higher costs than before.

Thus, performance is delivered through people, but they must have the right processes and resources at their disposal. They also need to be directed and focused in what they do, which is the role of the performance measurement system.

1.7 THE ROLES OF A PERFORMANCE MEASUREMENT SYSTEM

There are five basic roles of a performance measurement system: to establish position, communicate direction, influence behaviour, stimulate action and facilitate learning. We will explain these in more detail next.

1.7.1 Establishing your current position

This may seem obvious but many organisations rely too much on anecdotal evidence to establish their current position. Statements like 'we value our employees' or 'we offer the fastest delivery times in our business' become ingrained to the point that it is heresy for any senior manager to disagree. These statements may well have been true once but no longer stand up to close scrutiny in the face of the evidence. It can be a hard lesson, but establishing your true position is vital to avoid complacency and to understand what action is needed.

Unless you have some data to know where your starting point is, how will you establish progress, compare performance of similar departments or products or benchmark with competitors? You need to measure accurately and consistently from a solid base line.

1.7.2 Communicating direction

If you measure a particular activity you are indicating immediately and forcefully that this is an important activity. Therefore the very act of creating a performance measurement system communicates the new direction to the business. Let us take Tesco as an example of this. Their ethos is to keep things simple. They have used a measurement process which they call the 'steering wheel' based on a balanced scorecard (which we will describe in some detail in the next chapter). Through the steering wheel they are able to communicate very clearly to all employees what is important to the business. In 2006 they added a new category for measurement, reflecting the change in the environment in which the company was operating. They were aware of the pressure from the media, government and from their customers on businesses to become more 'responsible'. Responding to this they added an array of actions and measures such as reducing packaging and reducing carbon emissions through the use of bio fuels and trucks carrying double loads. The act of measuring these factors showed very clearly how important they were.

1.7.3 Influencing behaviour

You should not underestimate the strength of influence generated by measuring something. That is why it is so important to measure the right things, in the right way, and to reward people against the right criteria. If you do not, you can encourage the wrong behaviour. For example, pure financial targets can create too much risk-taking in investment banks or too much focus on efficiency rather than customer responsiveness in a manufacturing plant. However, if you define your measures carefully you can influence people very significantly to achieve the goals you have set for the organisation. Not only have you set a clear direction, you have also motivated people and created a sense of purpose by showing the progress they are making.

1.7.4 Stimulating action in the most important areas for your business

Few organisations have unlimited resources, so the resources you have should be directed as efficiently as possible towards fulfilling the most important requirements of the business.

Firstly, the process of setting up a measurement system can help you to do that because it helps you to identify what the critical actions are for success in your business. It also makes you aware of what is not important. Here is an example. It was not until they started to discuss the structure of their performance processes that the senior management team in a training business realised just how much their business relied on freelance management trainers. These people were in direct contact with their clients and presented the face of their business. In the past they had assiduously measured the quality of the courses as seen by attendees but had not taken any action to engender loyalty in the freelance trainers or even to ensure they were up to date.

Secondly, the process of reviewing performance should stimulate action. When performance starts to deviate from what is planned, root cause analysis needs to be done and corrective actions made. Taking the training business example, after each programme the freelance management trainers were assessed through participants completing a questionnaire. Every trainer has an off day, but a declining trend immediately triggered a review and action.

1.7.5 Facilitating learning

Using a good set of measures should provoke debate about your business strategy and provide information for making better decisions. Two important questions are:

- Are the things you are doing being done in the right way?
- Are you doing the right things?

The first question should make you reflect on your corrective actions. Are the actions you are taking having the impact you expect? If not, are they being undertaken effectively? The second question is at a higher level; it asks whether the actions you are taking are the right actions to take. However, you have to ask both questions before you can come to a conclusion. The performance may not be improving because your actions have not been completed or done correctly. Alternatively, the actions may be completed correctly, but they turn out to be the wrong actions.

The greatest benefit of a measurement system is the opportunity it gives you to learn. Measurement systems are so often used to drive performance, but the value of understanding how your business works and the feedback a measurement system can give you is invaluable, especially if you can get everyone in the organisation to use it that way.

1.8   THE FOCUS OF MEASUREMENT

In the last section we explained the five roles of measurement; next we highlight three dimensions on which a performance measurement system should focus. These are the external environment, internal performance and strategy implementation.

1.8.1 External environment

With the sophisticated ERP and EPM systems (enterprise resource planning and enterprise performance management) available today, it is very easy to become internally focused. Every element of your business can be measured and reported. However a business only survives if it can compete effectively, so the most important information you need to track is in your environment.

We stated earlier that all performance is comparative. Understanding how you compare in terms of financial performance, brand preference, market share, customer satisfaction, product rating, cost base, process excellence, employee satisfaction and employer brand can give you a feel for how your competitive position is improving or declining. The more time you have to react to changes in the market place or competition the more successful you will be. Being caught by surprise can be both painful and costly.

1.8.2 Internal performance

Internal performance should be tracked too, but most companies are awash with internal performance information. You will need to focus on what is collected and reported. You should also consider the management process so that people at the relevant levels in your organisation receive the information they need and make appropriate and timely decisions.

1.8.3 Strategy implementation

By measuring your environment and monitoring your internal performance, you will have a good feel of how the organisation is performing, but there is one last step. You need to track that your strategy is being implemented so that you can assure the future of your business.

How many organisations spend time and money devising a strategy that then remains sitting on the shelf, known only to the elite few at the top of the organisation? Even if employees know what the key elements of the strategy are, how many of them understand what it means for their jobs and how their work contributes towards its success? We have visited companies where employees claim to understand what the strategy is, but are clearly not taking the actions that lead towards achieving it. In other words, the strategy exists but what is actually happening is something quite different. The reasons for this may be valid – those 'at the sharp end', close to the customer, perhaps, or with a very good understanding of a particular market – know the strategy will not work but are unwilling to put forward their case to more senior managers. They carry on doing what they believe to be necessary. On the other hand, the reason may simply be that people do not want change.

Crystallising the strategy into a set of measures can help to align action with the strategy. However, it is vital that the factors you measure really are those contributing towards your strategy. We cover how you create measures in more detail in Chapter 2, but it is worth including a small example here. A certain training business had two product lines – a programme of open courses that they marketed primarily to HR managers as a means of building relationships with them and encouraging them to buy from their second product line, the more expensive in company training. The open courses were profitable in themselves and they also acted as a showcase for the company's services. The senior management team believed the company should be more profitable and agreed that moving towards the higher end of the market with more customised training would be the way to do this. They could charge a premium for the customisation and present their services as being a higher quality than most of their competitors. In setting measures, however, profitability became confused with volume. One measure set for the team running the open programme was 'the number of delegates per course'. To meet their targets that team set up a programme of cheap and cheerful management skills courses, which attracted large numbers of attendees by virtue of the price but which detracted enormously from the company's declared intention of moving upmarket. This action was directly opposed to the strategy and worked against it, but the managers of that section of the business were only doing what they could to achieve their target.

Performance measurement should make goals and objectives explicit and bring the strategy to life. If communicated in the right way, it should be possible to create a culture of achievement in which individuals no longer work in the dark but are clear about their roles and what their contribution is to be in creating a successful organisation. A good performance measurement system will act as a motivator, showing people what is expected of them and how they are progressing.

1.9   THE ROLE OF MANAGEMENT AND LEADERSHIP

Creating good performance is not an exact science. You can set out what needs to be done, agree standards and you can measure progress. You can have an excellent process in place but without good leadership you will not achieve sustainable results.

Leadership is about creating the culture and environment in which good performance is delivered. This includes setting the tone for the organisation. By this we mean the standards of behaviour expected from everyone working within it. It includes setting values – how staff, customers and suppliers will be treated. Finally, it includes setting the direction of the organisation and creating a vision of success.

In the first section we pointed out that the definition of success depends on your viewpoint. Leaders have to balance the often conflicting needs of various stakeholders, current demands and future success and they have to propose a way forward. This sometimes involves making difficult decisions and saying no to certain courses of action. Having done this they have to get commitment to their proposals, even from those whose personal interests may be adversely affected by the decisions made.

Leaders have to support management in their development and use of any performance measurement system. Performance measurement has to be at the heart of everything the organisation does and managers should be encouraged to use the system to evaluate performance and make decisions. We are not talking here particularly about the performance of individuals, but about the whole spread of information generated on how things are working. However, such a system can become too mechanistic and it is the job of leaders to ensure this does not happen. A performance system will provide data and information but it is up to the judgement of managers and leaders to decide what will be done with it.

One of the critical tests of a good leader is how they deal with failure, remembering that if you set stretching targets you must expect failure. An innovative organisation needs people who have ideas and take calculated risks, and inevitably some of these will fail, but the company still has to support the risk taking. Something may fail because the circumstances change and the target has simply become unattainable.

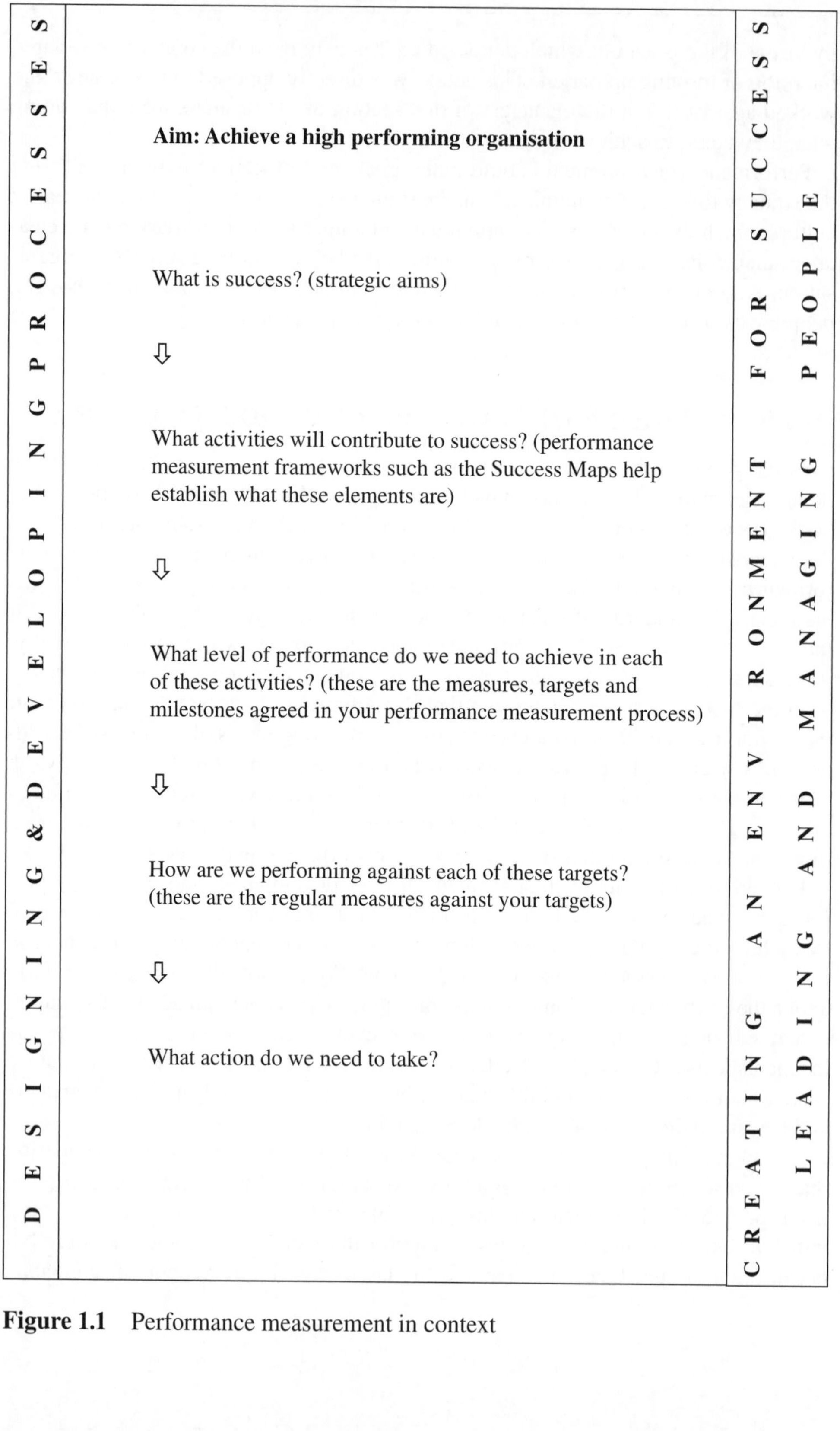

DESIGNING & DEVELOPING PROCESSES

CREATING AN ENVIRONMENT FOR SUCCESS

LEADING AND MANAGING PEOPLE

Aim: Achieve a high performing organisation

What is success? (strategic aims)

⇩

What activities will contribute to success? (performance measurement frameworks such as the Success Maps help establish what these elements are)

⇩

What level of performance do we need to achieve in each of these activities? (these are the measures, targets and milestones agreed in your performance measurement process)

⇩

How are we performing against each of these targets? (these are the regular measures against your targets)

⇩

What action do we need to take?

Figure 1.1 Performance measurement in context

A good leader should recognise this and act accordingly. Failure can be caused by processes not working or projects being underresourced and a good leader should be able to judge if this has happened. Finally, failure can be caused by an individual through lack of experience, capability or application. A leader needs to judge which of these is the case and what action should be taken.

Leaders need to see the wider picture and not just react to the simplistic logic coming from what the measures are telling them. Good leaders consider the decisions they make in the wider context and in particular they think about the message the decision sends externally and to the rest of the organisation. One business services company decided not to deal with clients whose behaviour was unacceptable to their staff, although in some cases these were lucrative contracts. This sent a clear message about the way leaders in that company valued their employees. A window producer, Kayplan, had the policy of only selling through builders' merchants and so no matter how large the incentive to win an order by selling directly to a customer, this was never done. This created a great deal of loyalty from builders' merchant customers.

A performance management process is only ever that - a process. It is a very useful tool to help leaders run their businesses. However, how they use it will determine whether the system is seen as a bureaucratic impediment to performance or as a mechanism for guiding action and gaining employee commitment to achieving the goals of the business.

1.10   IN SUMMARY

In this chapter we have given an overview of what performance is and of the benefits of setting up a performance measurement and management process. We have looked at the role of leadership and management in that process. The diagram (Figure 1.1) is a straightforward summary of the thinking process. In the next chapter we will look in detail at some of the frameworks and tools you can use.

FURTHER READING

Collins, J., and Porras, J. (2005) *Built to Last: Successful Habits of Visionary Companies*, Random House Business Books, London.

Practical Tools for Measuring Performance

2.1 INTRODUCTION

Having looked at the nature of performance and the benefits of measuring it, we will now describe some practical tools to help you. We will set out the key elements of a performance measurement system and then take you through the tools that companies find most effective when designing their performance systems.

2.2 ELEMENTS OF A PERFORMANCE MEASUREMENT SYSTEM

A performance measurement system will typically include a framework, objectives, measures, targets and initiatives for improvement. We will take each element in turn.

2.2.1 Frameworks

Performance measures enable you to calculate and report the level of performance you are achieving. However, as you have seen from Chapter 1, they should do much more for you than this. One of their prime benefits is in communicating to all employees what is important for the business and for this reason it is essential that your measures are closely related to the organisation's strategic objectives. Increasingly, companies and public sector organisations are using frameworks to help them to ensure there is a strong link between strategic objectives and to organise their objectives in a useful way. Frameworks such as the Balanced Scorecard and Performance Prism are particularly useful for doing this.

Frameworks are the organising structures used in measurement systems. Each framework has a slightly different focus. The Balanced Scorecard will help to focus more attention on the nonfinancial elements of performance; the Performance Prism will focus attention on the requirements of different stakeholders and the EFQM (European Foundation for Quality Management) framework helps in differentiating between the drivers of performance and the result.

People can only remember between five to seven things so the ideal is for an individual to have no more than five objectives. Unfortunately, most organisations are more complex than that, but with the help of a framework you can arrange the objectives in a way that deals with that greater complexity.

Frameworks are useful because they simplify the way an organisation's objectives are presented and they help focus attention on the most important factors for the success of the business.

2.2.2 Objectives

Objectives are descriptions of what has to be achieved in order to fulfil the strategy of the organisation. They are usually cascaded down from the top levels through various departments to individuals. They can be very specific, such as Pepsi's objective of wanting to 'overtake Coca Cola's market share in the US', but often they are described in more general terms, such as 'improving customer service levels' or 'reducing waste', which is fine at this level. Choosing the objectives your organisation needs to achieve is the most important activity in developing your measurement system and we believe it is one that many managers give insufficient thought to. Much as we may want to, it is just not possible to *focus* on everything and having too many objectives is a recipe for disaster. Later in this chapter we will present the concept of the success map, which is an excellent tool for establishing which objectives are critical for your business and which are not. It helps you to apply Ockham's razor, cutting away complex and sometimes unnecessary courses of action and focusing on the clearest and simplest approach.

2.2.3 Measures

Performance measures (or performance indicators) quantify performance and enable you to assess progress towards achieving an objective. Unlike objectives, where a general description is fine, measures must be precise. They are only meaningful when they have a clear formula of how they are to be calculated and are attached to the target to be achieved.

The performance measure record sheet described below is a useful tool for ensuring your performance measure is precise and usable. We will describe later on in this chapter just how you design appropriate measures.

2.2.4 Targets

Target setting is neither an art nor a science – but a blend of the two. In essence, targets specify the level of performance to be achieved and are used for a variety of purposes, including making objectives and measures meaningful and tangible to everyone working in the organisation. We will discuss two issues with target setting later in the chapter and you can find a target setting process (the target setting wheel) in Chapter 6.

2.2.5 Improvement initiatives

Improvement initiatives are changes made to the operation of the organisation in order to improve performance. Remember that measurement itself does not improve performance; it simply focuses people's attention on what is important and provides feedback on trends and changes in performance. Sustainable improvement comes from improving the processes or resources employed, so it is important not only to measure and fix targets but also to build in a plan to implement changes and improvements when they are necessary. We will discuss how you do this later on in this chapter.

For a performance measurement system to be effective there should be alignment between the various elements (see Figure 2.1). The organisation's purpose and strategy should be captured and represented in the performance measurement framework by a few key objectives. Each objective should have a performance measure that defines how progress is to be quantified and each measure should have a target that explains what has to be achieved by when. This alignment clearly communicates what the organisation is trying to achieve. These objectives, measures and targets should be underpinned by a few carefully selected initiatives for improving performance. Some initiatives will support the achievement of more than one objective, but all initiatives should support at least one objective, and all objectives should be supported by at least one initiative if performance is to be improved.

Having outlined the relationship between frameworks, objectives, measures, target and initiatives, let us move on to discuss the tools needed to develop a performance measurement systems, starting with a discussion of two frameworks, starting with the Balanced Scorecard.

2.3   THE BALANCED SCORECARD

The Balanced Scorecard was first used in analogue devices in the United States in the late 1980s and was popularised by Kaplan and Norton in 1992. The big idea behind the Balanced Scorecard was the need to reduce reliance on financial measures. Bob Kaplan pointed out that by only using financial measures you may encourage undesirable behaviour. Managers, for example, may delay important capital expenditure to meet short term financial targets. While this may cut costs in the short term, the longer term consequence will be a delay in improving the business and loss of competitive advantage. Training costs, for example, are easy to defer as they are a cost in this financial period with payback coming only in the longer term. However, cutting your training budget may damage the capability of your company, undermining performance in future periods. Delaying recruitment is often seen as a means of saving money and improving financial performance but being short-staffed may result in lowering of customer service standards and ultimately in loss of customers.

The underlying principle of the Balanced Scorecard is that no one single factor can provide a clear indicator of performance. This immediately moves away from

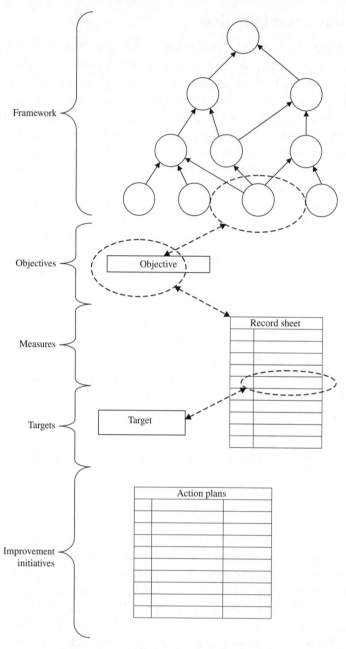

Figure 2.1   The key elements of a performance measurement system

the idea that measuring performance is about financial results – which are nearly always measured retrospectively anyway. If you are genuinely focusing on the most important factors to make your business successful then you will be spanning several fields of activity. Activities within any organisation do not stand alone. They are interrelated and what happens in one field of activity will almost certainly have an impact on another. This is true even in the simplest of businesses. Success in one area such as speed of production is not enough. If you do not have a commensurate volume of sales then speed of production may even be a liability as you will be accumulating stock. It is all too convenient for us to think in 'silos', to compartmentalise, even to set targets based on performance in one field of activity alone, which could be at the expense of other important activities.

Kaplan and Norton devised four perspectives for their Balanced Scorecard (see Figure 2.2):

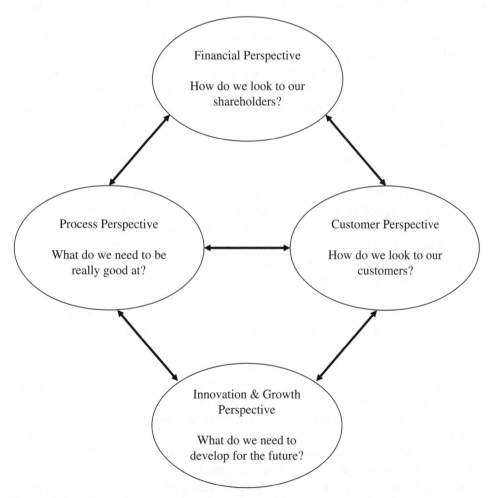

Figure 2.2   The Balanced Scorecard (adapted from Kaplan and Norton, 1992)

- The Financial Perspective – How do we look to our shareholders?
- The Customer Perspective – How do we look to our customers?
- The Business Process Perspective – What must we excel at?
- The Innovation and Learning Perspective – How can we continue to improve and create value?

The Balanced Scorecard is about measuring activities, processes and outputs that are essential for the success of the business. As well as balancing financial and non-financial measures, it aligns internal processes with external needs. For example, it identifies what is most important for customers and then creates processes that deliver what customers want. In any business the needs of the customer conflict with the needs of the owners. The former want the best products and services for the least outlay. The latter want to make better returns. The Balanced Scorecard helps by including both perspectives.

Current success does not necessarily mean success in the future. High street stores selling DVDs were once popular and successful but with the advent of easy downloads and changing consumer buying habits, they have struggled for survival. Competitors are always developing their own capabilities and customer and employee needs and wants change. The Balanced Scorecard balances the past with the future. The financial performance of today is balanced by measures of innovation and learning, an indication of future success.

The Balanced Scorecard has a number of benefits, notably that:

- It puts strategy rather than control at the centre of business performance (Kaplan and Norton argued that financial measures were purely for control, whilst the Balanced Scorecard should be developed from business strategy).
- It provides information on disparate elements of a company's performance in one report, and even on one page at a glance.
- It forces managers to consider all the key operating measures together and how improvement in one area may be at the expense of another.
- It involves managers from across the organisation – not just financial managers – bringing different perspectives to the discussion of a company's performance.

There are of course critics of the Balanced Scorecard. Some consider it to be too simplistic and dismissive of the external business environment. Others say it ignores stakeholders such as employees and regulators. In practice, the Balanced Scorecard may be simplistic but its simplicity forces one to think very clearly about what is really important and makes the framework eminently usable. The original four perspectives as set out by Kaplan and Norton may seem restrictive but they can be adapted to meet the needs of different types of organisation. In the UK, for example, Tesco have used a Balanced Scorecard type of framework (which they called the 'steering wheel') to measure their performance and more recently added an extra dimension to measure their corporate responsibility, which was becoming increasingly important for them.

2.4   THE PERFORMANCE PRISM

The Balanced Scorecard has become the framework of choice for many organisations. However, there is an increasing requirement to pay more attention to the needs of various stakeholder groups within the performance measurement process. Understanding stakeholder needs and weaving these into a comprehensive view of what the organisation is trying to deliver necessitates a different approach. The Performance Prism (Neely *et al.*, 2002) was designed with this in mind. It is a sophisticated performance measurement framework with a multistakeholder and multilevel approach, developed jointly between Accenture and The Centre for Business Performance. It has five facets: stakeholder requirements, strategy, process, capability and resources, and requirements from the stakeholders (see Figure 2.3). With the Balanced Scorecard

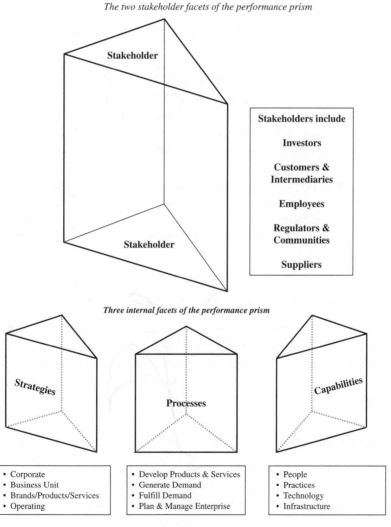

The two stakeholder facets of the performance prism

Stakeholder

Stakeholder

Stakeholders include

Investors

Customers &
Intermediaries

Employees

Regulators &
Communities

Suppliers

Three internal facets of the performance prism

Strategies

Processes

Capabilities

- Corporate
- Business Unit
- Brands/Products/Services
- Operating

- Develop Products & Services
- Generate Demand
- Fulfill Demand
- Plan & Manage Enterprise

- People
- Practices
- Technology
- Infrastructure

Figure 2.3   The five facets of the performance prism

Questions to ask when developing a Performance Prism

Stakeholders	Who are our stakeholders? What do our stakeholders require?
Strategy	Which stakeholder needs are we going to meet? What strategy are we going to pursue to satisfy our stakeholders?
Processes	What processes do we need to deliver the strategy?
Capability and Resources	What capability and which resources do we need to make processes perform effectively? Are we developing and sustaining these capabilities and resources?
Stakeholders	What do we need from our stakeholders?

your starting point is the strategy, although you also look at the stakeholder needs. With the Prism, your starting point is the stakeholder and for this reason it is particularly suitable for public sector organisations. It incorporates both stakeholder needs (what the stakeholder needs from the organisation) and stakeholder requirements (what the organisation needs from stakeholders) at corporate, business unit and functional level.

The Performance Prism also provides a series of questions you should ask to establish what is critical to the success of your organisation.

Once you have answered these questions you can go on to develop objectives and from those to derive your measures and targets in the same way as you would with the Balanced Scorecard.

2.5   OBJECTIVES AND SUCCESS MAPS

In the preceding sections we described two of the leading performance measurement frameworks. In this section we will present the concept of success maps. A success map is both a framework for capturing your business objectives and a process for deciding what to measure. We will start by describing the process of creating a success map before illustrating the approach with an example.

2.5.1 The success map process

The start of the process is the simple question, 'What do we need to do?' For a commercial organisation, this may be to 'increase our financial return'. For a humanitarian agency, this may be 'reduce the incidence of malaria in Africa'. Once you have established a question, the next step is to ask, 'How are we going to do that?' The answer to the 'how' question will identify your objectives at the next level. Once you have identified your objectives at the next level, they then become the 'what do we need to do?' followed by 'how are we going to do that?' again.

In Figure 2.4, stage 1 identifies 'what' as 'increasing our financial returns' and 'how' as 'increasing sales' and 'reducing costs'. In stage 2, you make the 'increasing sales' and 'reducing costs' as your 'whats' and ask the 'how' question again. This is continued through further stages until you have an initial success map.

The 'what/how' process takes you down a success map. However, there is a second question you should ask to check your logic, 'why?' The why question takes you up your success map. Therefore, in the example shown in Figure 2.4, 'Why does the company want to increase sales?' the answer is 'To increase returns'. Similarly, for 'Why does the company want to reduce costs?' again the answer is 'To increase returns'.

When you have finished your initial draft of a success map using the 'what/how' process, the first test should be to apply the 'why?' question to check your logic from the bottom up. 'Why?' is the question your people will ask, so although you may have a success map that delivers what you want the organisation to do, the first question a staff member will ask is 'why?' By answering the 'why?' question you are explaining to them how what they do links to what the organisation is trying

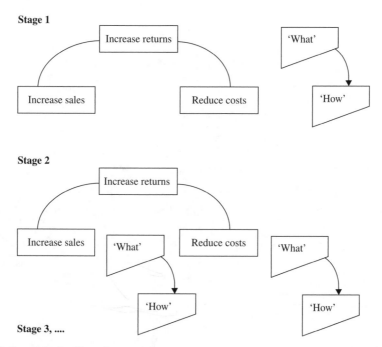

Figure 2.4   A 'what/how' example

to achieve. When people know how their work influences the performance of the organisation, they understand and appreciate their role and there is evidence that they will perform better as a direct result. If the link seems unconvincing, then you should think carefully about whether your success map is correct.

The success map created in this way is a logical set of objectives linked to the organisation's core purpose.

2.5.2 Success map examples

Let us now give an example of a success map for a training company wanting to improve their profit. They have been operating successfully for some years running short courses at their own training centre, but shareholders now want a better return on their investment. The management team has looked at various ways of doing this. One possibility would be to increase the volume of business, but their training centre is at full capacity and, although they could hire facilities, they are not sure there is enough demand to increase volume sufficiently to justify this. Their research has led them to believe the best way of improving profitability is to increase the price of their courses. They believe by doing this they could keep many of their existing customers and tap into a new market, but they would have to manage the process carefully. The success map reflecting their thinking is shown in Figure 2.5.

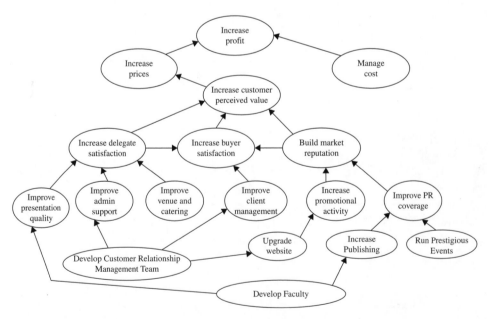

Figure 2.5   Success map for a training company

If they are to retain existing customers – and attract new ones prepared to pay more – then they will have to increase their customers' perception of the value the training is providing. They understand that in increasing prices they will lose some customers and in order to boost profitability they will have to replace those, so they will also have to reposition themselves to appeal to a new segment of the market.

They divide perception of value into two parts – perception of delegates attending the courses and perception of those buying the courses – often the training managers of larger companies. How could they add to the satisfaction of delegates? They could do this by improving the facilities at their training centre and by improving the catering. They could also develop the skills of the trainers to ensure presentations are more lively and interesting. How could they improve the satisfaction of the buyers? One way would be to ensure their business is 'easy and pleasant to deal with'. How would they do this? One way would be to create a client management team.

Then they must think how they are going to attract new customers. They decide the key action here will be to build their reputation in the market, which will not only attract new clients but will reinforce their standing with the customers they want to keep. How will they build their reputation? They will undertake some public relations and raise the level of promotional activity. How will they do that? They will run some prestigious events. They will produce articles for professional journals and so on.

In checking the success map logic, they must also ask the 'why?' question. For example, why are they developing faculty? The answer is to increase publishing and to improve the presentation quality. Why do they want to improve the presentation quality? The answer is to increase delegate satisfaction. Why do they want to increase delegate satisfaction? To increase customer perceived value, and so on. In this case, the answer to each 'why?' question is the objective above.

Seeing the logic of these actions and how they are linked is much easier in the form of a map. As well as helping to clarify and simplify thinking it is much easier to communicate what is being done and why to the people involved in doing it.

2.5.3 The success map process in practice

We will finish this section on success maps by explaining the process in practice. The ideal team to create your success map is the senior team itself. They need to do this so that they check their understanding of what the organisation is trying to achieve and how the strategy will be translated into action. The process is as important as the final success map itself, because it is the time when the team debate, argue and finally agree the key objectives for the business. Let us take an example.

At a builders' merchant, the senior team established that the top level objective was to increase their profitability. How were they going to do this? This would be achieved by selling more and controlling their cost base. How were they going to sell more? They decided that they would sell more to existing customers and find new customers. How were they going to sell more to existing customers and find new customers? There was a whole series of actions proposed.

However, when the success map was reviewed bottom up, they asked the question, 'Why do we need more new customers?' The managing director then pointed out that the company already dealt with every major builder in the UK and every major local authority. 'Who are these new customers?' he asked, and then went on to answer his own question: 'Are they people just starting out in business or are they people who have run out of credit with our competitors? There are not any new customers out there that are size-able and that we do not already know. If a new customer comes into one of our branches and asks to open an account, of course we will do it, we want their business, but I am not targeting new customers or incentivising our sales force to look for them as they will clog up our sales ledger and they will be only marginal contributors to profitability. We need to double the percentage of business that we have with our existing customers, not look for new ones.' At this point, the whole branch of attracting new customers and the associated actions was cut off the success map. All the directors at the meeting knew the benefit of looking after and increasing the business with their existing customers, but it had never been articulated so powerfully or communicated so clearly before.

In every success mapping process it is moments like this that make the difference. These are the moments when an element of strategy becomes crystal clear or a long running argument is finally resolved. People taking part remember these instances years later and the lessons learnt become almost part of folklore.

2.6 DESIGNING MEASURES

A success map helps you to consider what your objectives should be. The next step is to decide which aspects of that objective you are going to measure and how you are going to measure them so you can track your success. Making the correct decision on what you measure is critical, as people will put their effort into improving whatever you are measuring. Here is an example from a training session with a group of senior police officers. It became apparent during the discussion that the force was being targeted on reducing the total number of crimes committed. This meant that solving the theft of a mobile phone had the same weight as solving a murder. Tracking down a few petty thieves could significantly reduce the number of crimes as a rela-tively small number of thieves were responsible for many instances of crime and this looked good against performance targets. The police officers then looked at what they should be focusing on, using the success map process. They created a performance measure (using the record sheet we will describe below) around reducing the murder rate in their jurisdiction. They agreed the key was to focus on domestic violence and in doing so they believed they could reduce the murder rate by 30%.

This example raises some difficult policy issues, given that resources are always limited, and highlights interesting differences between requirements of stakeholder groups. If you are a member of the public living in an area plagued by petty theft or antisocial behaviour you will be delighted if the police spend more time catching the perpetrators. The government of the day will be pleased to announce that clearup rates for crimes have increased. However, although a murder will touch fewer people, it is such a serious crime most people would claim that finding the murderer should take precedence over finding several petty thieves. Putting more time into dealing with domestic violence, although time-consuming, could save a life.

In this example, it is clear that there is a need to see the impact of thinking through the link between your objectives and how you define your measures. It also shows the importance of consulting those who actually do the job about what the priorities should be. Individual police officers understood how important instances of domestic violence could be but the measurement system was pushing them to put attention elsewhere. When this happens in organisations, the effort of individuals to do their jobs effectively is thwarted and the result is lower performance than could be achieved if priorities were different.

On a more light-hearted note there is another (possibly apocryphal) example of a company producing nails in the former Soviet Union. The workers were given a target of producing a certain tonnage of nails in the year. As it was easier and faster to make fewer bigger nails than lots of smaller ones, they created one enormous nail weighing the requisite amount but which was of no practical use to anyone. They had achieved their annual target!

What you measure will influence behaviour and allocation of resources. Therefore ask yourself if the measure is really measuring what you want and what the consequences will be if you measure it.

Measures establish your position. If they are defined incorrectly (for example cause and effect are not linked) they will give a misleading picture of what is happening and can lead you in the wrong direction. If they are inconsistently calculated, you will lose the trends, you will not be able to make any internal comparisons and arguments will occur over their validity.

Measures should stimulate action and result in learning through regular review of what is working and what is not. Therefore, in designing your process you need to ensure someone is taking responsibility for reviewing both individual measures and the overall performance. If there is no individual or collective accountability and no regular review process, actions are likely to slip and there will be no learning from the time and effort you have invested.

Above all you must make sure you can measure what you want. It may seem desirable to measure a particular factor but if you cannot access data to measure it, you will have to weigh up the costs of designing a process to collect those data against not measuring that factor at all. If data are not readily available people often 'fudge' results, which is obviously undesirable and meaningless.

Performance Measure Record Sheet

Measure	
Purpose	
Relates to	
Target	
Formula	
Frequency	
Who measures?	
Source of data	
Who acts on the data?	
What do they do?	
Notes and comments	

Figure 2.6   The performance measure record sheet (adapted from Neely *et al.*, 1996)

2.6.1 The performance measure record sheet

The performance measure record sheet (see Figure 2.6) provides a means of thinking through and recording each measure. It is useful because it shows clearly how each measure is calculated, how often it is measured, who is responsible for it and the sources of the data so that you can ensure consistency over time. It also helps by connecting performance measures to top level objectives and thus to your strategy. Finally, it helps ensure action is taken because it names the individuals responsible.

Title	Select a title that captures the essence of what is being measured, but be precise. Customer service, for example, could cover a whole range of factors from delivering on time to number of complaints received.
Purpose	What is the purpose of measuring this aspect of performance? If there is not a good reason, do not use this measure.
Relates to	To which top level business objective does this measure relate? Make sure this measure is contributing towards delivering your strategy. It is not unknown for managers to slip in measures because they know they can achieve them rather than because they are measuring an important activity within the business.

	It is better to have too few measures than too many, so take care that the measures you choose are the most critical.
Target	This can be difficult, particularly at first. The target must be sufficiently stretching without being demotivating or creating an unrealistic expectation of performance, and we discuss this below, but the whole process of target setting is described in Chapter 6.
Formula	How is the performance measure calculated? Be precise. There is a wonderful example of an airline measuring the performance of baggage handlers where the measure was the time it took for the first piece of luggage to be delivered to the carousel. When a 'plane arrived, one baggage handler would rush to get the first case to the carousel in the quickest possible time. The target had been achieved despite the fact it took rather longer for the rest of the baggage to arrive.
Frequency	Different measures require different frequencies – you will have to decide not only how frequently you measure but also how frequently you review your measures.
Who measures	It is important to name an individual rather than to give responsibility to a big team.
Source of data	Specify the source of the data so that the measure is made consistently.
Who takes action	Again, it is important to allocate responsibility to a particular individual.
What do they do	Specify in outline the types of action people should take to improve the performance of this measure. Remember there are aspects of performance that are outside the control of the organisation. In reducing time lost through accidents, for example, you can take control over health and safety within your premises but you have less influence over how your staff drive to work and no influence over the actions of other drivers.

2.6.2 Target setting

A target is the level of performance to be achieved by a fixed date. However, when you set targets you will use them for different purposes. For example:

- Stretch targets – high but achievable targets designed to stretch people in the work they do.
- Minimum standards – base level targets that should be consistently achieved all the time.
- Realistic targets – targets that reflect the most likely outcome.

In performance measurement people regularly set high but achievable targets to move the organisation forward, but if you do that you must be clear that not all the targets will be met. If they were, your target setting would have been less high and more achievable. Target setting is so important that we devote a whole chapter to it later in this book (Chapter 6) but it is worth noting here the two basic questions to ask:

1. Is the target realistic based on our knowledge of the external environment and the changes we can reasonably foresee?
2. Are the current processes capable of delivering the targeted level of performance?

To answer the first question you will need to be able to forecast levels of activity and be able to react to changes in the environment. To answer the second question you will need to measure your process performance and use the Statistical Process Control tools we discuss in Chapter 8. Targets only motivate when they are appropriately set; otherwise they can simply annoy people. Therefore, getting the target right is critical.

2.6.3 Initiatives for improvement

In order to improve performance you have to do something differently or adjust or change the resources you use. This requires time and effort and should be planned in advance. When you create your measurement system we strongly recommend that you capture your performance improvement initiatives along with the objectives, measures and targets. There are two reasons for doing this. Firstly, you will need to track the progress of the initiatives to ensure that they are completed, as performance is not expected to improve until the changes are made. Secondly, organisations only have a limited capacity for delivering change. By recording initiatives you can check whether you are in danger of overloading the organisation with too many new activities and, if you do find too many initiatives, you can discuss how you will prioritise what you do next.

There are many ways of displaying your initiatives alongside the performance measurement system. Figure 2.7 shows one approach, drawing on a subtheme from the training centre example above. It also shows the link between the success map, specific objectives, measures targets and the initiatives planned to deliver the improvements expected.

Figure 2.8 gives an alternative perspective and one we use in companies to review their initiative portfolio. In this example, we use the appropriate scorecard perspective to group objectives and the chart to link objectives to initiatives. When reviewing this chart, you should ask:

• Should we continue with the initiatives that are not linked to specific objectives?
• How will we deliver sustained improvement to objectives that have no associated improvement activity?

Success map	Objectives	Measures	Targets	Initiatives
	Increase Profit	Gross profit before tax	£500,000 by end of 2012	
	Increase prices	Average price per delegate after discounts and concessions	20% increase by end 2012	
	Improve customer perceived value	Decision maker survey value score	0.3 point improvement year on year	Account management programme
	Improve delegate satisfaction	Delegate course survey overall satisfaction score	0.3 point improvement year on year	Satisfaction measurement & improvement initiative
		Delegate course survey survey scores		
	Presentation quality	Presentation	Average 4.3 by 2012	Faculty development programme
	Admin quality	Administration	Average 4.0 by 2012	Admin process re-engineering
	Venue quality	Venue	Average 4.0 by 2012	Facilities outsourcing initiative
	Develop faculty	% of faculty engaged in development	80% by 2012, 100% by 2013	Faculty development programme

Figure 2.7 Linking initiatives, targets, measures and objectives to the success map

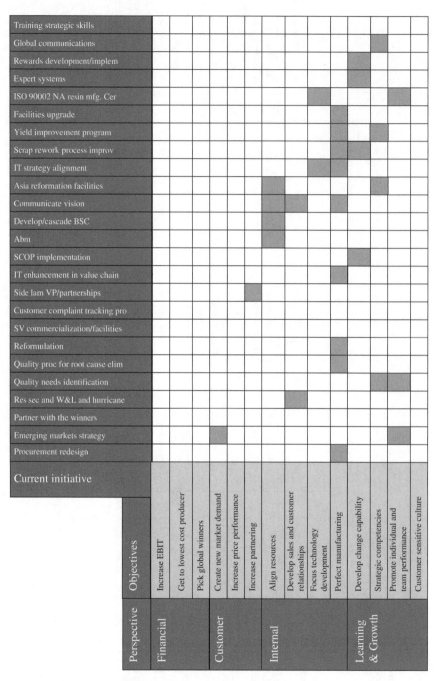

Figure 2.8   Mapping initiatives to the success map

- Do we have the capacity to deliver the initiatives planned?
- What are our priorities and does our planning activity reflect these priorities?
- Are we expecting too much from any single initiative?

2.7 SUMMARY

In this chapter we have introduced the key elements that you would expect to see in a performance measurement system and some of the most important tools that companies use to develop their systems. Unfortunately a measurement system is only as strong as its weakest link, so if an element is missing or is not working well, the system will not operate as you expect. Try to separate the different elements in your own mind and test the strength of each of them. This will enable you to see more clearly how the different elements fit together and it will also enable you to identify problems more quickly.

FURTHER READING

Kaplan, R. S. and Norton, D. P. (1992) 'The balanced scorecard – measures that drive performance', *Harvard Business Review*, **Jan./Feb.**, 71–79.

Neely, A. D., Mills, J. F., Gregory, M. J., Richards, A. H., Platts, K. W. and Bourne, M.C.S. (1996) *Getting the Measure of Your Business*, Findlay, London.

Neely, A. D., Adams, C. and Kennerley, M. (2002) *The Performance Prism, The Scorecard for Measuring and Managing Business Success*, FT Prentice Hall, London.

3
Designing the System

3.1   INTRODUCTION

In the last chapter, we presented the key elements of a performance measurement system and the tools you can use to build it. However, a performance measurement and management system goes far beyond the tools you use. Studies have shown that nearly 70% of measurement and management systems are not implemented successfully. That represents a great deal of wasted time and effort, not to mention the many disgruntled and demotivated people you leave behind. Understanding the tools and how they are used is only half the battle; *how* you implement your system is crucial to your success.

In this chapter we will take you through the essential 'softer' elements of designing and implementing a performance measurement and management system. We start by outlining the life cycle of a performance measurement process and then focus on design and implementation.

3.2   A FOUR PHASE LIFE CYCLE

There are four stages in the life cycle of a performance measurement and management system (see Figure 3.1), which we will outline below, before going on to describe in detail the design element.

The design phase focuses on developing the key elements of your system: creating the success map, determining the key objectives, defining the measures, setting the

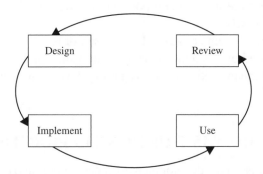

Figure 3.1   Four phases of a performance measurement and management system life cycle

targets and identifying the actions needed for improvement. This phase may also involve considering the link to rewards. You can find more detail about this in Chapter 7.

The implementation phase involves introducing the success map, objectives, measures, targets and initiatives and beginning to use them in the organisation. This is much more easily said than done as it begins to have an impact on people and resources and often raises tricky political issues concerning the running of the organisation.

The next phase – the use of the measurement and management system post-implementation – should be the period when the organisation begins to derive real benefit from all the time and effort invested. This is the phase when the system is used throughout the organisation, with individuals and their managers getting feed-back on what is being achieved, evaluating the information and taking appropriate action. People can now see the benefits and even the critics should perceive the value of the exercise.

The fourth phase is review, ensuring the measurement and management system remains relevant in the light of changing circumstances, both internally through progress towards achieving objectives and externally through evaluating develop-ments in the business environment. This may lead to a re-design and starting the cycle again.

3.3   DESIGN

How you design and implement anything has a big influence on its likely adoption within an organisation and hence on its success. This is particularly important in the design of measurement and management systems. During the design process you need to focus on creating a system that is appropriate for your organisation. For a successful implementation you will need to ensure that:

- the performance measurement and management system is **understood** by senior management both in terms of its purpose and the way it works - understanding is critical to its success;
- the elements of the system are **agreed** by the senior team;
- the system is **owned** by the senior management team – and 'owning' goes beyond 'commitment'; it means taking an active part in developing the system, reviewing and improving it.

3.4   HOW IS THIS DONE IN PRACTICE?

In Chapter 2 we discussed the development of success maps and definition of the indi-vidual performance measures. Now we will build on these elements to describe how the process creates the understanding, facilitates agreement and fosters ownership.

We explained in Chapter 2 the 'what/how?' and 'why?' questions used in developing the success map. You can use these questions on your own to create a success map for your organisation – or indeed for your function within it – but it is much more effective if you can involve others with this process. If you ask each member of a senior management team to create their own version of the success map, in virtually every case each success map will be different. Each member of the team will have their unique perspective based on their experience and their views on how things should run. It is the process of working together to create a common success map that creates the understanding, facilitates agreement and fosters ownership. That does not mean that the team will not have heated arguments and debate along the way. These disagreements are healthy as they ensure there is a true debate about the factors that are important to the future success of the organisation. In fact, the quality of the debate is one of the most important factors in determining a successful implementation.

3.5   THE DEBATE

Why is the debate important? The debate is important because:

- It allows every member of the team to express their position and understand the position of their colleagues.
- The different perspectives for the debate will mean that issues are raised and ideally resolved.
- The conclusion of the debate invariably produces an answer that is better than any of the individual contributions.
- The conduct of the debate creates what is known as procedural justice, whereby members of the team will be happy to accept the outcome if they perceive that the means by which it is reached is fair.

A good debate is created, not stumbled upon by accident. The following four elements will help you achieve this.

Point of departure   You need to think about why you are embarking on a new or revised performance measurement and management system, how you are going to obtain agreement from those who need to be involved and how you are going to tell the organisation about it. Some organisations like to signal this well in advance and have a lot of promotional activity at the very outset of the process. Other organisations like to work on the system until they have fashioned something that they believe will be sufficiently tangible and acceptable to show the rest of the organisation. Both approaches have their

	advantages and disadvantages so you should pick the best approach for the culture of your organisation.
Participation	Who will be involved? Who will participate in the debate? Ideally you should try to involve the whole top management team of the organisation. You should not exclude anybody. If they are part of the team they should be there. We have encountered several organisations developing a new system precisely because they perceive they have a problem with the performance of a particular function whose management teams have, bizarrely, failed to invite the head of that function to take part in the debate. This approach does not work.
Process	You will need a good process. Be explicit about the timing and the order of what is to be discussed and decided. This focuses the debate and stops the conversation wandering off the topic in question. You will need to specify the number of meetings, when they are going to be run and the focus of each meeting. Ideally you should spread the meetings out so there is a break between them. In that way, you make the process part of everyday work and not something where the team goes away for a weekend for a discussion and then forgets about it on Monday morning. You should also allow time for reflection by providing time in between meetings.
Project management	Professional running of the meetings is essential. Simple things, such as gathering the outputs from one meeting and turning them into an easily read document for reviewing at the start of the next meeting, are of great help but are often ignored. You will need to decide whether you are going to run the process yourself or have an external facilitator. An external facilitator will not be an expert in your business but they will be an expert in the process. They will know how to ask difficult questions that need to be asked, when to challenge, when to take a break to reflect and, most importantly, they will be impartial. However, if you do decide to use an external facilitator for meetings it is useful to have an internal project manager. This will be someone who understands the internal workings of the organisation and who will communicate with the group between meetings and pick up any feedback from them.

As you can see from the above, involvement of the management team is at the heart of this approach. This is very different from just giving the project to a group of external consultants or to the strategy team, in which case it can seem to the rest of the organisation like a 'bolt-on extra'. Drew Morris, UK Business Process Director of DHL, once said about performance management and measurement systems: 'You can't go out and buy one of these off the shelf or from a consultant.' In this he was emphasising the personal involvement required from the senior team in the design, implementation and operation of the system. By doing this you help cement the system into the everyday working of people in the organisation.

3.6   DEVELOPING THE SUCCESS MAP

There are various approaches that you can take to developing your success map and they all use the basic questions 'what/how?' and 'why?' Our preferred approach is to start by understanding who the key stakeholders are and what they are looking for from your business. Once you know who they are, you can go about creating a success map for each of the stakeholders.

In doing this we are not entering the debate about what the purpose of a business is – most (but not all) businesses exist to make a return for the shareholders. However, to make a return for the shareholders, the company has at least to satisfy the other stakeholders to survive, and sometimes you can use the requirements of the other stakeholders to make significant improvements to the performance of your business.

The key stakeholders you should consider must include:

- shareholders for whom you need to make a return;
- customers and consumers – if you do not provide products and services they want to buy, the business will not have a future;
- the regulator, if there is one, as it gives you your licence to operate and without that the business will be closed.

You should also think about:

- employees who are, after all, a major source of your competitive advantage and underpin everything the business delivers;
- business partners who may contribute knowledge and expertise critical to your success;
- suppliers because, although many are replaceable, a few will be essential;
- the community – it is difficult to operate in an environment where you do not have the local community's backing. Take the example of a small manufacturing company located in a village. The local community objected to the company's plans for expansion and these had to be put on hold. However, the company began to build closer links with local people. They took pains to explain more about their business and they used and supported local services. After a while they revisited

their plans for expansion and this time fewer objections were received and planning permission was granted.

Be careful in defining who your stakeholders are. It is important to be precise. Take the example of the toyshop owner considering her stakeholders. The customer is the parent and the consumer is the child. The child is looking for colour, softness and adorability in choosing a toy. The parent is thinking about health and safety, cost and probably noise level. If you are the toy manufacturer, you will have a different perspective. Your customer will be the toyshop owner who will be adding in considerations such as storage and availability of display space, so the chain is even longer.

By working through the requirements of each stakeholder in turn, you will build a rich picture of the environment in which you operate. Members of your management team may know what the needs of your stakeholder groups are – but you could also meet with your stakeholders and ask what they want of your organisation. It is a useful thing to do because it is easy to make assumptions about what your stakeholders need and assumptions can be misleading. However you choose to establish the needs of your stakeholders, you will find conflicting requirements and there is usually no simple way of resolving them – it has to be done by discussion and agreeing priorities. Take heart, though, because this is useful in itself in that it brings to light some of the contradictions and conflicts that often lead to fudging and to misunderstandings. Sometimes compromise is possible but sometimes difficult decisions have to be made and needs cannot be met. At least the way ahead is clear.

There is a difference between identifying and understanding the different stakeholders' needs and acting upon them. For each stakeholder you must decide:

• how important they are to the short, medium and long term success of the business;
• how powerful they are now or may be in the future.

Only then can you devise your strategy appropriately. You cannot please all the stakeholders all the time, so you will need to create a balanced set of objectives that allows your business to survive and prosper while satisfying the different stakeholders' needs as far a possible.

You can use a process similar to Figure 3.2 to think through possible conflicts, consider how they may be resolved and create objectives from them. In the simple example below we have looked at customers' needs and the needs of the business owner. Some of these needs match and some appear at first sight to be in conflict. As you can see, customers need high product reliability to minimise the inconvenience caused if the product is faulty. The company has the same objective in order to minimise warranty costs and thus there is no conflict.

However, customers are also looking for quick delivery. The owner is looking to meet return on investment targets (ROI) and sees reducing stock levels as critical

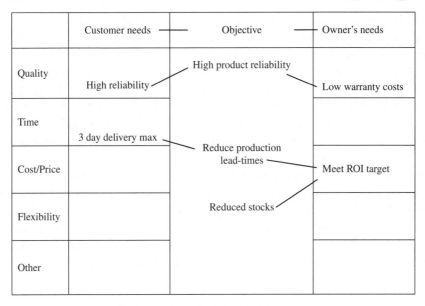

Figure 3.2   Developing business objectives

to achieving this. The customers' need for quick lead-time and the stock reduction objective may therefore conflict. As a consequence, one of the resulting objectives may be drastically to reduce production lead-times.

You can see from this example how the various stakeholder needs can be translated into business objectives.

An alternative approach is to create a success map for each stakeholder in turn. This is useful because it will allow the team to view different perspectives and will enable them to see where demands on the organisation conflict or coincide. Having done this, you need to create a single success map for the business. You can try to do this in a group, but it is usually easier to let one or two members of the team have a go first and then let the whole team work on the first draft. The key here is to keep moving forward, allowing the team to discuss and agree each step.

3.7   DEVELOPING THE MEASURES

Once the various success maps have been refined into a single success map for the organisation, you need to develop appropriate performance measures. Do this by allocating the objectives appropriately across the senior team who developed the success map, asking them to work on the design of the measures against each objective with their staff. You can use the performance measure record sheet described in Chapter 2 for this purpose.

However, you cannot develop measures in isolation. Members of the senior management team need to be involved because they will know *why* the objective is important. Staff need to be involved in designing the measures because they have knowledge and experience of *how* the measures will be used in practice. Finally, it is important that the completed measures are presented back to the senior team for their approval. The design of the measures is important for communicating strategy because it is through the measures that everyone in the organisation knows what has to be achieved. This can only be fully confirmed by the senior team responsible for the design of the system.

Surprisingly, it is the seriousness of this final review of the measures that will give you the first indication as to whether they are going to be implemented successfully. Teams that simply run through them playing lip service to the review are showing their lack of commitment to the future deployment of the measures. Teams that argue and typically send half the measures back for serious redesign are showing the commitment that is a good predictor of a successful implementation.

3.8   THE NEXT STAGE

Unfortunately the process of design is the most enjoyable and the easiest part of developing a performance measurement and management system. Everything at that stage is exciting and new. The hard slog starts as soon as the development meetings are over, the decisions have been made and all that is left to do is to implement. We are going to look at the thorny issue of implementation in the next chapter.

FURTHER READING

Bourne, M. C. S., Neely, A. D., Mills, J. F. and Platts, K. W. (2003) 'Implementing performance measurement systems: a literature review', *International Journal of Business Performance Management*, **5**(1), 1–24.

Bourne, M. C. S., Neely, A. D., Mills, J. F. and Platts, K. W. (2003) 'Why some performance measurement initiatives fail: lessons from the change management literature', *International Journal of Business Performance Management*, 5(2/3), 245–269.

Platts K. W. (1993) 'A process approach to researching manufacturing strategy', *International Journal of Operations and Production Management*, **13**(8), 4–17.

4
Managing Implementation

4.1   INTRODUCTION

In the last chapter we discussed the softer side of designing your measurement and management systems, particularly looking at how to develop ownership of and commitment to the process. In this chapter we will focus on how you implement the system you have designed. We will start by explaining how the phases of design, implementation and use overlap before going on to discuss the reasons why performance systems succeed and fail. We conclude by identifying the factors you need in order to implement your processes effectively.

4.2   PHASES OF IMPLEMENTATION

Figure 4.1 shows the overlap of phases around implementation. During the design phase, as we discussed in the last chapter, the meetings can be handled discretely (hence the bars on the chart). Managers have to make time available for meetings, but that time is bounded, and by careful use of a facilitator the meetings can be easily managed. True implementation starts at the end of this phase when other people become involved. The new performance measurement and management system has to be communicated to the rest of the organisation, measures have to be made, the IT department will invariably be involved in data gathering and manipulation, surveys have to be created and so on. During this phase the amount of effort required increases substantially. That is true not only for the initial management team involved in the design but also for others around the organisation who must now put effort into the implementation process. It is not surprising that most failures occur during this phase.

However, once the back of this work has been broken and the measures are being produced automatically, management time starts to move from the creation of the measures to their use, results are being generated and people are beginning to see the benefits. It is useful to reflect on the relative intensity of management effort required in each of the phases shown in Figure 4.1. Most performance measurement processes fail in the difficult phase between design and use, where the most effort is required. Next, we will discuss the reasons for success and failure.

4.3   WHY DOES IMPLEMENTATION SUCCEED OR FAIL?

There are two main reasons for success and four main reasons for failure and we will look at each of these in turn.

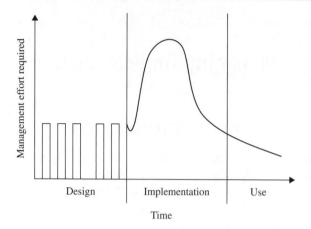

Figure 4.1   Implementation in practice

4.3.1 Top management commitment

When writing about change management people invariably cite top management commitment as being essential for any change programme to succeed. However, if senior managers are so clever, why do they not just give their commitment and make change happen? Unfortunately, it is not as simple as that.

Many writers on change assume that top management commitment is a constant. It is not. The senior management team may initially be committed, but this commitment can, and probably will, fluctuate over time and it can dissipate altogether when some more important priority emerges, as it inevitably does. So you must not only secure top management commitment at the outset, you must find a way to maintain it during the implementation phase and beyond. This is probably best done by keeping top management out of the day-to-day implementation of the project and making sure they have an important role to play in the big occasions or whenever their show of support is really necessary.

Top management commitment is an essential ingredient. Manage expectations from the outset so that those involved know how long it is going to take. Then find ways to manage expectations through the process and keep the momentum going.

4.3.2 Benefits of performance measurement and management

Performance systems are implemented more successfully when people perceive benefits arising from them and this is most likely to happen when the design is right. That is a very good reason to put time and effort into designing a good system to start with rather than making lots of adjustments later because certain parts do not work. When the design phase has gone well, people who have been involved change the way they perceive the business and think differently about what it is important to measure.

They gain a clearer idea of the most important factors for success and gain more insights into the dynamics of the business. When this happens, they perceive benefit coming from the process and they have the incentive to carry on towards implementation so their new approach can be shared with the rest of the organisation. The opposite happens after a bad design process. When nothing new comes out, people are reluctant to implement the measures because they feel it is a waste of time.

Again, the benefits have to be managed throughout the implementation. This means making quick wins where possible so that momentum is sustained. Implementation always takes longer than you would expect, so it is a matter of sustaining the pressure to implement, showing benefits when they occur, but emphasising the need for the whole scheme to be implemented to maintain a balanced system.

In a study of scorecard implementations, one of the first differentiators between companies that implemented their performance measurement and management systems successfully and the rest was their reason for doing it. The companies whose managing directors talked about 'improving their measurement system' failed. Those who talked about improving 'the way they managed the business' succeeded. What seemed at the time to be a very subtle difference turned out not to be the case. One group of managing directors were looking at their scorecard processes as, simply, a set of tools. The other group looked at their scorecard processes as an essential part of running their businesses.

4.3.3 Fear of measurement

Fear of measurement goes beyond people in the organisation not liking to be measured. It happens where there is an extreme blame culture and managers use measurement solely as a means of identifying 'who' was responsible.

One of the worse cases we encountered was an engineering firm in the east of England. The project did not start well when the managing director announced that he knew all about performance measurement and left the team of directors and senior managers to get on with the process. Although it was possible to get the measures agreed, there was absolutely no commitment to implement them. It finally reached the stage where the managing director made the announcement at a board meeting that he would fire on the spot anyone who had not implemented their measures by the next meeting. The next board meeting came and no one had implemented their measures. It turned out afterwards that there was a long history of abuse of the measurement system. The managing director's style was to turn up to the monthly management meeting, tell the senior team how badly they were performing and then storm out, leaving them with the information on their 'poor' performance. They were so frightened of the measures that they preferred to lose their jobs rather than comply. Obviously, the managing director could not sack everybody, so the project was quickly forgotten. His career with the company did not last much longer either.

Before you embark on a performance measurement and management project just reflect on the cultural climate in your organisation. Do you have a managing director who will abuse the system? Are there other managers who might do the same locally? If there are, you will need to think about management training and development. Luckily most organisations do not fall into this category any more.

4.3.4 Parent company interventions

New initiatives and interventions by parent companies represent the biggest cause of failure. You often find, during the design phase, that local managers understand how their organisation works and really get to grips with what they need to achieve. Then comes the problem of the parent organisation launching its own initiatives. In one example, a machine shop producing components for all the sister factories in Europe had just completed the implementation of a Balanced Scorecard process when the parent organisation decided it was implementing a benchmarking project using specific measures and tying the senior management team's bonus to these new benchmarks. Inevitably the Balanced Scorecard project that had been worked on so diligently over several months simply stopped.

Parent companies have the habit of doing this in the private sector, but public sector organisations suffer a very similar fate. All the work that has been done to meet one standard is suddenly undermined and thrown away as a new set of targets or a new regulatory regime is devised by government. The argument is always that if ministers do not inject change, public sector organisations will become complacent. However, if change is injected too often, all the organisation ends up doing is chasing the change rather than delivering a good service to its users.

It is possible to build a performance process that fits both with the parent company and with the subsidiary. At Schering Health Care in the UK, head office had communicated to all their subsidiary companies the five groupings of objectives they required. In working with the UK operation we built their performance system by examining their key business processes, working out what success looked like and developing performance measures appropriately. We then took these output and outcome measures and put them into the five head office groups (under headings such as finance, market and so on). The parent company even imposed a reorganisation during the project, but because we had built the performance system around the fundamental business processes that applied throughout this part of the business the reorganisation had almost no impact on the system or the measures we had designed.

One question to ask yourself before you launch into any project is 'How much local discretion do I have?' If you do not have a great deal of discretion, you need to ask for it or create it. Many years ago, working on implementing a Balanced Scorecard at instrument manufacturer Ai Qualitek, we believed that implementation was far from assured as the company was taken over just the day before we started the project. Four years later, when Mike Ophield the MD was asked about this he told us that the two new owners had turned up and asked him what he wanted to do with the business. He explained that he wanted to do two things: he wanted to reduce the cost base by using less of the factory so he could rent out the rest and he wanted to implement a Balanced Scorecard project. They told him to get on with it. Apparently five other companies were also bought that day as part of the same takeover, and when they did not have an answer to the question, they were given no option and were simply told what they had to do.

4.3.5 Lack of time

This is a serious and widespread problem. Most managers claim they are under time pressures and many projects of all descriptions fail (or take longer than necessary to implement) because people simply do not have sufficient time to devote to them. A well thought out performance system will add significant value to a business but it does take time. This has to be recognised and accounted for. One of the most important differentiators between high and average performing companies is that high performing companies undertake fewer change initiatives but finish them. The rest start many initiatives but far fewer come to fruition.

In Chapter 5 we will describe how you can assess the pressures on management time and how this will impact on the success of your project.

4.3.6 Poor IT infrastructure

Increasingly performance systems are dependent on IT support for their implementation. It is therefore critical to realise this at the outset and commit the IT resources required to make the implementation happen.

Most companies we have worked with have complained about their IT infrastructure and the amount of effort required to make things happen. Companies that succeed invest time and effort to overcome these problems; companies that fail do not.

4.4   HURDLES AND BLOCKERS

As you can see from the above, there are hurdles and blockers. The *hurdles* are the issues that all companies face. Management time and effort and IT infrastructure are hurdles on the way to implementation. You can jump them if you want to succeed, but they can bring you down if there is not sufficient commitment to the project.

The *blockers* are more serious and may prevent you from embarking on your project in the first place. They include fear of measurement and parent company initiatives. When these issues exist, performance measurement projects are extremely likely to fail. Fear of measurement should be something you identify and address before you start the project. It will be an issue if your company has a 'blame' culture and you will need to think how you are going to tackle it. Whatever you do it is unlikely to be a 'quick fix' – fear of measurement is something that will have built up over a long period of time. Parent company initiatives, on the other hand, are often bolts from the blue. If it is possible to involve the parent company in some way it may help, as they will have a greater understanding of and commitment to what you are doing. However, much will depend on the relationship and you may simply have to take your chances.

Chapter 5 will provide you with tools for assessing your chances of success and failure. Tools (such as a force field analysis) will highlight issues around the blame culture and may identify issues with your IT infrastructure. The implementation audit tool in Chapter 5 is particularly useful for assessing management commitment and the time pressure on your managers. It also explains why parent company initiatives are so damaging, but, of course, it cannot always identify when these will occur!

4.5   STEPS TO SUCCESSFUL IMPLEMENTATION

4.5.1 A long march

Chairman Mao spoke of bold strokes and long marches. Implementing an effective performance measurement and management system is a long march. It takes time to gain top management commitment, it takes time to run the design workshops and involve the right people and it takes time to implement and settle down.

Figure 4.2 shows the elapsed time taken for three successful implementations. As you can see, it took between 9 and 13 months between the agreement of the objectives and measures and the point at which we believe that they were properly implemented. That only happens when the success map, objectives, measures, targets and performance are displayed around the company for all to see. This may be on the canteen wall or on the intranet, but until everyone can see them (and not just management) they are not embedded. Once measures and performance are displayed, the company moves into a new position. Now everyone can see the performance, be it good or bad. Also everyone can see whether the measures are up to date or not and it is immediately obvious when managers are no longer interested in the measurement system as the performance reported by the measures becomes out of date very quickly.

It takes time to design and implement a performance system and time to use it properly and keep it up to date. It should not be rushed. This means you need to think about the best time of year to begin the design process and the best time to start the implementation. Can the busy times be avoided? Can you avoid the period when everyone is tied up in the budgeting process? Do not use a performance system for managing a crisis because it will not work. It is also difficult to implement during

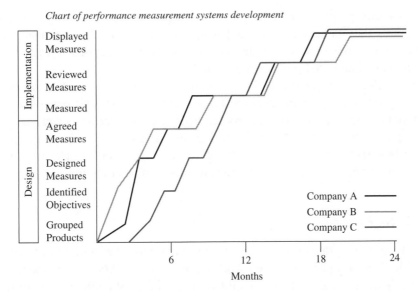

Figure 4.2   The development of three different performance systems over time

a period of turbulent change. However, it can be used to great effect in reinforcing planned change. Our point here is that timing is everything.

4.5.2 Culture

Having a receptive culture is important both within the senior management team and within the organisation as a whole. We have already talked about the problems associated with having a blame culture.

When you embark on the process you do not know precisely what the outcome will be. It is a learning process and the outcome cannot be determined in advance, so there is an amount of uncertainty. The managing director or leader has to be comfortable with this and it can be quite difficult for them as there is a certain amount of personal risk involved. If you are leading a project team in these circumstances you need to have the confidence to let go and let the process proceed. The whole team needs to understand about the element of uncertainty and be prepared to accept it.

The following example shows just how important culture is. Four business units from one company were all sharing the same site. The local director responsible for all four businesses had signed up to developing a performance system, but suddenly halfway through the process he decided he was going to dictate what the measures were going to be. This did not go down at all well with the four general managers who complained bitterly that the approach had been usurped. It took another two meetings to work out the compromise, whereby the managing director justified some of the measures he was proposing and the general managers had their chance to incorporate the measures they believed were needed for the success of the organisation. The director's sudden desire to dictate the outcome of the process created a great deal of bad feeling and hampered progress on a number of fronts.

Interestingly, it is these crises that often are long remembered after the event. If there has been some pain in creating the performance system it can really create commitment to the consultative approach. That does not mean to say you should deliberately set out to create the pain. It does mean to say if you have an open and honest debate there are likely to be difficult issues to be resolved. Do not shy away from discussing them even if they cause some discomfort at the time.

4.5.3 Integrate

Finally, try and integrate your performance system into other initiatives wherever it is possible. One company had been working on Total Quality Management (TQM) for many years. Instead of throwing all that away, they called the new performance project 'TQM with bite', by adding the KPIs to their quality management system. This had the benefit of building on, rather than losing, what had gone before. Taking another example, a company started their performance project after reformulating their strategy and the process became the vehicle for making the strategy explicit in the organisation. When the next piece of strategy development happened, we ensured that the measurement and management system was realigned with the new direction. Similarly, when the appraisal system was reviewed, we linked this in as well. Each time a change was made, we built capability by incorporating what was done before as well as increasing alignment within the organisation's new strategy.

4.6   CONCLUSION

In this chapter we have identified the main reasons why performance measurement and management initiatives fail and given some further guidance on the factors you need to consider when taking this approach. In the next chapter we will provide you with a tool for conducting a pre-implementation audit so you can have some indication in advance of the likelihood of success or failure.

FURTHER READING

Bourne, M. (2005) 'Researching performance measurement system implementation: the dynamics of success and failure', *Production, Planning and Control*, **16**(2), 113–124.

Bourne, M. C. S., Neely, A. D., Platts, K. W. and Mills, J. F. (2002) 'The success and failure of performance measurement initiatives: the perceptions of participating managers', *International Journal of Operations and Production Management*, **22**(11), 1288–1310.

Neely, A., Mills, J., Platts, K., Richards, H., Gregory, M., Bourne, M. and Kennerley, M. (2000) 'Performance measurement system design: developing and testing a process-based approach', *International Journal of Operations and Production Management*, **20**(9), 1119–1145.

5
Assessing and Managing Change

5.1 INTRODUCTION

Before you embark on implementing any large project, you should conduct an assessment to understand both your chances of success and the factors that could cause you to fail. It is often called a 'pre-assessment'.

In this chapter we are going to explain two approaches to pre-assessment of the implementation of your performance measurement and management system. Firstly, we will discuss a number of the traditional change management tools you can use. This will serve as a useful reminder of tools and techniques you have encountered before. Secondly, we will look at a methodology developed specifically to assess the design and implementation of performance measurement and management systems. This will build on the issues raised in the last chapter using the concept 'return on management'. The basic premise is that management time and effort is not infinite, leading to the conclusion that not all projects can succeed and that success is dependent on their context.

5.2 CHANGE IN CONTEXT

The first thing to understand is how change affects people. Change at work may not be the only change happening in people's lives and we all have a limited capacity to deal with change. This is why good managers are always very interested in what else is happening with their people. Personal change can be emotionally draining. Dealing with the day-to-day elements of the job may be relatively easy to accomplish as they are routine, planned and require a limited emotional commitment. However, dealing with change, either as an instigator or recipient, may take the individual beyond what they can satisfactorily cope with.

The change roller coaster is often used to describe the personal emotional side of change that those going through the process feel (see Figure 5.1). It all starts with denial, moves on to blaming others, then yourself, which can result in despair. You are then helped, or find your own way forward, trying new things. As this works, confidence comes back and self-esteem grows through achieving results.

However, you also need to consider change from the perspective of the initiator. Most change is a step into the unknown. You may start by being optimistic, but usually have no idea what you have launched into. Conner calls this uninformed optimism (see Figure 5.2), which can quickly lead to informed pessimism as the reality

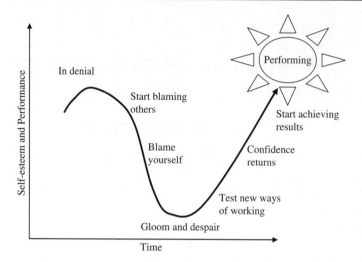

Figure 5.1 The change roller coaster (adapted from Carnall, 2007, and Coyle and Page, 2006)

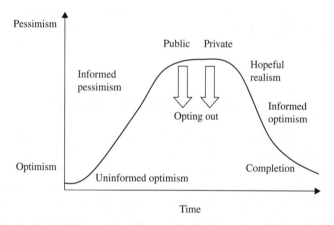

Figure 5.2 The initiator's response to change (adapted from Conner, 1992) reprinted with permission from John Wiley & Sons, Ltd.

bites. If things go well, you move on to hopeful realism and informed optimism, leading finally to the successful completion of the change.

However, it should be noted that management often *opt out*. That can happen in public, when senior managers start to voice their concerns about whether or not the change is going to work, or in private, by withdrawing their support from the project. In both cases, the change in sentiment will often cause the change to fail, leaving the organisation in the situation where it has spent time and effort trying to move forward and that has been wasted. Worse, it can breed a cynicism about change, that 'here we go again' mentality, when many veterans of the organisation smile wisely not really expecting anything really to alter. This cynicism makes change very difficult to achieve in the future.

People often avoid change because of the emotional turmoil it creates. Worse still, the turmoil can be for nothing if the change never happens after all, but this is not the only reason to avoid change. The change may not be perceived as being personally beneficial. It may be fine for you and all those who are going to be the team leaders in the new structure, but what about the rest who now have additional work to do?

5.3   ASSESSING RESISTANCE TO CHANGE

One of the oldest and most widely used approaches to assessing resistance to change is Kurt Lewin's force field analysis. It is a simple diagrammatic representation of the elements that can be mustered in support of a change initiative and the elements that may well be mustered against the change (Figure 5.3). The idea is to shore up the forces for the change while distracting, reducing and removing the people, issues and barriers to the change.

More recent approaches have taken the classic 'two by two' matrix approach. In Figure 5.4, we have two elements, the impact of the change and the energy of the response. There are normally a number of change agents who see positive benefits from the change and are highly motivated and energetic in their drive to implement the change, but there will also be those who will be adversely affected and may be in powerful positions, making them change resistors. Traditionalists and bystanders cannot be completely ignored. This is partly because they may be large in number, simply creating inertia, and partly because as the change unfolds and they see what it really means for them, they may find ways through their union or other forms of representation to become change resistors.

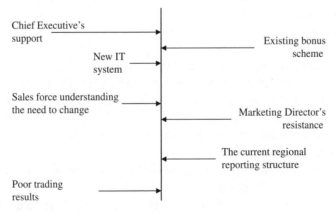

Figure 5.3   An example of a force field analysis

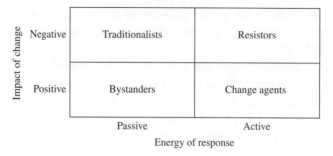

Figure 5.4   The four change categories

We recommend that you start any change initiative by thinking about the impact it will have on those involved. Who are the obvious change agents and who are the change resistors? Assess the other two boxes as well. Bystanders will not help you implement a change, but can easily become traditionalists. Traditionalists can be antagonised by the change and provide effective resistance. You should at least have all these elements in the back of your mind before your proceed.

5.4   RETURN ON MANAGEMENT

Strassman created the concept of return on management. His argument is that in today's corporate environment the scarce resource is not money – it is management time and effort. This means that organisations need to focus management time and effort on the things that give them the greatest return.

We will show you how you can use this within your own organisation to predict the success or failure of your performance measurement initiative, or any other change you may be considering. This approach has been tried and tested, so it is not simply an academic theory, but we think it is important you understand the assumptions behind this tool.

The assumptions are:

1. That managers have limited time and effort available.
2. That managers endeavour to use their time and effort effectively.
3. That managers focus their own effort on delivering the day-to-day performance before they focus on change.
4. That there are several change and improvement initiatives happening in the organisation at any one time.
5. That managers prioritise their time and effort, focusing on what they perceive will give them the best returns.
6. That those projects for which there is insufficient time and effort fail to progress.

This approach is useful when looking at real organisations, where there are usually several change projects going on at once. Now, with the assumptions above, we have a situation where different projects are competing for management time and effort. If there are too many projects, it is inevitable that some will fail. This is not because of resistance to the change, but simply because there is not sufficient management capacity to deliver everything that is required of them.

5.5   ASSESSING LIKELIHOOD OF IMPLEMENTATION

From experience, many senior managers, in their enthusiasm for progress, attempt too many change initiatives at the same time and overburden their managers. What they should be doing is controlling the number of change initiatives they have in progress at any one time and prioritising their actions. This is as true at the senior levels of the organisation when launching change initiatives as it is lower down the ranks, where improvement projects are prioritised for implementation.

We will start by describing how the assessment tool is used and then we will present the tool itself. We finish by highlighting some of the insights it can provide and one significant blind spot.

5.5.1 How to assess

You need to know how busy your managers and directors are. Are they already over-loaded with things they are doing, or do they have the time, effort and motivation to be involved in yet another project? The traditional way of asking for support is by going to each individual manager in turn and discussing the project with them. At the end of the discussion you can ask for their support. If you are the project manager, you may get a truthful answer. If you are the chief executive, the answer to offering support is invariably 'yes'. You therefore need to ask a different set of questions.

The starting point is to ask the managers to list their own change and improvement projects and initiatives that they are personally going to be involved with over the next three to six months. When you have done this, you will find that managers tend to have between one and ten initiatives. You then ask them to list the initiatives in order of priority. It is important that you ask the managers to consider their own order of priority as they are the ones juggling different demands on a day-to-day basis. Sometimes managers can give a clear list of priorities; sometimes groups of projects all have equal priority.

By this stage, you should have a good idea of what each individual has on their plate. The next question to ask is how much effort these projects are going to require. You focus on effort here, because it is not just time that you are interested in. Writing a report and firing somebody from the organisation may in fact both take the same amount of time, but in terms of effort, the latter is far more demanding than the former. As there is no uniform measure of effort, you ask people to allocate 100 points of effort across the list of projects provided (see below).

Now you have a list of projects in order of priority and an indication of the comparative level of effort required to complete each of them. Next you ask how much effort is required to deliver the day job – all the things that the manager needs to do to keep the everyday performance up to scratch. You will find typically that this can vary from zero (e.g. a project manager who only does change) to 500 (e.g. an operations manager overseeing activity with only a small element of change).

The final 'killer' question, which usually brings a smile, is 'how much effort do you have available?' Now you can compare each manager's available effort with the effort required to deliver day-to-day performance plus the change work.

5.5.2 The assessment tool

On the table and graph below:

1. List your key improvement projects in the first column.
2. Rank your projects in priority order.
3. Consider the amount of effort required over the next 3 to 6 months for each project. Then split 100 points of effort among your projects
4. If your improvement projects will take in total 100 points of your effort, estimate the number of points of effort required for the day-to-day aspects of the job.
5. Calculate the total effort required (improvement projects plus day-to-day).
6. Estimate your total effort available.
7. Complete the graph.

Title of improvement project	Priority	Effort required
(A) Total project effort required		100
(B) Day-to-day job effort required		
(A+B) Total effort needed		
Total effort available		

- Complete the graph on the right-hand side, starting at the bottom with the improvement projects with the highest priority
- Add in the effort for the day-to-day job below the zero line
- Calculate where the time and effort available line cuts the graph and draw this in

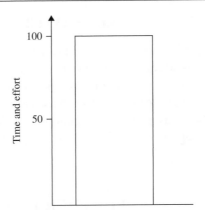

5.5.3 Insights from the assessment tool

When managers have capacity to complete an initiative it is usually completed. Initiatives that fall above the line, into the zone where the demand on effort exceeds the estimate of effort available, are rarely completed. Our studies show that this predicts success and failure of projects very accurately. However, there are a few issues:

1. Initiatives that have not yet been launched will not appear on the manager's chart and so the response can be distorted. The main source of these unforeseen initiatives is head office or the parent organisation. They tend to arrive without notice, along with a high priority. That is why parent company initiatives are the major cause of failure of performance measurement and management system implementations. They are not foreseen by local management. This the main blind spot.
2. Occasionally, managers overestimate what they are capable of delivering, but this is rare and happens only in about 2 % of projects overall.
3. Be aware of games being played. These can be identified by the priority given to the initiative. Some managers will signal their lack of support for a project by giving it an inappropriately low priority. This is useful in itself because it should give you an early indication of a major issue with that individual.

Therefore, given the proviso of the issues identified above, doing the assessment should give you:

1. An overview of all the change and initiatives being undertaken.
2. An assessment of how heavily loaded managers are.
3. A feel for the level of commitment to the project as reported by its relative priority.
4. An indication of bottlenecks – managers who are overloaded.
5. An indication (if nothing else changes) of the likelihood of success.

5.6   CONCLUSION

In this chapter we have provided some insights into how to assess the chance of success of your new performance system. You should use the tools at the outset, but realise that management commitment changes over time. It is a good idea to apply the tools at key stages of the project to assess progress and commitment to the next steps. You should pay particular attention to the launch of any new initiative, as this could push managers over their capacity and cause your project to falter and finally to fail.

FURTHER READING

Bourne, M. C. S. and Bourne, P. A. (2002) *Change Management in a Week*, Hodder & Stoughton, London.

Carnall, C. (2007) *Managing Change in Organisations*, Fifth Edition, FT Prentice Hall, London.

Conner, D. R. (1992), *Managing at the Speed of Change: How Resilient Managers Succeed and Prosper Where Others Fail*, John Wiley & Sons, Ltd, Chichester.

Conner, D. R. (1998) *Leading at the Edge of Chaos: How to Create the Nimble Organization*, John Wiley & Sons, Inc., New York, USA.

Coyle, M. and Page, C. (2006), *Managing Change*, Kogan Page, London.

Lewin, K. (1947) 'Frontiers in group dynamics', *Human Relations*, **1**(1), 5–47.

Lewin, K. (1951) *Field Theory in Social Science*, Harper, New York, USA.

Simons, R. and Dávila, A. (1998) 'How high is your return on management?', *Harvard Business Review*, **Jan./Feb.**, 70–80.

Strassmann, P. A. (1985) *Information Payoff: The Transformation of Work in the Electronic Age*, The Free Press, New York, USA.

6

Target Setting

6.1 INTRODUCTION

When you think about setting targets the words 'high but achievable' probably spring to mind. You need to set targets at a high level to stretch people, but the targets need to be perceived as achievable if people are going to accept the stretch. However, in real life the world is much more complex than this. Many companies use performance targets for influencing the behaviour of their employees, but the results these companies obtain are not always the ones they expect.

There is often justifiable concern over the impact of targets on behaviour and ultimately on organisational performance. Managers implicitly believe that setting targets works, but the BP Gulf oil spill disaster and other related events make some people question the benefits of target setting. This is exacerbated by disagreement in the academic literature, where researchers who specialise in motivation stress the fact that performance targets are key mechanisms for improving performance while those researchers from a *Total Quality Management* background suggest that the use of performance targets can be detrimental as they generate stressful work environments, a low trust culture, data manipulation and poor performance.

As you can see, target setting is fraught with difficulty. It becomes even harder when you use targets as part of the reward system. Suddenly, targets take on an even greater personal importance to individuals and the incentives to manipulate and cheat increase.

In this chapter we will start by looking at why and how you set targets. We will illustrate a number of common problems that occur in target setting and provide you with a framework – the target setting wheel – to help you through the process.

6.2 WHY DO YOU SET TARGETS?

At first glance, this may seem a banal question, but actually if you sit down for a few minutes and think about it, the reason why you set targets is not always clear.

You set targets to stretch people. It gives them something to aim for, a benchmark against which to judge success and failure. The motivation literature and fifty years of research shows that having a target creates higher levels of performance than not having a target. It gives staff clarity and purpose. It is good for communicating objectives.

You set targets to communicate and before long you are using these targets to communicate between departments. Let us say you have set your sales targets, so production need to be aware of those targets because sales activity generates orders and they will need to be prepared for the increase you are expecting. Now you have forgotten that the sales targets were stretch targets, not the level of performance you actually expected but figures agreed because you wanted to motivate the sales team and it was just possible they may achieve these with extra effort. By communicating the stretch target from sales to production you risk production gearing up to produce more goods than you would normally expect to be needed. You may incur additional costs by doing so.

Your finance people, though, will have a very different view of targets. They prepare the budget and need to look at figures as if they are certain and not some whim. For finance, targets are often the least that is expected, so that the company can plan its cash flow and manage within these constraints. Suddenly you are in the situation where targets are three things:

1. Your stretch goals
2. Your estimate of what is likely to happen
3. Your estimate of the least you expect to achieve

and that is before you have attached targets to the compensation system, which brings additional complications.

6.3   TEN COMMON PROBLEMS

During a recent research project into the use of target setting in organisations conducted by the Centre for Business Performance at Cranfield, 10 common problems were identified:

1. *Targets were mainly based on past performance*, which means people were careful not to overachieve. Overachievement meant that the next year's target was going to be so much harder – referred to as the 'ratchet' effect. In the worst cases it was found that really good sales people worked themselves out of a job. Here their targets became so difficult it was easier for them to go to a new company and start again. Past performance is important, but is it not also good to know how individuals are performing against their peers?
2. *Targets were allocated inappropriately* so some people were overwhelmed because they were given too much to achieve while others had an easy time. This was because managers did not fully understand the level of work necessary to achieve the target. Besides the obvious impact on individual motivation, this will undermine the performance of the team, as the process will be seen as unfair. How do you allocate your targets across your team or teams? Could it be done better?
3. *Targets were perceived to be too high or too low* so people were not motivated. Low targets mean that performance can be achieved with little effort and you

have to be careful to ensure people feel sufficiently challenged so they do not stagnate. High targets, on the other hand, are not perceived to be achievable and so people do not even bother to try. You need to be good at setting just the right targets in order for them to work. It is also important to know whether you can detect that the target has been set at the wrong level. Just knowing this gives you a chance of doing something about it or learning for the future.

4. *Some targets were based on the wrong performance measures*, resulting in performance not being related to what the organisation was trying to achieve. You may think this is absurd but many companies fail to link the strategy to objectives, measures and targets. This is often referred to as 'hitting the target and missing the point'. You should periodically just work through the different links and ask yourself if they are still valid.

5. *Targets were based entirely on financial indicators* even when other factors were important. Financial targets are usually clearly defined and easily measurable and so they are the type of targets managers like to set. However, they can encourage inappropriate behaviour in the short term, with people taking certain actions just so they reach their target and in this way can undermine longer term performance. You need a balance of financial and nonfinancial targets to compensate for this. When thinking about financial targets ask yourself whether they are being met at the expense of longer term sustainable performance.

6. *The data analysis process on which targets were based was poor and lacked rigour*. To do target setting properly takes time and many organisations do not invest that time. Analysing the data thoroughly should not only give you better targets but should also provide insights into the factors that really affect business performance, providing benefits beyond that of target setting. It should also be said that we have come across some companies that set targets for their employees without having adequate systems to measure them!

7. *Targets were not periodically reviewed* so were overtaken by events. Big changes in the business environment can make targets inappropriate overnight. If you want to keep your people focused and on the ball you should be ready to re-set the targets when this happens. At the very least, this will communicate to the rest of the organisation that you are on top of the situation. Ask yourself, what level of change can be tolerated before we need to review the targets?

8. *Targets were 'given' to people* and so did not create ownership. Targets without ownership are ineffective. You should ask, how am I going to involve people in the target setting process? How am I going to monitor commitment to the targets that have been set?

9. *The interrelation between targets was not considered*, causing inconsistency. What happens if you set a target for a number of leads generated by your marketing department? They generate leads, but are they the best leads for your sales teams to follow up? You should look across the different work groups in your company and ask yourself, do the different targets support each other or do they just create effort in one area at the expense of another?

10. *Agreed action plans were the exception and not the norm.* When you set a target there should also be a plan of how that target is going to be achieved. Targets invariably go up, but the question you should ask is how are you going to achieve more with the same resources? If there is a plan, then you may have some belief that the target will be met. If there is no plan, are you really managing the business?

6.4   THE TARGET SETTING WHEEL

There is a process for target setting that you can use to overcome the difficulties outlined above. This process starts by integrating the targets into the wider requirements of the stakeholders and the organisation, before you even consider the measures to be used and the actual target for performance. The complete process is shown in Figure 6.1, the target setting wheel.

Figure 6.1   The target setting wheel

The point of departure should be the stakeholders, whether they are the external stakeholders for the organisation at the top level or the stakeholders inside the organisation who have requirements from the department or the individual. Determining the underlying stakeholder requirement should come before the strategic objective setting. As with the Performance Prism (described in Chapter 2), the wheel makes the assumption that organisations and functions exist to satisfy the needs of different stakeholders. The setting of strategic objectives therefore comes after determining what the stakeholders need.

Setting strategic objectives means making choices. This is the point at which you decide how to balance the stakeholder requirements and make clear decisions about your priorities. Ideally, you should then summarise these into a success map so that people in the organisation understand what you are trying to achieve and how you plan to deliver it. Part of the success mapping process will focus on identifying the priorities and the aspects that you need to focus your attention on.

The next step is to define the KPI or performance measure. You should use the performance measurement record sheet from Chapter 2 to ensure that you create and document an appropriate performance measure.

Creating the measure gives you the definition of what you are measuring and guides data collection. Once the data are collected you will need to analyse them to obtain an understanding of the current levels of performance being achieved and to allow you to start to forecast the future.

The data analysis stage in the process is critical and should include two distinct elements – establishing capability and forecasting. To begin, you should establish the level of performance that the process is currently delivering. This should be done by looking at the data over time and using techniques such as SPC (statistical process control; see Chapter 8). All processes have natural levels of performance and those natural levels are not easily changed. Understanding the level of current performance is critical, as your current process may not have the capability of delivering more than it does at present. Having established the capability of your processes, the second stage is forecasting. There are a whole range of approaches that you can take here, but start with the question 'Is the past a good predictor of the future?' If it is, then you can predict forward from the levels of performance that have been achieved, but often this is not the case. There may be step changes happening. If you are making a new product launch this may increase volumes significantly; however, if your competitor does the same you may have the opposite outcome. Similarly, going into or out of a recession should be factored into your forecast to make it realistic or, for those to whom the target is being applied, more believable.

It is only now that you should set the target level to be achieved. However, that is not the end of the matter; you will need to plan how the target will be delivered. Performance does not simply change because a target has been set, so you will need to change the things you do, the way you act and possibly the resources you commit in order to improve performance significantly from current levels.

The final element in the wheel is the communication and discussion of the target and the plan to achieve the target. Much of the academic literature on motivation centres on the need to involve people in agreeing the target because it creates commitment. However, the reality is often very different. Targets are set at a high level in the organisation and cascaded, so individuals have very little say in the level set for them or their department. They can, however, have a considerable say in how the target will be achieved. Involvement in target setting involves not only setting the figure to be achieved but also the plan to achieve it. Agreement to the plan is the critical element.

Table 6.1   Target setting questions

1. *Review stakeholder expectations*
   - What do the external stakeholders expect from this organisation?
   - What do the stakeholders expect from your department or process?
2. *Strategic objectives clarification/selection*
   - What are our key objectives?
3. *Define the organisation's success map*
   - What does success look like?
   - What are we trying to achieve and how will we deliver it?
4. *Prioritise objectives*
   - What are our priorities?
   - Which objectives are key to success?
5. *Operationalisation*
   - How do we measure progress against our key objectives?
6. *Data collection*
   - What data do we need?
   - How often do we need to collect the data?
7. *Data analysis*
   - What is the current level of our capability?
   - What is the forecast for the future?
8. *Set targets*
   - What targets should be set?
9. *Action plan design*
   - How are we going to achieve the targets?
   - What actions need to be implemented?
10. *Action plan discussion and agreement*
    - How are we going to communicate the target and plan?
    - How are we going to gain commitment to the targets and plan?

As a final comment, it should be noted that one of the key elements in gaining commitment to a target is the perception of its difficulty. If the target is perceived as being too difficult, the whole value of the process is lost. Similarly, if the target is perceived as being too easy, then the objective of stretching people in the organisation is not achieved. There are three things you can do to alleviate this problem:

1. Ensure that people have a clear understanding of what their roles are and the precise target. Clarity is vital.
2. Create a supportive organisation where risk-taking, continuous learning and improvement are encouraged. This environment promotes greater ownership of the targets, which in turn positively affects perceptions about how difficult these targets are.
3. Ensure that there is involvement in the target setting process. This may not be specifically about the level of the target to be achieved, but people should know why that level has been set and the thought processes behind it. They should, however, be involved in planning how the target is to be achieved.

Table 6.1 gives a succinct list of questions to guide you through the target setting process.

6.5   CLOSING REMARK

After reading this chapter, you may be thinking that this is a lot of work to set a target. This is true, but the consequences of setting poor targets can adversely affect the performance of individuals and the business for several years. If you cannot spare the time and effort, then maybe the best resort is not to set targets at all!

FURTHER READING

Franco-Santos, M. and Bourne, M. (2009) *The Impact of Performance Targets on Behaviour: A Close Look at Sales Force Contexts*, CIMA Research Executive Summaries Series, Vol. 5, Issue 5.

Franco-Santos, M., Marcos, J. and Bourne, M. (2010) 'Hitting the mark: the art and science of target setting', *IESE Insight*, **7**, 34–41.

7
Linking Rewards to Performance

7.1 INTRODUCTION

The number of companies we have worked with who think the ultimate solution to improving performance is to link their measurement system to rewards is only slightly outweighed by the number of companies who regret doing so!

It is much easier to criticise a reward system than to design one. Designing a reward system requires you to make a complex series of interrelated decisions about targets, measures and rewards, with elements of judgement and assumptions added in, and a mistake in any one of these elements will create problems. On top of this you will have to keep the system up to date whenever strategy, objectives, measures and targets change.

Before we launch into the detail of creating a reward system linked to performance it is worth pausing to think about the link between money and motivation. On an executive development course participants were asked what motivated them. 'Money' was the response from most people. 'OK,' said the tutor, 'If that's the case, why aren't you working in the City?' 'I don't want to commute', 'You have to sell your soul to the bank', 'I need a little work/life balance' were some of the responses. So, the draw of a large City salary was outweighed by factors such as living where you want to live, not feeling you are on call for your employer all the time and spending time with the family. While most people felt money motivated them, when put to the test it just was not true. Having said this, it is important to feel valued and to be recognised for what you do and good managers know this. Just receiving praise in the form of an email or a phone call makes a difference and it costs nothing except a little time. We explore the issue of motivation in more depth in Chapter 18.

In this chapter we start by highlighting a series of issues that occur when you link pay and performance and then provide you with a framework for thinking about how to create a reward system. We will end by giving you a few examples.

7.2 PITFALLS

The first question to ask is why you want to link reward to performance. Most managers will say it is in order to motivate people to perform better and, of course, creating better performance is ultimately what it is about. They then go on to consider what targets should be set. However, before you leap ahead to think about targets, one of the first things you should think about is behaviour. What behaviours do you want to encourage in your employees to help make your organisation successful? How will linking performance and reward help you do this? Do you want people to work together as a team or can you survive with unbridled individualism? Team bonuses create the former, but have the disadvantage of not rewarding individual effort, while individual bonuses are very clear, but can undermine the team. If you try to combine both are you creating a system that is too complicated to handle?

In practice, one principal use of reward systems is to communicate the objectives of the organisation. People want to know what they are being rewarded on and that is where they will concentrate their effort. It is quite possible to achieve a great deal with a very simple and low cost reward system.

Let us consider the pitfalls of linking performance and reward:

1. The loss of information caused by the change in dynamics in the target setting process
2. The behavioural consequences
3. The level of influence people have over performance
4. The need to constantly change and evolve.

We will look at each of these in turn.

7.2.1 Information loss

When reaching your own target affects your reward it makes it even more important that you achieve it. That sounds good in principle. However, in practice it may create other problems. When negotiating your own targets, it will be in your best interests to make those targets as low as possible. From the organisation's perspective, however, managers are looking to achieve the most they can from the process and are looking for higher targets. As a consequence, both sides guard their own information. The employee does not want to let on how much he or she can deliver because this will weaken their bargaining position, and the manager does the same.

Here is an example from a pharmaceutical company we were working with recently. The UK sales director for one of the major selling lines had suggested to her boss that she could increase sales by 50% in the year. Her boss accepted the goal without question, and he failed to pay her the bonus when, after a cracking year's performance, she only achieved a 45% increase in sales. Having been stung by this, she was suggesting a 2% increase for the following year's target, and her boss was trying to increase this to 5%. By now the trust in the negotiation had been destroyed.

In this example, the initial trust created by an open discussion about what could be achieved was completely destroyed once the consequences of not achieving became apparent. Therefore, if it is possible, you should try to separate targets used for calculating reward from the indicators used to provide the information needed to manage the business. This is difficult to achieve but it can be done by setting targets through external comparison. BP do not always pay bonuses based on achieving a budget figure or, say, hitting a cost reduction target. Because of the volatility caused by world oil prices their bonus is based on how well their people have performed against their major competitors.

Transparency of information is the lifeblood of any performance measurement system. It can be very damaging if data are distorted because of the 'negotiation game'. The organisation can lose touch with reality and will be unable to respond quickly to changes if they become necessary.

7.2.2 Behaviour

The behavioural consequences of linking pay and performance are legendary. Take the example of a friend trying to buy an expensive car in Germany who went into a showroom near work looking forward to making his purchase. He was astonished when no one showed any interest in him after finding out where he lived. Eventually he discovered the sales team were paid a bonus on all cars sold in that particular state. As he lived in the next state they were not going to receive any reward for selling him a car. What was worse, they would be doing work for which someone else would be rewarded!

Closer to home, it could be argued that large bonuses paid to some people in financial services encouraged them to take too many risks with dire results.

It is essential to think carefully about the effect your reward processes will have on your employees' behaviour. If you simply pay on hitting a target it focuses attention on the short term – winning the next order. What does that do for longer term customer relationships? On the other hand, if you include all the behavioural elements in the bonus system, it can become unwieldy and you lose clarity.

7.2.3 Influence

Just how much influence does an individual have over corporate performance? Research evidence suggests that, in general, they have very little because most individuals are part of wider processes.

In most manufacturing or service operations, the role of an individual is to work with others as part of a team to deliver the process. In many situations the individual has virtually no control over performance on his or her own. Paying an individual bonus should be restricted to those situations where people are acting independently, where the additional effort can be measured or where it is clear they have made an outstanding achievement.

In a sales context, it is often argued that the salesperson has considerable influence over performance. This may be true, but do not forget that the sales person is also part of a wider process. They are given leads to follow up, products and services to sell, a price list and a discount structure to work from. Of course they have a major impact, but it is not a solo operation. A sales person is usually working at the end of a sales process.

People know what they can influence in their work, so talk to them about it and when you are designing the reward system, think about both the individual and the group element.

7.2.4 Change

There is always a tension with processes and systems between flexibility and keeping some element of continuity and stability. Reward systems are personally important and individuals value stability and continuity in their operation.

When you first create a success map it is based on your assumptions about how you think the organisation works. These may all turn out to be true, but often some elements will be wrong and you will have to revise your success map. If you have already linked the success map to reward then you will also have to revise the reward system. We know that the most lamented action is linking objectives to rewards too early in the cycle before the measurement system has been embedded and any problems ironed out.

However, you do need to make changes sometimes. Strategy will change over time and if you do not change the reward system accordingly, you will find the new strategy is in conflict with what you are paying people to do! It is difficult to change a reward system quickly once it is in place so there is a danger that you will prevent your new strategy from being implemented.

When things change, your reward system can become out of date very quickly. One bank went from being competitive on their mortgage rates to being uncompetitive over the period of a weekend. When this happened the targets became unattainable. However, within a year the situation had completely reversed and everyone could hit the target. If you are using targets to motivate people you should adjust them as circumstances change or the reward system loses traction. Then there is the thorny question of whether you are paying for effort or results? Typically, in hard times people have to work so much harder to get anywhere near their targets, but they are not rewarded, whereas in good times they may be rewarded just for turning up to work. Rewarding on effort seems to make sense then – but if you decide to take this approach, you will end up having to justify paying bonuses when the organisation is struggling financially.

As you can see, there are a number of pitfalls for the unwary. However, there is one further question. Do you have the discretion to change the incentive system? In many large organisations the systems are now designed at corporate level, leaving very little discretion to local managers trying to run their part of the organisation. Smaller companies are seeing reward practice as a source of competitive advantage.

If they can create a reward system that supports the behaviours they want in the business while their large competitors cannot, then they have a distinct advantage.

Let us now look at the way you can link performance and reward.

7.3   LINKING REWARDS TO PERFORMANCE

As we stated at the outset of this chapter, to influence behaviour you need to consider the way in which incentive pay is linked to the targets and targets to the performance measures. Performance targets, incentive plans and performance measures cannot be considered in isolation – they are all inextricably linked. We call this the *pay for performance chain*. Like any chain, it is only as strong as its weakest link, so a mistake in one element will undermine the whole approach.

Figure 7.1 presents the key factors you will need to consider in linking performance to reward. It shows the factors that are important for the incentive system, performance measures and targets, as well as those that are common. For example, the factors completeness, agreement and reliability are common to both the measures and targets. The factors communication, clarity, review and fairness are common across all three elements (incentive system, performance measures and targets).

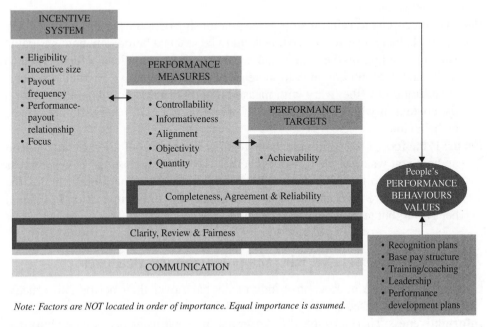

Note: Factors are NOT located in order of importance. Equal importance is assumed.

Figure 7.1   Important factors for the design of a reward system

7.3.1 Factors associated with the incentive system

Eligibility: Who is eligible to share in the reward? Everyone with the same role should be included on grounds of fairness, but has everyone who has had an influence on performance been included? On what basis are people included or excluded from the bonus system?

Incentive size: How big is the bonus pool or what proportion of salary is the incentive? How does this compare with other companies in your industry? Is the size of the incentive appropriate and equitable against other people in your own organisation? How much personal effort is required to earn the bonus? Does the incentive generate the right behaviours? Does the incentive build the team or cause disruptive internal competition? What are the risks involved? Is the bonus simply based on industry norms or can you create a competitive advantage from being different? Is the incentive simply a way of risk sharing, so people get rewarded in good time and costs are kept low when the business is struggling?

Payout frequency: How often is the bonus calculated and how often is it paid? The frequency of payout to sales people should be in line with the sales processes. Similarly, in operations, the target should be set and the bonus paid for an appropriate period. However, there are circumstances where the results of the effort have an impact for many years to come. A banker making loans will fall into this category as will a chief executive making an acquisition, so this needs to be considered carefully.

Performance–payout relationship: Is the relationship between performance and pay linear? Is there a performance threshold to be reached before any bonus is paid? Is there a ceiling on the bonus paid, so that over a certain level of performance the bonus does not continue to increase? The way incentive payments are calculated and how they vary with measured performance should be aligned with the context in which the organisation operates, as it will have different effects on behaviour.

Focus: Is the focus on the individual, the team or the organisation? This will depend on how you want people to work together. The more diffuse the bonus the less relevant it is to the individual and their motivation, but the more it builds the team. The more focused the bonus, the greater the direct impact on individual behaviour, but team work could be undermined as a result.

7.3.2 Factors associated with the performance measures

Controllability: The more control individuals have over their performance measures, the more effective the process will be.

Informativeness: There are typically two groups of people using performance information: the individuals who are being rewarded on their performance and the managers overseeing the activity. It is important that the performance measures provide the correct information to the decision makers (managers overseeing the activity) as well as giving individuals a clear indication of how they are performing.

Alignment: Performance measures need to be aligned with strategy in order to encourage the required behaviours and avoid the well-known issue of 'rewarding A, while hoping for B' (Kerr, 1995).

Objectivity: Measures used for pay purposes need to be perceived as objective by their users. If people think the measures are too subjective it will create doubt and may have a detrimental impact on their behaviour and performance.

Quantity: In order to keep people focused, the number of performance measures needs to be relatively small. Following Miller's (1956) advice, the magic number is five, plus or minus two, as this is the maximum number of things people can keep in their heads at one time.

7.3.3 Factors associated with the performance targets

Achievability: To be motivating, targets need to be perceived as being achievable. If they are not you will lose commitment and this one element will undermine the whole process of linking reward to performance.

7.3.4 Factors associated with the performance measures and targets

Performance targets are intrinsically related to performance measures. Selecting the most appropriate performance measures for compensation purposes is a critical decision. If your compensation system is based on the wrong measures you will encourage dysfunctional behaviour, undermining business performance.

In reviewing individual performance, two types of performance measures are typically used. These are behaviour-based measures and outcome-based measures. Behaviour-based measures are associated with behaviours rather than results. For a sales team, examples of behaviour-based measures could include product knowledge, client relationship management and selling skills. Behaviour-based measures are by their very nature more difficult to measure and are oriented towards the longer term. In fact, their effects may not be fully realised for many years to come. These characteristics make them less appropriate for target setting because specific and accurate targets are difficult to create. On the other hand, outcome-based measures have high measurability and are oriented towards the short term; therefore, their impact can be fully realised during the incentive period. For this reason, these types of measures are seen as more appropriate for target-setting purposes. Some examples of these measures in a sales environment may be: number of orders won, value of orders placed and sales margins achieved.

Most organisations use both types of measure in order to influence behaviour and performance. However, be very careful if you decide you only want to reward one type of measure. If you reward solely on outcome (e.g. financial target) you risk people acting inappropriately in order to achieve their target. If you reward only on behaviour (e.g. *how* things are done) you risk not achieving your results.

Besides the issues of controllability, informativeness, alignment, objectivity, quality and achievability discussed above, when linking performance measures and targets you should also consider:

Completeness: The measures and associated targets used for evaluating performance and determining reward should reflect both behavioural and performance aspects. Achieving your bonus by upsetting all your colleagues or at the expense of irritating your major customer is damaging for everyone in the long term.

Agreement: You should, whenever possible, involve people in setting and agreeing performance measures and targets so they will be more committed to achieving them. It also means you are more likely to elicit the behaviour you are looking for. If you are not able to involve people in setting the level of the targets then, as we explained in Chapter 6, you should at least involve them in the process for planning how the targets will be achieved.

Reliability: Performance data must be reliable. If people do not accept it, they will not behave as you would like. If your performance data are distorted or manipulated in any way it will have a negative effect and you will lose your employees' trust.

7.3.5   Factors associated with the incentive system, performance measures and targets

There are four factors that cut right across all the elements:

Review: When will the whole system be reviewed? You should review the system at least every two years to ensure that you keep up to date and in line with market/ industry practices. You will also need to review your performance measures and targets when there is a change in strategic direction and in response to external events.

Fairness: Is the whole approach perceived as being fair? A system that is perceived as being unfair will cause disruption to the smooth working of your team. It will be a running sore turning up at exactly the wrong moment. If your organisation is in the public eye you will also need to think very carefully about how bonuses will be perceived externally. Recent publicity concerning bankers' bonuses has shown the importance of managing external perceptions of fairness as well as internal perceptions.

Clarity: How clear are the goals and targets that have been set? How clear is the link between effort and reward? People need to understand what they are being paid for and how they are being paid, but remember that the clearer the target the more focused people will become in trying to achieve it and the more likely it is that they will ignore the wider context.

Communication: How are targets set? How are the targets allocated across teams and between individuals? How will targets be measured? How are they going to be achieved? How are people going to be paid? Motivation theory tells us that people will exert effort if they perceive that their effort results in higher performance and this higher performance results in reward. People need to know how their incentive system works and the more communication and transparency there is with information about incentives, the more satisfied people will be, which will have a direct effect on their behaviour.

Communication is the Achilles heel in many organisations. To communicate properly, you need to present your approach in open forum, so all participants can hear and ask questions. You will need to give regular updates on the size of the incentive pool, the targets and how close people are to the target. You will have to talk about plans and listen to your staff's feedback and comments. It is important to use multiple channels of communication, so people not only hear and see your presentations, but also have access to the information again on your intranet or noticeboard. Most managers in companies believe they have explained well how the reward system will work, but when you ask the staff, most people believe the communication has been inadequate.

7.4   EXAMPLES

We usually like to give good examples, but sometimes it is helpful to see a few bad ones:

- The banking and insurance industry's problem with mis-selling of pensions was partly caused by paying bonuses on the value of the pensions sold without sufficient safeguards.
- Sales bonuses paid on achieving quarter end sales targets for orders placed, while not adjusting for orders cancelled in the following month. This is particularly common when the bonus is not a continuous function of performance, so an additional order received will take the bonus over the next threshold.
- A design office bonus scheme designed to encourage designers to be productive and calculated productivity based on the size of the drawings produced. The outcome was that all drawings were produced on the largest schematic and everyone consistently hit their bonus target within a couple of weeks.
- A production incentive scheme that paid bonuses on the weight of material processed during the month. The output bonuses was always met as the product was produced in two passes through the process instead of three passes, causing high levels of scrap.

However, scrap levels were not deducted in the bonus calculation, and this practice continued for many years until management finally realised that the cause of their problem was high levels of scrap.
• Banking bonuses paid on the value of loans approved with no recognition of the quality of the lending.

All the above are real examples, some of which continued for many years. With hindsight the problems with these schemes are clear to see and most should never have been implemented. Paying incentives based on a single measure of performance always has dangers, but as soon as you add additional elements or caveats, the message becomes blurred. Thus a balance has to be struck. All approaches have their own advantages and disadvantages, and you will have to decide whether the benefits outweigh the shortcomings. This will always be a judgement call. Remember that over time people will get better at manipulating the bonus system, so you should review your approach regularly and update it when necessary.

You can see below some examples of more balanced approaches, with a brief comment about how the approach was seen by both management and employees. They are not supposed to be best practice but simply examples to show you the types of benefits and shortcomings that occur.

7.4.1 Service company individual bonus scheme

Fitters' bonus

A service company employed fitters, who mainly worked on their own at their customers' premises. The company moved from a high basic wage to a scheme where the basic was significantly reduced but supplemented by a bonus paid on productivity. Fitters earned points for jobs completed. The bonus payments started after a certain number of points were earned in a week and there was no upper limit. To ensure quality was maintained, fitters had to rectify their own faults or have points deducted.

The employees liked the scheme as they had the opportunity to earn significantly more than they were previously earning. The company overall was pleased as it improved productivity and profitability. However, the bonus did cause an element of perverse behaviour. Fitters would either work hard to maximise their bonus earnings or take it easy if they were going to have a poor week. Therefore, if a fitter had a day off ill or took a holiday, their productivity would be low as there was no incentive to perform for the rest of the bonus week. This occasionally gave the branch managers a headache as they struggled to get the jobs completed and there was some concern about the impact the bonus system was having on customer service.

Branch managers' bonus

In this service company the branch managers had a bonus system based on their branch profitability. The focus on profitability was partially offset by the annual pay review, which focused on a wider set of measures including customer service, levels of rework and performance on company audits. Some people saw the two as creating a good balance, but some believed the bonus made managers too financially focused.

7.4.2 Manufacturing company group bonus scheme example

Business-wide bonus

A medium sized manufacturing company created a business-wide bonus based on customer satisfaction. The organisation was paying in the order of £200 000 a year in credit notes to their customers to compensate them for goods damaged in transit and for product faults. The customer satisfaction bonus was created to focus the whole company's attention on this problem. A bonus pot, equal to the value of the previous year's credit notes, was created at the beginning of the year. Each credit note issued reduced the amount available in the bonus pot. Finally, at the end of the year, the value of the pot remaining was split between all 100 or so employees, creating an incentive to look after the customer. The scheme had the advantage of being cost neutral, for if the company improved on the previous year's target, the cost would be the same, but the customer would benefit from better service. In the first year, the incentive system appeared to be working well as the size of the pot remaining each month was widely discussed and scrutinised. The concern was that the size of next year's pot could be much smaller and this would reduce the incentive to focus on this particular aspect of customer service.

Operator bonus

In the factory, the operators were given an incentive through a team performance bonus. Each week the team had to deliver against five objectives – output, adherence to schedule, quality, safety and housekeeping. Each time the team met one of the five objectives, an element of the bonus was added to the pot paid out at the end of the month. The scheme kept employees focused on what had to be delivered and it rewarded teamwork for meeting the goals. Although this was a team bonus, the incentive system did make it very clear which individual's actions had caused the loss of the team bonus. While the system focused attention on the five key objectives to be achieved, it was also seen as a punitive system for noncompliance. Managers believed the bonus worked, but were conscious of the tensions it sometimes created.

Management bonus

Managers in the company had two bonuses. They had a six monthly bonus paid
on meeting their departmental objectives and an annual profit share. Each year, the
managing director (and major shareholder) set a profit target and shared any amount
achieved above this with the management team. This was welcomed as it was seen
as sharing in the success of good years, but it was not clear what direct impact the
reward had on behaviour.

7.4.3 Handlesbanken's staff bonus scheme

At the Swedish bank, Handlesbanken, bonuses are based on beating the competition.
Bonuses are calculated on the amount that the company has outperformed the rest
of the Scandinavian banking sector. A third of this additional performance is paid as
bonus and split equally between all the staff. However, this is not received as salary
but put into the individual's pension scheme. Many individuals working for the bank
since the 1970s now have significant sums invested.

7.5 SUMMARY

In summary, you cannot consider using performance targets, performance measures and incentive systems in isolation. They are all interrelated and their specific
design must be aligned with the circumstances of the company and the environment
in which it is operating. Many reward systems are based on individual performance,
but some of the best reward systems we have seen are team based. This may mean
that some so-called 'stars' will think they are undervalued, but the teamwork it engen-
ders is usually far more beneficial.

Finally, do not forget that there are other ways you can motivate your people (see
Figure 7.1 again). You can use recognition plans, such as employee of the month or
sales person of the year. You can make increases in base pay to reflect performance.
You should think about leadership and management style as well as training and
development opportunities, which are not only motivational but develop the skills
to enhance performance. These other options also need to be considered, even if it is
just to ensure they do not clash with your reward approach.

FURTHER READING

Gomez-Mejia, L., Berone, P. and Franco-Santos, M. (2010) *Compensation and
Organizational Performance: Theory, Research and Practice*, M. E. Sharpe,
Armonk, New York, USA.

Kerr, S. (1995) 'On the folly of rewarding A, while hoping for B', *The Academy of Management Executive*, **9**(1), 7–14.

Miller, G. A. (1956) 'The magic number seven, plus or minus two: some limits in our capacity for processing information', *The Psychological Review*, **63**, 81–97.

Managing with Measures – Statistical Process Control

8.1   INTRODUCTION

One of the trickier aspects of using measures to manage performance is deciding what type of action to take and when. In this chapter we will discuss how you can approach these decisions and, in particular, when and how to intervene. The underlying approach we will be taking is based on the principles of Statistical Process Control (SPC). Walter Shewhart invented SPC in the Bell Telephone Laboratories in the 1920s, so it is not a new concept. The approach has been refined in high volume manufacturing processes, but SPC is applicable to most repetitive operations and situations, in fact to any situation where there is a process. It is important to understand the concepts behind SPC. If you do not understand them you may take action when it is not needed and that will undermine performance.

Problems tend to arise when people either ignore or misunderstand variations in performance so we will start this chapter by talking about variation. Performance is never completely consistent; there is always a slight variation. You need to understand this and be able to differentiate between what is known as 'common cause variation' and 'special cause variation', as these two different types of variation need to be managed differently.

We will then present an overview of SPC, which is a simple visual approach for identifying the difference between common cause and special cause variation. With SPC you can use time series data to calculate the normal limits of variation. This allows you to differentiate between the causes of variation and to predict (within limits) the level of future performance. We will explain how SPC should be used in management and give examples of how it is used in practice. Finally, we will link SPC with target setting and process capability.

8.2   VARIATION AND OUR REACTION

There is always variation, but sometimes the variation is more obvious than it is in other cases. Take a class of school children. They will all be about the same age but there will be a difference in height that is immediately obvious to anyone seeing them standing in a row. Take a box of pencils. When they first arrive the pencils will be very nearly the same length. However, with an extremely accurate measuring device you will be able to see slight differences. Give the pencils to the class of children for a week and the differences will be much more visible. These differences in things occur in all situations but are particularly important in operations. For example, the service in restaurants takes a little longer or is quicker depending on the number of customers and the number of staff working. Similarly, queues at airport check-ins and post office counters come and go. Even manufacturing processes vary slightly. You can reduce variation in an operation or a process significantly, but you cannot remove it altogether.

There are some variations you can live with and some you cannot. In a restaurant you chat to your family and friends while waiting for service. On some occasions the service will be quicker than on others and it is only when the waiting time becomes unacceptable that you start hassling the staff. Similarly, you allow time for the airport check-in and the post office queue – you cannot predict exactly how long it is going to take but you make an estimate based on past experience, perhaps, or on the time of day. These are everyday variations, which are usually manageable. However, if the front door to your house sticks in wet weather and you cannot unlock it easily, it becomes a real problem. All of us deal with variation on a daily basis – we cope with it – but the smaller the variation and the more predictable the process the better it is for us all. So it is important to understand how to identify variation and how to reduce it.

Let us take an example. You are doing target practice with a rifle. The first shot misses the bull, so you decide to correct for this error. One way of doing this is to adjust the settings on your sights to compensate for your error. You do this by moving the sights so that you aim for a spot exactly on the other side of the bull from where your first shot landed. This may mean you take two clicks to the right and two clicks upwards. You then take another shot and find that you miss again. The correction is now three clicks to the left and four down. If you continue in this way, what will be revealed is a pattern of shots in the target that become progressively wider and wider, making the result worse not better. What is happening in this example is that you are correcting on each shot and each shot has a small (or if you are not a good shot, a large) degree of error. Every time you make a correction, you compensate for this error, but if the error was a simple case of a small random variation, you are now setting the rifle to put the shot in the wrong place. As you continue to do this, the spread becomes wider. In practice, marksmen fire a number of rounds into the target. They can then see their grouping, how spread it is and how far from the bull it sits. Once this has been inspected, marksmen can then move the grouping to be clustered around the bull by adjusting the sights. The actual size of the grouping can only be improved by practice, that is to say by improving the accuracy of your shooting. By operating in this way you are making adjustments appropriately and only after you have understood the impact of the variation.

Here is a second example based on driving to work. If you time your journey, you will find that it does not take the same length of time each day. The drive from our house to Cranfield University takes about an hour, but it can take as little as 50 minutes if the journey is on a Saturday morning and it once took five hours in the snow! On the whole, the journey is very consistent. It takes between 54 and 60 minutes with an average of 57 minutes. Therefore, to be in a meeting for 9.00 a.m., we need to allow 60 minutes for the drive. If you only leave 57 minutes (the average length of time that it takes to get to Cranfield) you will be late for the meeting on about half the occasions you do this.

Now let us consider the reasons why the time of the journey varies. There is other traffic on the road, farm vehicles, queues at roundabouts, traffic lights and differences in the weather. There may also be other factors. Your car may break down or you may have a puncture; there may be an accident and there may be major road works. So what do you do when you drive to work and find the journey takes longer than expected? Do you start that much earlier the next morning? That is one possibility, but you should also think about why you were delayed. Was it caused by an increase in some of the normal things you encounter, such as a little longer queue, a bit more traffic, etc.? If that was so, starting a little earlier may be the right response. However, if you were delayed two hours by a major accident what would you do the next day, leave two hours earlier? Probably not, because an accident is not a common event (well not on the road to Cranfield anyway). You do not expect an accident every day and so you do not allow for it in your timings.

Your approach for dealing with the time it takes you to drive to work will depend on whether the delays are caused by normal issues (what we call *common causes*) or exceptional issues (what we call *special causes*). We will now look at how the difference between normal and special causes can be identified in processes where the issues are not as transparent as they are when you drive to work.

8.3   STATISTICAL PROCESS CONTROL

SPC was developed in the early years of high volume manufacturing at Bell Laboratories in the United States. Walter Shewhart and his colleagues found that the harder they tried to improve the quality of their telephones the worse the results were. This was because they were dealing with the variation inappropriately. This often happens in management too, but people do not always realise the damage they are doing. The approach Shewhart developed was based on measuring the variation in the process and using a chart to help those analysing performance to differentiate between special and common cause variations.

There is software available that will create an SPC (control) chart for you but it is worth knowing the underlying principles of SPC. You start to create a control chart by plotting time series data. That is to say, you plot the performance you are measuring on a graph in the time order of occurrence (see Figure 8.1). Once you have 10 to 12 points, it is useful to calculate the average performance and plot this through your data. Upper and lower control limits (UCL and LCL) can then be calculated (see box below). The upper and lower control limits represent the upper and lower levels of normal variation that is expected from the data you have collected.

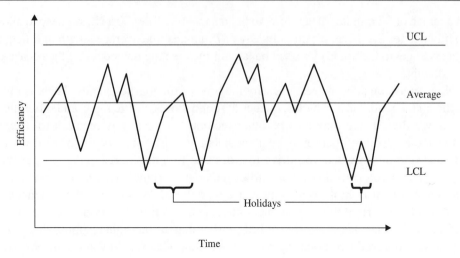

Figure 8.1 SPC chart of planning efficiency over time

Creating an SPC chart

You can use software to do this for you and if you have a significant amount of data or want to do a detailed analysis, this is the route to take. However, we will illustrate the calculations in a simple exercise below. The table shows the number of late trains each month. Figure 8.2 shows the completed chart.

Month	Number of late trains	Variance
Jan	19	
Feb	21	2
Mar	18	3
Apr	15	3
May	15	0
June	22	7
July	30	8
Aug	25	5
Sept	19	6
Oct	17	2
Total	201	36
Mean	20.1	4

1. Calculate the mean per month from the number of late trains you have observed. In this case it is 201/10 = 20.1
2. Calculate the variation between each of the two results. This should be an absolute variation, so all the results are positive
3. Calculate the mean of the variation. In this case it is 36/9 = 4
4. Multiply the mean of the variation by 2.66 (2.66 is the constant used to calculate control limits – or, for statisticians, the 3 sigma limit). In this case 4 × 2.66 = 10.64
5. Calculate the upper control limit by adding the 10.64 to the average, giving 30.65
6. Calculate the lower control limit by subtracting 10.64 from the average, giving 9.37

Number of late trains

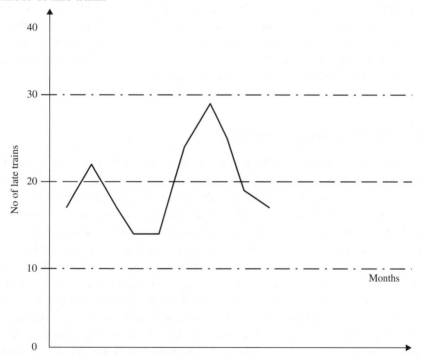

Figure 8.2   A statistical process control chart

This example shows quite clearly that there were no special causes over the 10 months of the report. So how many late trains would you expect in the final two months of the year? Given the results above it would be reasonable to

(*continued*)

expect between 9 and 31. That is assuming you run the network in the same way and that there is no special cause event, such as heavy snow.

To summarise: special causes are those that are economically worth while in identifying and separating for management action. You can identify these through statistical techniques and the points lying outside your control limits are those you should investigate first. The variation inside the control limits is normal variation. To reduce normal variation you must work on the whole process.

In practice, we assume that any data point that falls within the upper and lower control limits is normal variation, while any data point that falls outside the control limits has a special cause. In fact, it is only economic to spend time and effort looking for special causes, for points that lie outside the control limits. Once these special causes have been identified, they can be dealt with to ensure that they do not happen again. For the data points that lie in the area of normal variation, the way to reduce this variation is to improve the process as a whole.

8.3.1 SPC examples in practice

We will start this section with two examples showing how special cause variation can be identified and eliminated. We will then give two examples of common cause variation, where improvement can only be managed through understanding the process as a whole. Finally, we will give an example of how you can monitor process improvement and measure whether or not the improvement is sustainable.

Dealing with special cause variation can be relatively simple if you can find the source of your problem. Unilever had a problem with quality some time ago. It was significant but only occurred on a monthly cycle. Detailed analysis revealed that the problem happened on a precise lunar cycle and some bright spark had the idea that they needed an astrologer to help with their problem! Then they realised the problem was always associated with a high tide, an insight that finally led to the cause being identified as salt water ingress to the underground pipes during the high tides, which could then be eliminated.

However, special causes do not always happen on a regular basis. While investigating fluctuations in the planning efficiency of a paper mill a significant pattern was found. It comprised one week of low performance followed by one or two weeks normal performance followed by a week's poor performance (see Figure 8.1). There appeared to be no rational cause until you plotted the planner's holiday schedule on to the graph. Basically, the week before the planner's holiday and the week afterwards, performance was poor. We found that the planner created shorter schedules in these two weeks to get through her work quickly and efficiency suffered as a direct result. The solution here was more complex as a change in behaviour was required, but identifying the reasons for the poor performance in those weeks started the conversation with the planner about what could be improved.

Let us now turn our attention to common cause issues. A UK quoted company found that it had a significant problem with central overheads. There was a great deal of variation and it was so bad that the whole company had to issue a profit warning to the City. A major contributor was travel (see Figure 8.3). When analysts saw the figures, they wanted to understand what was causing the problem. They broke travel expenditure down into the different categories, the two biggest categories being air travel and land travel (predominantly car and train journeys). This gave Figures 8.4 and 8.5. Now it could be clearly seen that land travel was extremely consistent and the real problem

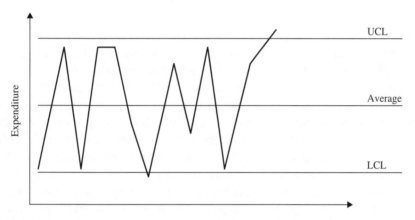

Figure 8.3   SPC chart of total travel overheads by month

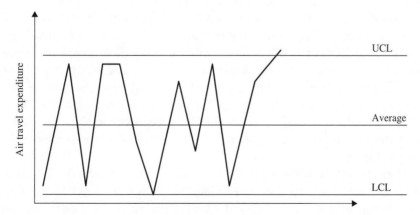

Figure 8.4   SPC chart of air travel by month

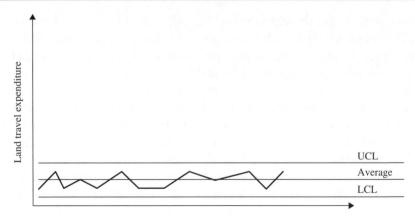

Figure 8.5   SPC chart of ground travel by month

was with air travel. The company's solution was to change the whole air travel process by subcontracting the management to a specialist travel agent and within a short period they were able to reduce the variation and get the costs under control.

   The example above demonstrated the use of SPC with an issue with a company process. However, the term *process* can cover a wide variety of repetitive events, such as dealing with drunks outside a pub, truancy from school or prisoners reoffending. For example, a pub in the South of England had a poor reputation with the police for drink related problems after hours. When the law on drinking hours was changed, the pub applied to the magistrates' courts to extend the drinking hours. The police were not happy, and nor were local residents, but the argument was made that if people could drink for longer, they would drink more slowly and leave at different times causing less trouble. Without real evidence either way, the application was granted, but residents kept complaining. A local councillor then plotted the graph of police incidents (see Figure 8.6) before and after the change in drinking hours. The graph showed a relatively consistent number of incidents in the period before the change in hours. After the change in hours there was also a relatively consistent number of incidents but at a higher level. The councillor, armed with these data went back to court to have the decision overturned. He successfully argued that there was a stable process (a predictable number of incidents) up to the point of the hours changing. He then argued that the change in hours created another stable process, but at a much higher level of incidents and that this was unacceptable. The court agreed and the hours were reduced; unsurprisingly, the number of incidents then fell back to their original level.

   SPC often shows how stable a process is when it is left to its own devices. However, the job of management is to intervene to improve things, so in most situations processes are being reviewed and changed on a regular basis. This does not stop you using SPC, but the graphs need to be interpreted alongside the information about

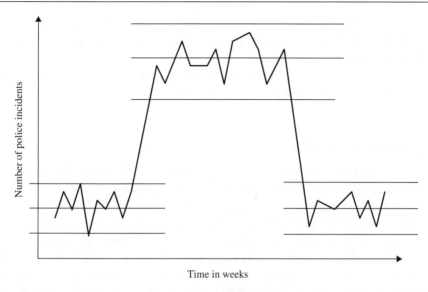

Figure 8.6   SPC chart of recorded police incidents outside the public house by week

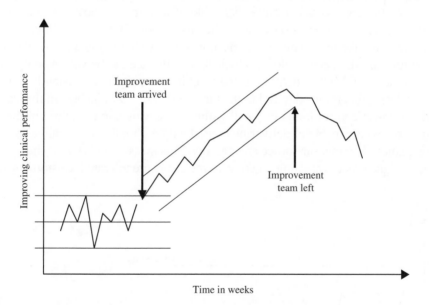

Figure 8.7   SPC chart of hospital clinical performance by week

the changes being made. Let us take the example of an NHS hospital. For many years, operations had been carried out in the same way (see Figure 8.7). However, improvement was deemed necessary, so an improvement team arrived from outside the hospital and made a series of changes. As you can see from the chart, the performance improved. The chart also shows that the improvement was relatively stable (see the lines drawn either side of the actual improvement). However, once the team had left, people reverted to their old ways and performance started to deteriorate again. For process improvements to continue, the changes needed to be embedded in the process so they could not easily be reversed.

8.3.2 SPC and targets

When a process operates between its upper and lower control limits it is predictable. You can expect that if no changes are made it will continue to operate in the same manner. However, the level of performance being delivered by the process may not match the level of performance required. Here are two examples.

A restaurant may have an average customer waiting time of 20 minutes between the food order and food service, with a variation of plus or minus 15 minutes. In the high street, this may be acceptable, but if the restaurant is situated in an airport and people only have a short time before their flights are called, this will be inadequate. A more appropriate target could be for all orders to be served in 20 minutes. Figure 8.8 shows how the process is currently incapable of meeting the target. In fact, in this example, the current process only meets the target about 50 % of the time.

Now we will take the example of a machine making shafts (Figure 8.9). The specification for shaft diameter could be 3 inches, with the need to be within an upper and lower tolerance of 3.005 and 2.995. If the machine runs highly consistently, it is possible for the shafts produced to fall in the range 3.002 to 2.998 inches. In this case the upper and lower control limits fall well within the specification required of the shaft and the process is capable of delivering consistently within the target range specified.

Companies often measure process capability. This measure tells them what the likelihood is of the process creating an error. Some errors are tolerated. Customers put up

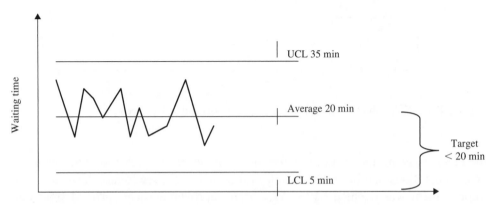

Figure 8.8   SPC chart of customer service waiting time in order of customer served

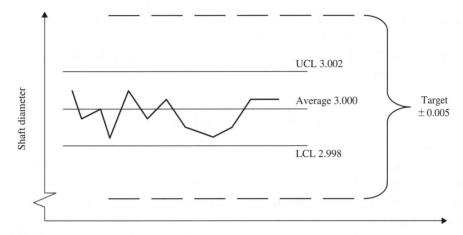

Figure 8.9   SPC chart of finished shaft diameter over time by shaft produced

with some goods not working or services not being delivered as they would have liked. Providing the numbers and consequences are small, the company supplying the goods and services can survive. However, if you are the National Blood Service, errors can cost lives. That is why organisations such as the National Blood Service work hard to ensure their processes are as capable as they can possibly be.

8.4   PERFORMANCE AND PERFORMANCE IMPROVEMENT

As you can see from the chapter so far, we are talking about two dimensions of performance. The first dimension is the level of performance; the second is the consistency of that performance.

When making performance improvements, removing or reducing the special causes of variation will make the process perform better. Firstly, special causes are the issues with the greatest impact on variation as they lie outside the control limits and therefore at the points furthest away from the average. Removing these outlying points greatly reduces the spread of variation. Secondly, their removal changes the average performance. If the special cause is a problem, then removing the outlying special cause will improve the average. As special causes are the only issues that have a single identifiable source, their removal is usually a good first step in making improvements.

Having removed the special causes, the next step is to work on the process as a whole to improve performance. This will have two effects. Firstly, the variation will reduce and, secondly, performance will improve. This type of continuous improvement refines the process over time, making the outputs better and more reliable.

It is useful to remember that besides continuous improvement, the process can be totally re-engineered by re-designing the process from scratch. However, once you have done this you should measure the process to establish its natural rhythm. You should use an SPC chart to do this and establish the average and upper and lower control limits. Only then can you see the real difference between your original and the re-engineered process.

FURTHER READING

Shewhart, W. A. (1931/1980) *Economic Control of Quality of Manufactured Product*, ASQC, Milwaukee, USA.

Wilcox, M. (2004) 'Principles for management by prediction', Chapter C8 in *The Handbook of Performance Measurement* (Bourne, M., editor), Third Edition, Gee Publishing, London.

9
Using Measures – Performance Reviews

9.1 INTRODUCTION

The measures you use to manage your business look to the future (feedforward) and to the past (feedback). When you set your objectives, measures and targets you are communicating to the whole organisation what is to be achieved and the direction in which the business is going; you are looking forward. When actual performance is reported against those objectives, measures and targets you are receiving feedback on what has been achieved, but you are also receiving information that can help you make a judgement about what may happen in the future. If you talk to people, it is the feedback role of measurement that most will instinctively talk about. However, the direction setting, feedforward, role is the other half of the circle and so is at least as important.

As we have said earlier in this book, performance measures influence behaviour. However, you will not ensure that the organisation performs well just by creating an objective, specifying a measure and setting a target. Performance comes from people doing things well, computer systems working smoothly and effective processes guiding activity. As we have already seen, a process will have a natural rhythm and within that rhythm there will be natural variation in performance from period to period. To improve the performance of a process you have to do more than measure; you have to change some aspect of the process itself. All measurement gives you is the feedback on what is happening and, ideally, some insights into what you need to change in order to improve.

In reviewing performance, the first task is to understand what is happening. Once you understand that, you can go on to decide what to change. In Chapter 8 we discussed the use of statistical process control in reviewing performance. In this chapter we will look at reviewing performance in groups. Reviewing performance in a group provides significant opportunities for gaining insights and taking decisions, but there are also real dangers that this does not occur because of the group setting.

We start by discussing the performance planning value chain, a tool to help you think about how you should organise your performance reviews. We will then give a case example describing the use of the performance planning value chain and finish the chapter by discussing how performance reviews impact on the performance of organisations.

9.2 THE PERFORMANCE PLANNING VALUE CHAIN

The performance planning value chain (PPVC) was developed by the Centre for Business Performance at Cranfield School of Management as part of a research project into managing with measures. The idea behind the concept was to document the stages you should go through when moving from receiving feedback to taking action. There are seven steps in the PPVC (see Figure 9.1), specifically:

- Creating the question
- Gathering the data
- Analysing the data
- Interpreting the data
- Engaging the decision makers
- Making the decision
- Taking action.

We will discuss each element in more detail next.

9.2.1 Creating a question

Your performance reviews should be centred around answering a series of questions. The questions form the first element in the chain, so it is critical to ask the right questions as they will guide everything that follows.

You could ask, 'How good is the service we provide to our customers?' or 'How do our customers perceive us?' Sometimes you will need to be more precise. For example, 'We believed our new call centre systems would increase customer satisfaction; is this actually happening?' The creation of the question, or hypothesis to be tested, is the first step in getting information from the data at your disposal.

9.2.2 Gathering data

The second stage is the gathering of data appropriate for answering the question (or testing the hypothesis) you posed in step 1. Data can come from multiple sources, from the existing performance measures, data mining for the exact information required or by conducting a survey.

In the data gathering phase, there are three tests you should apply. Firstly, are the data being gathered appropriate for answering the question set in the performance review? Secondly, are the data reliable enough for the purpose for which they are being used? This does not mean that the data have to be completely accurate, but they should be reliable enough to show movements and trends as and when they occur. Thirdly, are the data representative of the aspect of performance you are reviewing? In this test you are asking about the sample size and questions posed in surveys, but you are also asking about the period during which the data are captured.

Take the example of a road crossing for school children. What data would you need to collect in order to determine the level of risk? One element could be the volume of

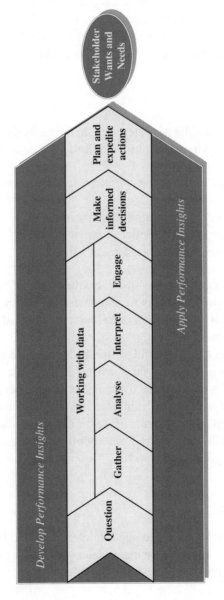

Figure 9.1   The performance value planning chain

traffic. However, that is not the only factor – it would be appropriate to know the speed of the traffic too. How accurate do the data need to be? Actually, you probably only need to know when the volumes of traffic are over a certain level and when drivers are travelling at speeds over 40 mph. Finally, are the data representative? That means you should look at traffic during the time children are going to or returning from school. This is usually morning rush hour and mid-afternoon outside the school holidays. Therefore, having average data of volumes and speeds from across the whole day is not appropriate. In fact, it would provide a misleading input to your decision making.

9.2.3 Analysing data

Having gathered the right data, the next step is to do the analysis. There are four basic questions you should be able to answer as a result of your data analysis:

- Is performance consistent – or is the variation in performance getting wider or smaller?
- Are there identifiable causes of variation in performance?
- Is there a trend – are things getting better or worse?
- Are there identifiable causes of the performance trend?

In reviewing data, it is a good idea to make frequent use of the question 'why?' People talk about the '5 whys?' This is to emphasise how many times you have to ask 'why?' to get to the root of a problem or to reach the level where you understand what is affecting performance.

The data analysis step is often one link in the PPVC that people skip over, but if it is not done properly, you will only be guessing at the causes of your problems. This means that all of the subsequent activity is based on a very shaky foundation. To really understand what is going on you often have to play with the data, cut it in different ways and look at it from different angles. This takes time and effort, but you will be surprised how much you can find out about what is really happening when you spend time analysing your data.

9.2.4 Interpreting data

Once you have understood the data, you need to interpret what they mean by putting the results in context. Data are actually meaningless without a context, so this is an important step. The questions you should ask include:

- How does this performance compare to previous periods?
- How does this performance compare to equivalent previous periods (e.g. this month or this quarter last year)?

- How does this performance compare to equivalent units within the organisation (e.g. other comparable stores, warehouses, call centres or factories)?
- How does this performance compare with our direct competitors?
- How does this performance compare with the best benchmarks available?

The choice you make for your comparison will colour how the data are interpreted, and it is likely you will have a very wide discretion in that choice. Take competitors; how do you decide whether a particular competitor is in direct competition with you? If you leave out all the multinationals who only provide a competitive service against part of your offering you may look very good against the remaining group. However, is it wise or justifiable to do that? If you compare retail outlets, their location makes a considerable difference to their performance. Placing one store in the next grouping, either a more affluent location group or a less affluent location group, can make that store look like a star performer or a dud!

The answer lies in showing multiple comparisons, so the decision makers can get a feel for the performance from different perspectives. A business unit may be the best in the group of companies you are working in and it may be performing as well as any businesses of its type in the country. However, the fact that it is performing well below international comparisons should be raised as a longer term concern. Senior managers often want immediate answers about comparable performance, but patience is needed. It is essential to ask and answer all the comparison questions first – otherwise you will only get a partial, and therefore misleading, view.

9.2.5 Engaging the decision makers

Let us face it, performance reviews are often extremely tedious and boring. There has to be something of interest to make people sit up and listen, so, if you are leading the discussion, you need to capture people's attention.

Rows and rows of numbers are often interesting to accountants, but most people respond better to visual representations of the data. This does not mean you should use every type of graph available in Microsoft Excel, but producing graphs with clear trends or clear comparisons can make all the difference.

Getting attention is critical. In one example, a company we were working with was very relaxed about the number of customer returns, until we showed a graph of returns as a percentage of sales. This shocked them and quality went to the top of the agenda. In another example, Jan Timmer, CEO of Philips, even went as far as issuing a hypothetical press release to his top team announcing the bankruptcy of the corporation to get their full attention. However, getting people's attention does not always happen. In the case of NASA, the *Challenger* space shuttle was launched despite the efforts of a subcontractor to prevent it. The subcontractor knew that the cold temperatures at the launch site would cause the O-rings to fail. However, in presenting their point, the subcontractor failed to get NASA's attention and understanding, leading to the explosion on take-off and the tragic loss of the crew.

If you are an analyst presenting the data, be as clear and as engaging as possible. If you are a decision maker, try to stay engaged. If you are losing your concentration then others will too, so it could be a good time to break for a coffee and come back to look at the situation again when you are fresh.

9.2.6 Making a decision

Sometimes, by the time the data have been presented you know the decision is obvious to all, but this is not always the case and the decision may require your judgement. Do not fall into the trap of thinking you always have to act on what you learn from your performance reviews. The decision does not necessarily mean taking action; deciding not to act is also a decision. In fact, delaying a decision to act can occasionally give you a better feel for which way to go. Sometimes, of course, it is a convenient way of ignoring a problem and it only puts you in a weaker position later on when you are forced to act. You will have to balance the risks and consequences, including the impact of the decision on the rest of the organisation and how that fits with the strategic objectives and organisation's values. The questions you should ask will include:

- Is action required?
- What are the consequences of not taking action?
- What will be gained if we wait a little longer before taking action?
- What will be at risk if we wait a little longer before taking action?
- What alternative actions are there?
- What are the risks and benefits of these different causes of action?

Getting consensus to act can be difficult, especially if the action has unpalatable consequences, and many companies can end up being like Charles Handy's frog, sitting in a pan of boiling water and not sensing the rise in temperature until it is too late. You can get round this by anticipating problems early and highlighting the issues to the decision making team. When you highlight the problems initially, there may be no agreement to act, but this could allow you to create a trigger point – a level of performance at which action would need to be taken. By highlighting the problem and setting a trigger point, you create a level of commitment to action in the future and with this approach you may be able to stop the company sleepwalking into a disaster. We have seen trigger points used effectively to decide the point at which the company has to initiate short time working, make redundancies and close a factory. Therefore you must identify the trend and set the trigger point early; otherwise it will be too late for you to act effectively.

9.2.7 Taking action

Performance review meetings usually create long lists of actions. Consider this list before the end of the meeting and prioritise them by splitting them into those actions that will be taken now and those that will be held over until next time. You need to ensure that actions agreed are completed, so, just like any meeting, you should specify what has to be done, allocate responsibility and timescales and ensure workloads are manageable. It is also a good idea to set out what you would expect the impact of the action to be. If you do this you will be able to go back and review your actions to see if they happened and if they had the desired impact. Do not forget that there will be a delay between the action being taken and performance improving. This delay may be minimal, but sometimes there is a considerable lag and the consequences could continue for several years. It is a common mistake not to consider how much time it will take for an action to have an impact.

9.2.8 Adding value

The intention of all this questioning, data gathering, analysis, interpretation, decision-making and action planning is to add value. You add value when your decisions and actions result in better performance, so always remember that this should be the purpose of your reviews. If this is not happening, you will need to look at what you are doing again.

The performance planning value chain outlines the steps you should take in undertaking a performance review. We have described it here in a linear form, but there will often be many loops when you go round again. The creation of a question may result in gathering some data, but the analysis may lead you to ask a better question, and so on. The PPVC is a simple and invaluable framework because it provides a certain discipline and robustness in identifying the steps that should be taken to arrive at good decisions. Too many companies shortcut the process and make flawed decisions as a result.

Having described the PPVC we will now look at how it can be used to help the development of performance reviews with a whole team taking part.

9.3 PERFORMANCE REVIEWS

How do you review performance in your organisation? A typical approach at board meetings is to have an agenda and receive a series of reports from heads of the functions represented. If the meeting is well conducted, these reports will be challenged and discussed, and proposed actions will be debated and approved. In those organisations using a Balanced Scorecard, another typical approach is to work through each of the performance measures or KPIs in turn, looking at performance against target. In a good meeting, you will consider aspects of under- and overperformance as well as the corrective actions and other activities taking place. In our opinion, board meetings that receive and review reports are generally too unfocused – they skim the surface without focusing sufficiently on performance. Board meetings that review KPIs resulting from, say, a Balanced Scorecard can become too focused on the measures themselves and people forget they are reviewing an indication of performance and not performance itself.

To overcome these two problems you have to steer a middle path. To do this we recommend creating an agenda based around a set of performance review questions that focus on the elements of performance that are important for the organisation. The board then needs to answer these questions using the performance data and other evidence available. The 'I' in KPI stands for 'indicator', so an overemphasis of the measurement results can be unhelpful. In many organisations, people focus too much on 'hitting the numbers'. This can lead to improving performance measures but (in the worst cases) at the expense of declining performance for the business as a whole.

We will describe next the approach developed by The Centre for Business Performance with DHL in the UK.

9.3.1 DHL UK

DHL has been developing and using a scorecard in the UK since the mid 1990s, but after many years of reporting their measures, they wanted to create a better focus in their board meetings. The company had a number of issues:

1. Board meetings often focused on the review of raw data and there was not sufficient time to really understand what was happening.
2. Board meetings were held monthly, but because the meetings were so frequent, it was not possible to see the impact of actions agreed at the previous meeting before board members were being asked to assess performance again.
3. Board members tended to act as heads of functions rather than as board members when they stood up to present their reports. This meant they defended their function's performance against any criticism raised.

The format of the board meetings was changed to overcome these problems. The first priority was to move away from reviewing raw data and towards reviewing information. Introducing the performance planning value chain enabled this. There were already a number of people working as analysts within DHL, analysing data and creating reports for individual directors. The analysts were organised into a team and given the job of presenting information to the board.

The board meetings were organised around a new agenda based on a series of performance questions. The framework adopted was the Performance Prism, so for each key stakeholder business the questions were formulated around the following:

Stakeholder needs
- What do our stakeholders want and need?
- How are they feeling and what are they doing, or planning to do?
- How do they perceive our performance?

Strategy
- What is our strategy?
- Are the different elements of our strategy working?
- Do we expect the strategy to continue to work in the future?

Processes
- Which are the key processes underpinning the strategy?
- Are these processes delivering the performance we need?
- Are the processes capable of delivering the performance we will require in the foreseeable future?

Resources and capabilities
- What are our key resources?
- Do we have the right resources to deliver the performance we currently require?
- Will we have the resources to deliver the performance we require in the future?

The questions then formed the backbone for the board agenda. The analysts were asked to collect, analyse and present information to help answer the questions, using the PPVC as the tool for guiding this activity. Getting the analysts to stand up and present while the board members remained seated dramatically changed the dynamics of the board meetings. Board members no longer felt the need to defend their function's performance; they started to act as a board looking at performance more dispassionately.

Board meetings became longer and less frequent. The format moved from a monthly day-long board meeting to a quarterly board meeting running over one and a half days. Quarterly board meetings were judged to be appropriate to reflect DHL's improvement cycle (see Figure 9.2). Thus, at a meeting held in March, the board would be able to review February's performance, agree actions that would be implemented in April, have an impact on performance in May and be visible at the next board meeting in June.

The board meeting agenda was constructed to allow time for reflection and prioritising actions following the review process. Not everything proposed in a review can be done because there are often insufficient resources or management time available. DHL therefore decided to concentrate very firmly on those actions that were important and needed more focus from the board itself. Other actions were either delayed or delegated. Having the analyst team available to support the board meetings meant that resources could be focused on the right activities and actions could be tracked following the meeting so they were not forgotten.

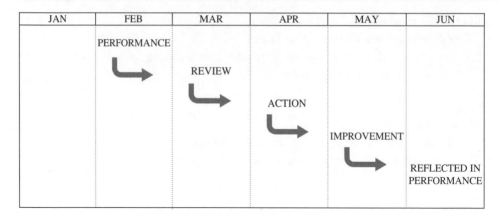

JAN	FEB	MAR	APR	MAY	JUN

Figure 9.2   The DHL performance review cycle

It is worth highlighting the role of judgement in the review process. By asking questions and reviewing information rather than looking at data, the board members were being asked to use their judgement to assess performance. This is in direct contrast to what is normally done at review meetings where people are simply relying on whether a particular performance target has been achieved or not. The idea of a performance review is that those responsible are able to understand the current level of performance, judge whether under the circumstances it is appropriate or not, and then take action when needed.

DHL adopted this approach in the UK and then went on to apply it in the management of their European Security Operation. They found it to be a useful way of focusing on real performance rather than on the impression created by the performance measures.

9.3.2 Key elements of a performance review

We will summarise here the key elements we believe are important for an effective performance review:

1. A clear understanding of what 'good' performance means for your organisation and a clear set of questions to ask.
2. A process for gathering analysing and presenting data to the decision makers.
3. A meeting where the data can be presented and discussed, insights gained and action agreed.
4. A process for reviewing past actions and prioritising new ones.
5. Sufficient resource so that the data analysis is done appropriately and there is sufficient time in the meeting for decision makers to reflect and decide.
6. Appropriately spaced meetings so that review reflects the natural cycle of the business.
7. An open culture to allow the process to operate naturally.

9.3.3 The importance of performance review meetings

Performance review meetings happen at all levels of the organisation, from the board to the shopfloor work team. Board processes are important, but so are the effective operations of all the other performance review meetings. It is easy to forget that while decisions made locally affect local customers and local people the combined effect of all the local decisions affects the organisation as a whole.

Research shows that the performance review meeting is the point at which the strategy is interpreted and implemented. Goals, measures and targets, cascaded down the organisation, influence the conduct and debate of the performance review meetings. People engaged in these meetings arrive with their understanding of what is happening in their part of the business. During the meeting, they share this understanding with their colleagues, discuss the organisation's priorities and craft a response. The response will include both feedback to senior management about what is happening and action plans for the team and their reports about what is happening next (see Figure 9.3). Therefore, the meeting transmits guidance both up and down the

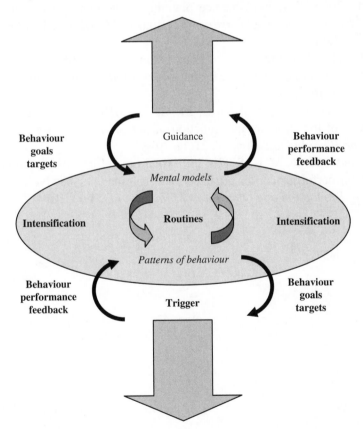

Figure 9.3   The role of performance review meetings in managing the performance of the organisation

organisation, intensifies the debate around performance and acts as the trigger for getting things done.

We know from studying performance review practices across the branches of one organisation that the intensity of the interaction can have a considerable impact on performance. At board level, it is important to see the information, but at a local level the performance measures often simply confirm to local management that they are achieving what they believed they were delivering. The closer you get to the front line, the more of a feel for performance you will have, but this feel always needs to be checked against something more objective, such as the performance measures. It is very important to review performance with front line teams, celebrating success and acting on failure. If you only review performance at the top of the organisation, the people doing the work will never feel truly involved.

FURTHER READING

Bourne, M. (2004) 'The performance planning value chain', Chapter D8 in *The Handbook of Performance Measurement* (Bourne, M., editor), Third Edition, Gee Publishing, London.

Bourne, M. C. S., Kennerley, M. and Franco-Santos, M. (2005) 'Managing through measures, a study of impact on performance', *Journal of Manufacturing Technology Management*, **16**(4), 373–395.

Martinez, V., Pavlov, A. and Bourne, M. C. S. (2010) 'Reviewing performance: an analysis of the structure and function of performance management reviews', *Production Planning and Control*, **21**(1), 70–83.

Pavlov, A. and Bourne, M. C. S. (2011) 'Explain the effects of performance measurement on performance: an organisational routines perspective', *International Journal of Production and Operations Management*, **31**(1), 101–122.

Using Measures to Manage – Challenging Strategy

10.1 INTRODUCTION

In the last two chapters we discussed the tools for analysing individual performance measure data and have shown you an approach to reviewing performance using the performance planning value chain. In this chapter we will look at a third element, how you use your performance measures to test your success map and challenge your strategy.

Success maps, described in Chapter 2, begin their lives as a model of how you think your organisation works. They start as an initial best guess of the strategic objectives for your business based on your team's knowledge and experience. Once the success map and associated measures are implemented, you will collect data that you can use to check and refine your initial assumptions. In this chapter we show you the tools for testing your success map, highlighting the difficulties and traps you will face when doing it in your own organisation.

There is a mantra: 'happy employees make happy customers make happy shareholders'. In the main, this is true, but you should test this belief and other elements of your success map with your own data. On many occasions when we have seen this testing done in real organisations the results are not as expected. Testing your own success map with real data gives you the opportunity to understand why your organisation does not function as expected and to get real insights about your unique set of circumstances. If you simply take the results of somebody else's work (be those pieces of academic research or studies by consultants) you will miss opportunities and, even worse, you may overlook threats to the future of your business.

We will start by presenting three examples of how companies have linked the different perspectives of the Balanced Scorecard.

10.2 COMPANY EXAMPLES

The classic example of a company building and testing a relationship is Sears, Roebuck and Company, the American department store business. They created the slogans:

- A compelling place to work
- A compelling place to shop
- A compelling place to invest

but they went further than simply using the slogans; they tested their understanding by comparing performance across their stores in the USA. The result was an understanding that:

- People's perceptions, measured by
  - Attitude about the job
  - Attitude about the company
- Drove customer perception, measured by
  - Perception of service helpfulness
  - Perception of the value of the merchandise
- Drove financial performance, measured by
  - Return on assets
  - Revenue growth.

They even went as far as calculating the relationship finding that a 5 unit increase in employee attitude resulted in a 1.3 unit increase in customer perception and a 0.5% increase in revenues (see Figure 10.1). This did not happen overnight. In fact, the senior managers worked hard on the development and testing of their success map for two years. This initially involved the top 65 managers in the business working together and rose to 150 by the end of the process.

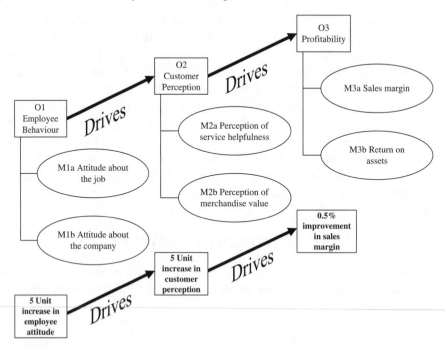

Figure 10.1   The employee–customer profit chain at Sears Roebuck & Co. (adapted from Rucci *et al.*, 1998)

If building the model was not difficult enough, rolling it out across the organisation was a challenge too. They had to overcome the prevailing culture. When managers asked their staff what their job was the answer in over half the cases was about 'protecting the assets of the company'. Satisfying the customer was not on their radar. People did not understand the business either. There was a widespread belief that Sears kept 45 cents in every dollar of merchandise sold, when the reality was nearer 2 cents in the dollar. A huge learning and development programme was needed. To do this they developed learning maps to present hard data about the business and to stimulate a frank discussion about the future. This activity was complemented by 'town hall' meetings to capture ideas and create local action plans.

The process did not stop there; managers also had to change the way they worked. To transform the organisation, Sears created a skills and leadership model that reflected their needs. This model was used for hiring and assessing suitability for promotion. In parallel, Sears University was created and 40 000 managers were put through a transformation programme. The approach was reinforced by the compensation system with the top 200 managers' bonus being readjusted to reflect the need to balance employee, customer and financial success measures. After four years, the company began to reap the benefits of their approach.

There is another interesting example from a retail business about the relationship between customers, sales staff and business performance that illustrates the importance of testing assumptions with your own data. A chain of convenience stores was concerned about losing market share to supermarkets. After considering how the problem could be tackled, the senior management team came to the conclusion that they should create the feel of a 'friendly local corner shop', which the supermarkets were unable to do. They believed the friendliness of staff would be an important aspect of this strategy, helping to create a group of loyal customers. The company embarked on an intensive training programme around the country, teaching staff about the behaviour that would make the customer feel special. They learnt about making eye contact, how to say 'good morning' and about a variety of other tactics designed to leave the customer with a 'warm' feeling about the store.

Following the training programme mystery shoppers were sent into a sample of the stores to check how the programme had worked. They measured the number of eye contacts, 'good mornings' and so on. When all these data were analysed, the management team was shocked by the results. They discovered the stores with the lowest 'customer friendly score' were the best performers in terms of sales per square foot. A further study was conducted and this showed that there were times of day when stores were particularly busy. At these busy times staff in the successful stores knew instinctively that customers wanted quick service with no 'chit chat'. They avoided making too much eye contact and greetings that encouraged conversation and slowed down service to customers. Staff in the less successful stores irritated customers by using their customer care skills when people were in a rush, slowing the flow through the tills and resulting in customers not bothering to wait for service. This understanding resulted in a drive to provide maximum staffing at busy times while still ensuring customer care skills were employed to the full outside those times.

You can probably understand the importance of the relationship between employee satisfaction, customer satisfaction and financial performance in a retail setting. Customers are with staff through most of the buying process, so if handled in the right way, the interaction can be a rewarding experience for everyone. However, let us give you a second example from a business-to-business setting. Milliken is a highly capital intensive manufacturer of industrial fibres including carpet tiles for convention centres and the fibres for car tyres. They found across their 13 European manufacturing sites that they could link their customer satisfaction to financial performance. This was not an immediate link. It took some 18 months for a fall in customer satisfaction to work its way through to having an impact on financial performance, but the relationship was clearly visible. Similarly, when they looked at employee satisfaction, they also found a link to customer satisfaction, not quite as strong this time and with a twelve-month lag (see Figure 10.2). Clive Jeanes, the managing director, kept a close eye on employee and customer satisfaction, as he understood the consequences for future performance.

Predicting success is one use of this approach, but linking the different perspectives together can also help predict failure. Our third example is from Marks & Spencer, which in the mid 1990s was Europe's most profitable retailer. Figure 10.3 shows the customer measures of customer attitude to service and value for money against the share price. The company lost the trust of its customers and as a result there was a slump in sales leading to the share price falling to around a quarter of its original value. Marks & Spencer has now recovered from this position, but for a while the company got into serious difficulties. Although these data were being collected by Marks & Spencer at the time and are now publicly available, there was evidence that this information was not being presented to the board to inform their decision making.

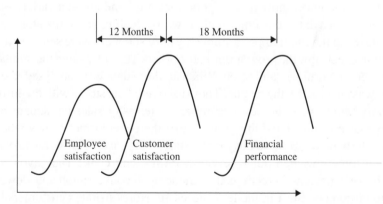

Figure 10.2   The employee satisfaction, customer satisfaction and financial link at Milliken

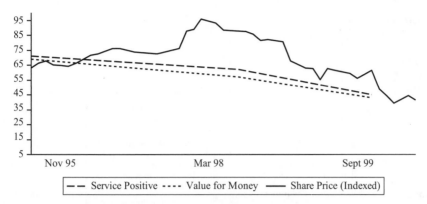

Figure 10.3   M&S customer perception and share price

10.3   TESTING SUCCESS MAPS IN PRACTICE

In this section we will look at the experiences of three companies who tested their success maps.

Shell had an interest in understanding the drivers of performance in their oil products business. Oil products is the business that sells petrol to the retail customer. Shell measured performance across a wide set of perspectives, including the strength of their brand, their environmental credentials, their employee satisfaction and, naturally, their financial performance. There was an interest in understanding the relationship between these different elements. Did the work the company was doing to improve their environmental credentials and citizenship have a positive impact on their brand? Did the brand have a positive impact on financial results? What impact did employee satisfaction have on the performance of the business? However, testing the links was easier said than done. Although Shell had very detailed information on each element of performance broken down by region and country across the world, the data was not in one place. The company had the financial results and the environmental and citizenship data were collected and managed centrally, but brand data were collected and managed by the brand agency. Similarly, employee data were collected and held by a third party survey company. Shell had the data and information it needed but it was not easily accessible. Establishing the data sources and negotiating access can be one of the first tasks in a large organisation, before you can begin the task of looking at the connections between the different performance elements.

Even companies that have all the data in one place often do not test their approach. BA had a strategy of delivering customer satisfaction. They believed this strategy would create a stronger willingness by customers to recommend the airline and make customers more willing to book again. These two outcomes in turn were expected to improve the financial performance of the company (see Figure 10.4). However,

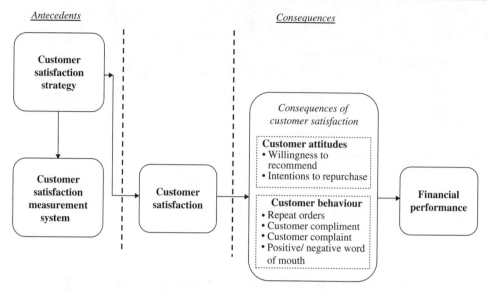

Figure 10.4   Elements in BA's customer satisfaction strategy

although BA was surveying approximately half a million customers a year, the beliefs had not been put to the test with their own data.

BA's customer satisfaction survey asked questions about:

- Initial contact with the airline
- Check-in service
- Departure time
- Cabin crew service
- Meal rating
- Aircraft condition
- Customer satisfaction
- Willingness to recommend.

When the data were interrogated, correlation analysis was used to test statistically the links between the different aspects being measured in the customer survey and the financial performance of the airline (as measured by turnover). Figure 10.5 shows the only statistically significant links found. Although this type of statistical analysis does not prove that one element drives another, it does start to generate evidence of the links between the elements, giving managers information on which to base their decisions. Therefore, although not theoretically correct, we will use the shorthand term 'driver' to describe the connections found.

From the analysis, there was only one significant driver of financial performance and that was willingness to recommend the airline. Similarly, the only significant driver of

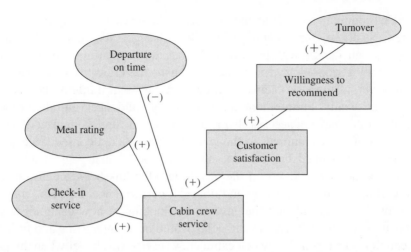

Figure 10.5   Statistically significant relationships found in testing BA's customer satisfaction strategy

willingness to recommend was customer satisfaction and the only significant driver of customer satisfaction was cabin crew service. However, when the drivers of cabin crew service were identified, there was a surprise. Two drivers were fairly obvious, check-in service and meal rating. If passengers have a bad experience on check-in, they are not predisposed to like the cabin crew and vice versa. Similarly, the mealtime is the most intense interaction between the cabin crew and the passengers, so finding the meal rating statistically correlated to cabin crew service could have been expected too. The surprise was departure time, as this was a negative correlation. What this means is that every time a BA plane left late, cabin crew service was better, customer satisfaction increased, willingness to recommend rose and turnover increased! How could this be?

As a result of further investigation, it turned out the effect was created by 'service recovery'; that is to say, the extra effort the cabin crew and other staff make when something goes wrong. If you think about departure delays, the first thing that usually happens is that the captain comes on the address system to apologise for the delay. He usually mentions the cause, which quite often is not the airline's fault. One of the more usual excuses is that 'air traffic control have lost the slot' and the captain goes on to provide an estimate of the delay to manage expectations. This is the cue for the cabin crew to go to work. They bring round magazines and drinks – anything to keep the passengers occupied – as they know an agitated customer will cause a disrupted flight. During the flight, passengers are expected to drink their drink, eat their meal, watch the film and go to sleep, so the cabin crew will do the best they can to relax the passengers. If the captain is good, he will be back to announce that the plane is leaving before the end of his estimated delay, leaving the passengers with the feeling that the delay was not quite as bad as they were expecting.

The added communication from the captain and the service recovery provided by the cabin crew usually has the effect of making the passengers feel more looked after and this increases satisfaction with the airline. It does not happen in every case, so when there is a really serious delay, no matter how hard the crew try, customers will be upset. However, as these problems are usually in the small minority the relationship still holds statistically. Furthermore, airlines usually build slack into their schedules, so a late departure may not necessarily mean a late arrival, and the impact of a delayed departure can often be minimal. In this way, the unexpected consequences of a late departure can be explained, but what does this mean for the management of the airline?

It was important to make use of the insight into the link between customer satisfaction, willingness to recommend and financial performance. Ensuring that all BA planes leave late is clearly not the answer, but looking at how cabin crew service might be improved when there is not a delay would be an interesting and fruitful first line of enquiry. The airline knew that cabin crew service was better when things went wrong, and considered how they could encourage this improved service more often, especially when things were going well.

Our third example is taken from a builders' merchant, a company selling building materials to a wide range of builders. Figure 10.6 shows the links the management believed occurred in their success map. They believed that if they could increase the length of time staff stayed with the company, they would be able to train them and increase their skills and knowledge. These skills and knowledge would lead to better customer service and better customer service would result in increased customer

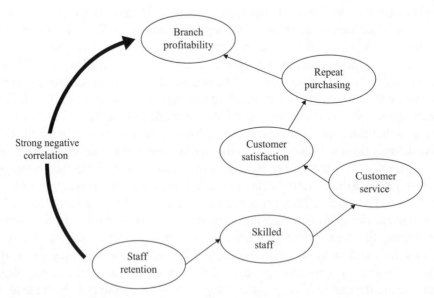

Figure 10.6   The testing of a success map for a builders' merchant

satisfaction. Customer satisfaction, in turn, would result in the builder returning to buy again, improving the financial performance of the business. However, when data were collected from across all their branches in the UK they found an unexpected significant negative correlation between the length of service of employees and the financial performance of the branch. This suggested that the quicker staff left the company the more profitable it would be!

Why was this so? Could it be that long term employees were paid more so were more costly, undermining profitability of the branch? Were longer serving employees lazier or less motivated than new employees? If these suppositions were true, there were serious repercussions for the business. However, further analysis revealed that there was nothing wrong with the success map itself, but it was swamped by the influence of another factor. The cause was economic activity. In the south of England, there was a high level of economic activity, combined with high levels of building work, so the branches were more profitable. There was also a strong labour market, which meant that if staff did not like their jobs they soon left the company, making the employee turnover higher. In the north, economic activity was at a much lower level, so there were not as many job opportunities, staff hung on to the jobs they had and staff length of service was higher. However, in the north, because of the low level of economic activity, building activity was lower and branches were less profitable. If the impact of economic activity was removed this spurious correlation disappeared.

The insight for the company was the size and impact of the difference in economic activity. They had not fully appreciated this. They had been judging all their branches as if they were facing the same economic conditions when, in practice, branches in the north were having to work extremely hard to make a profit, while in the south it was almost impossible not to do well.

The case examples above have highlighted:

1. Issues with data availability
2. Unexpected consequences resulting in new insights
3. Spurious correlations created by other external factors.

In the next section, we will describe other technical issues that you should be aware of when you use your data to validate your success map.

10.4   TESTING IN THEORY AND PRACTICE

There are four fundamental assumptions that most people make when they attempt to validate their success map using correlation analysis. These are:

1. The relationships are linear.
2. The objectives can be adequately measured.

3. The impact of a change is almost immediate.
4. The relationship is one way.

10.4.1 Linear relationships

The standard correlation analysis normally used when reviewing success maps assumes that the relationship between the variables is linear. For example, in the Sears, Roebuck and Company case above, the formula was stated as a 5 unit increase in employee attitude delivering a 1.3 unit increase in customer perception and a 5% increase in turnover. However, this is often not the case.

We will take a car as an example. An increase in the quality of the car, such as better reliability, may increase your satisfaction, but at the highest levels of quality, you will reach a point when additional quality does not increase your satisfaction, so the relationship stops being linear. Xerox found that customer satisfaction was a good indicator of whether or not customers would buy again. Customers who were in the top box (that is to say, they rated themselves *very satisfied*) were six times as likely to buy again from Xerox than those who were only *satisfied*. This is a nonlinear relationship.

You should expect that the relationship between your success map measures to be nonlinear as you reach the extremes and it is always useful to plot the data on a graph so you can see what is happening, as well as conducting the statistical tests such as correlation.

10.4.2 Measurement

In your success map you show links between the different objectives. You will show customer satisfaction resulting in repeat orders. How do you know what the level of customer satisfaction is? The only way you can establish the level of customer satisfaction is by measuring it. This is true of repeat orders too. Therefore, when you test your success map, you are not testing whether customer satisfaction is correlated to repeat orders, you are testing whether the measure of customer satisfaction is correlated to the measure of repeat orders.

Let us explain this by referring to Figure 10.7. You may assume that you are testing the relationship shown as X1, whereas in fact you are testing the relationship shown as Y1. This may seem just a little academic, but you must be sure that when you have a success map the measures are valid. This means that M1a is a valid measure for O1 and M2a for O2. In Figure 10.7, this will depend on the measure you choose. The customer satisfaction survey (M1a) may be a good predictor of repeat orders (M2a), but will customer complaints (M1b) be a good predictor of repeat orders, whether they be measured by their frequency (M2a) or their value (M2b)?

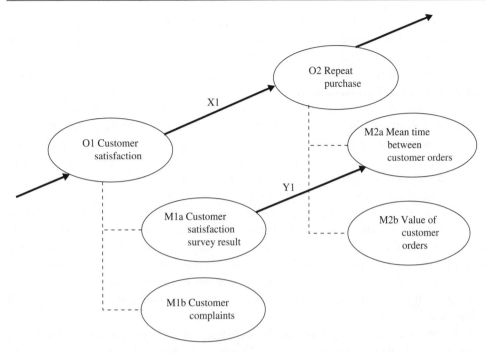

Figure 10.7   The links between objectives and measures in part of a success map

The message is that, when you test your success map, ensure that you have valid measures of your objectives. If you do not find the relationships you expect, check the validity of your measures before you do anything else.

10.4.3 Time lags

As we discussed in Chapter 9, there are delays between decisions and actions and between actions and performance improvement. In some simple circumstances, the change may be immediate. Once a new system is installed and the training is done, your call centre staff productivity may increase very rapidly. However, if you improve the quality of your product, it may take years for your customers to fully appreciate the change and adjust their buying habits. It may take even longer for others in the market who do not usually buy your product to react. You should try to estimate the time lags that you expect to occur, although this adds a further complication in testing your success map.

10.4.4 Cause and effect

When you test the links in the success map you assume the relationship goes one way. Sears, Roebuck and Company talked about employee attitude driving customer satisfaction. Are there situations where customer satisfaction drives employee satisfaction? This cause and effect relationship should always be on your mind and in fact some of these relationships can be circular.

In Figure 10.8, we show the result of a new designer being employed in a clothing business. This designer has a good eye for the latest trends and creates a range of products the customers really like. Customers flood into the stores to buy the goods and staff morale is lifted. Shops are filled with the buzz of activity. The increase in morale rubs off on the customers and a virtuous circle is created. However, also think about the management cycle. Management sees the result of the new designs and decides to spend more on designers and new products. If this works, these new designs and products may attract more customers, producing an even bigger virtuous circle.

However, these activities can go the other way. Figure 10.9 shows what happens when management decides their margins are too small. To save costs they decide to cut back on the design input. Customers are underwhelmed by the new season's offering and so stay away. Staff become disillusioned by the reaction of their customers and morale drops. This destructive cycle reduces profitability even further, so management cuts cost again and if the cycle is not interrupted, the organisation will spiral down to failure.

What we are describing here are the dynamics of the systems you are working with. System dynamic diagrams such as Figures 10.8 and 10.9 are effective tools to take you beyond the linear nature of your success map to the next level of analysis. You can use them with sophisticated software to predict outcomes, but when you map a complex system with all the positive and negative feedback loops and system lags (delays between the causes and effects) you will rapidly reach the stage where

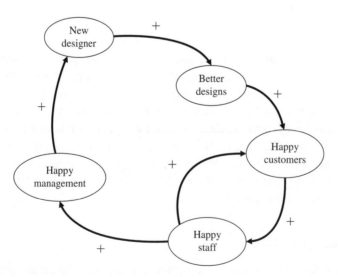

Figure 10.8   A virtuous circle of relationship

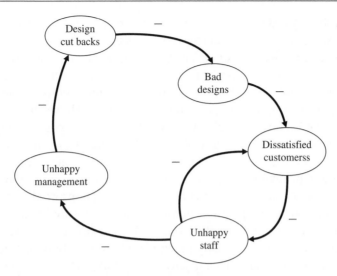

Figure 10.9   A destructive circle of relationship

you can see the result but not understand why it is happening. Our belief is that if you create a model that management does not understand, you will have difficulty in getting them to use it. We recommend you keep it simple. We also find that linear success maps are usually easier to use in order to communicate strategy across the organisation. System dynamic approaches can be extremely powerful, but use them appropriately.

10.5   BEHAVIOURAL ISSUES

Testing a success map is a learning exercise, so you will need to be careful how you act on what you have learnt. Your organisation is not a machine; it is more like an organism. The success map gives you some good insights but it does not give you a set of levers that you can pull.

Here is an example. A machine tool manufacturer detected a relationship across the following chain, from the number of customer visits made, to the number of quotations raised, to the number of orders received. This led the management to believe that if they could increase the number of customer visits, they would, in time, increase the number of orders. If all things are equal, this may be true. However, from the perspective of the sales force, they were suddenly faced with a real push to see more customers. The temptation was to slot in a quick visit just to increase the numbers. They ended up quoting for work earlier in the process than normal and, because customers subsequently changed their minds, they often had to quote a second time before the order was won. The consequence was that the quotation department was overrun with work, while the number of orders received remained unchanged. Eventually management realised what was happening and changed their focus.

Interestingly, some twelve months later, the market changed and there was a sudden increase in customer requests for visits. Now the sales force was really pushed to visit all their customers in time, the requests for quotations flooded in and the quotations department was again put under real pressure. However, on this occasion the orders followed. Thus a model may be predictive, but if your actions change the fundamental nature of the model, it will not always behave as you expect.

In practice, it is the 'hard measures' in your organisation that are often most susceptible to the type of behaviour or 'gaming' described in the example above. Measures such as the number of visits made, the number of quotations produced and the time to respond to customer complaints can all be easily measured and easily manipulated. Softer measures taken from attitude surveys, such as customer satisfaction and employee satisfaction, are less easily manipulated, especially if an external agency is used to do the measurement. That is why the big links between employee satisfaction, customer satisfaction and profitability are so often used.

10.6   CONCLUSION

Testing your success map can give valuable insights into how your organisation actually works, but you will have to do this cautiously. There may be people in the organisation who want to undermine your approach and finding an invalid link in your success map may be their perfect opportunity to attack it. Further, you cannot spend all your time testing, you need to be pragmatic and go with what you believe. Also, you should remember, the relationships you find will not last forever, so you should plan to re-test your success map at an appropriate regularity for your particular business environment.

FURTHER READING

Neely, A. and Al-Najjar, M. (2006) 'Management learning not management control: the true role of performance measurement', *California Management Review*, **48**(3) (Spring), 101–114.

Rucci, A. J., Kirn, S. P. and Quinn, R. T. (1998) 'The employee–customer profit chain at Sears', *Harvard Business Review*, **Jan./Feb.**, 82–97.

11

Keeping Your Measurement Process up to Date

11.1 INTRODUCTION

Once your performance measurement system is in place and yielding results it is tempting to let it become part of the woodwork. Resist the temptation, it is dangerous. Your measurement system must reflect the current situation – if it does not it will lose credibility and, worse still, it will mean that new strategies are held back by the old performance measures.

In this chapter, we will describe the different ways in which you can keep your system up to date and negotiate some of the barriers that get in the way.

11.2 KEEPING THE PROCESS UP TO DATE

There are four main ways of keeping your performance measurement process up to date (see Figure 11.1). Starting from the bottom up these are:

1. **Reviewing targets** on a regular basis and updating them to reflect changes in budgets, increasing performance levels and changing customer requirements, as well as the results from competitor analysis or external benchmarking.
2. **Developing the measures** – as measures affect behaviour they need to be revised from time to time to overcome any dysfunctional behaviour and to reflect new circumstances.
3. **Reviewing the success map and measures** arising from it in line with changes in strategy.
4. **Challenging the strategy** – the initial success map reflects the assumptions and beliefs of the people who created it. However, once the measures have been implemented and used, you should use them to challenge the success map and, through doing that, challenge your strategy.

We will describe these in turn and provide examples of these different methods in action.

11.3 WHEN DO YOU UPDATE TARGETS?

Accountants normally operate on an annual cycle, changing the budget at least once a year. This is minimum frequency for reviewing targets, as they should always be

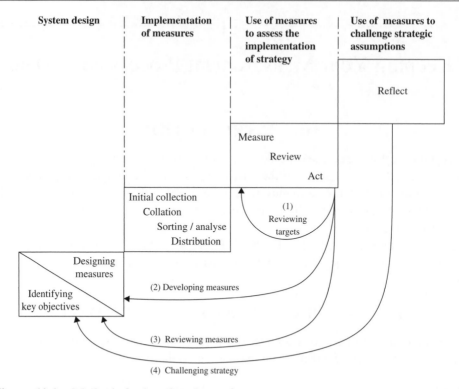

Figure 11.1   Methods for keeping the performance measurement process up to date

aligned to the budget. Many organisations have moved to quarterly rolling budgets, requiring targets to be reviewed and updated much more frequently. Targets need to be reviewed when an event triggers change, regardless of any other cycle.

11.3.1 Budgetary changes

Targets are updated annually during the normal budgeting process. It is usual for the sales income target for the next financial year to be reviewed, reflecting economic conditions, customer demand and competitor activity. The point here is that targets are interrelated. If you increase sales volumes, you will need to increase production output. This may require additional capacity or increased productivity. The budgeting round should prompt a series of changes through the organisation that reflect not only changes in the budget but also in the nonfinancial performance measures.

11.3.2 Performance improvement

Regularly attaining or surpassing a target suggests it needs to be reviewed and possibly revised, but it should not automatically trigger an increase in the target that has been set. All improvements have an associated cost and you need to balance the cost against the business and customer benefits.

The Jade Garden

A Chinese restaurant had a target of delivering all orders to the town centre within 25 minutes of the order being taken. They used the target as a selling point to customers, promising not to charge if the delivery took longer than 25 minutes. Having reached an almost perfect on-time delivery performance within the 25 minutes, the company did not reduce its target – 25 minutes was a reasonable time for the customer to wait and there was no overriding customer or business benefit from reducing the target. In fact, the costs of providing the extra resources to deliver more quickly were simply prohibitive.

11.3.3 Changes driven by customers

Customers will drive change in two situations: firstly, when an improved performance opens a new market opportunity for them and they require the better performance from you to exploit the situation, and, secondly, when they respond positively to competitor improvements, causing you to respond appropriately to keep their business.

11.3.4 Changes driven by external benchmarking

The sudden discovery that others' performance is better than yours will result in the review and possible change in targets.

Shock of benchmarking

The Danish plastics manufacturer, Borealis, used to set its cost targets based on the previous year's performance, as many companies do. When they conducted an external benchmarking exercise they realised their performance was not quite as good as they had thought. From then on, targets were set according to their performance against their key competitors.

11.3.5 Changes driven by need for competitive advantage

It can be hard to identify and secure competitive advantage for your business but it can sometimes be achieved by delivering very high performance on just a few specific performance measures. To do this, your target against those measures will require a step change, which will probably mean finding a different way of doing things. There is a limit to how much you can improve performance without changing the way you do something.

Delivering competitive advantage

Milliken's industrial carpet business relied primarily on gaining specification through architectural practices, the vast majority of which were located in central London. They wanted to improve their responsiveness to these architects as part of their drive to increase specifications. They had been achieving a good response by using an overnight courier service but they were finding that architects really wanted samples within a couple of hours of making a telephone call. Their overnight service did not provide a significantly better performance than their competitors' and if they could respond faster, they would achieve a competitive advantage, at least in the short term. Using motorbike couriers for key accounts was an option, but that would be expensive. The solution was to employ a van and driver. The van was stacked with all the samples and simply drove around central London all day responding to the latest requests. Architects were impressed that they could call in the morning and have their sample when they got back from lunch. This service was very well received by architects and encouraged them always to request samples from Milliken, resulting in increased specification of their products.

11.4   REVISING MEASURES

There is a conflict in performance measurement between the need to have a stable set of measures to track longer term trends and changes in performance over time and the need to change scope and definitions as circumstances change.

Change is needed when the measure is simply wrong or can now be improved in the light of experience – when people are 'playing games' in order to achieve it or when it must be adapted to meet changing circumstances. In fact it is quite common for measures to be found wanting when first installed. There is a classic example of this from the airline industry. At the end of their flight the last thing passengers want is to have to wait a long time for their luggage to be delivered. Conscious of this the company decided to improve the speed of delivery of bags from the hold of the aircraft to the luggage carousel in the airport and they introduced a new performance measure to support this aim. On the first day a team of baggage handlers was seen chatting while they awaited the arrival of the baggage carts from the plane. When the first cart arrived the team leader leapt into action, grabbing a bag and rushing to place it on the conveyor. Then he ambled back to the group. After that the whole team began to unload the carts at their usual speed. What caused this strange behaviour? The company had chosen as its measure 'the time taken for the first bag to reach the conveyor'.

In some cases you cannot immediately leap ahead to measure what you really want. You have to use the measures to create a certain behaviour and then build on that. Here is an example from a Japanese car manufacturer whose management team felt they needed a greater number of useful suggestions from their UK workforce.

The company implemented a measure of the number of suggestions received and this worked well. Over the next couple of months, the number of suggestions increased, but there was now a bottleneck in the engineering department, which had to review all the suggestions. As a result, the key measure was revised to 'the number of suggestions reviewed'. Doing this moved the focus of the measurement away from the workforce making the suggestions to the efficiency of the review process. The review process started to improve, but in time the company realised they needed to do something about the quality of the suggestions they were receiving. The definition therefore changed again. The measure became the 'percentage of suggestions accepted'. A suggestion may have been accepted but that did not mean it was implemented, so a further redefinition was required. The 'number of suggestions implemented' became the key measure. Finally, someone questioned the real purpose of increasing the number of suggestions and suggested that the measure should relate to the benefit accrued to the company in terms of cost saving.

If the company had started with the final measure they would never have created the behaviour that allowed them to reach their final goal. Therefore, start with a measure that is appropriate for your circumstances but be prepared to refine it as the situation changes.

11.5   REVIEWING THE MEASURES IN LINE WITH YOUR SUCCESS MAP

It is essential to review your success map at least once a year to check that your assumptions are correct and to ensure that measures and strategy are still aligned. When your strategy changes, your measures need to be changed accordingly.

Here is an example. If a company is moving from competing on price to competing on responsiveness to customers, the set of measures must change. The new measures will need to focus on activities and levels of performance required to achieve quicker response levels rather than on reducing cost. Some existing measures will be dropped and new ones introduced, a few of which may even be at odds with the originals. In this case you will have to make sure you do not have a whole set of entrenched performance measures that will work against the new strategy. In manufacturing, machine utilisation and labour efficiency are essential elements in cost competitiveness. This can be achieved by introducing longer production runs, minimising the changeover costs and gaining all the benefits from stable production. Responsiveness, on the other hand, requires excess capacity and, at times, underutilised resources to provide the flexibility the customers now need. It requires smaller job lots and batch sizes.

If you introduce a measure of responsiveness, such as 'reduction in average lead-time' at the top level, it may well look as if you are implementing your strategy when, in fact, you are not. If you do not remove the supporting process measures such as 'labour utilisation' and 'machine efficiency', the behaviour in the production area will not change and the old strategy will prevail. The lower level measures must align with the new strategy and if they do not, the chain in the success map will be broken and the strategy will remain virtually unchanged.

It is essential to work through your success map again and rebuild it, asking 'What do we want to achieve?' and 'How will we achieve it?' occasionally challenging your analysis by asking 'Why are we doing this?' and 'Does this link to what we are trying to achieve at the higher level?'

11.6   REFLECTING ON YOUR STRATEGY

On an assignment to a west of England manufacturing company we asked the Managing Director what he wanted from his proposed new performance measurement and management system. After a long debate we discovered the business was reasonably successful (our factory visit showed it was very well run) but not fulfilling its true potential. Finally, the MD asked us to meet his senior management team, which had gathered in the room next door and left us to debate the merits of the new system with them. 'Why are you here?' asked the HR Director. 'We're here to implement a new performance measurement system linking directly to your strategy,' we said. 'Well, that's a great idea,' she replied. 'And it would be good if we had a strategy.' Six out of the eight directors did not think the company had a clear strategy. When we returned to the MD's office we discussed this with him. 'We do have a strategy!' was his response and he took a ring binder from a shelf in which was a document headed 'Company Strategy' and the document was signed by the directors.

In most organisations the strategy is not understood or communicated. It is often written, forgotten and brought out again the next year when it needs to be updated. In this case the Managing Director had gone further than this. He had written the strategy, asked his directors to read and review it and then sign it. This they had duly done. But had they understood it? Had they agreed to it? Or had they simply done as they were asked? Certainly from our conversation, they appeared either to have forgotten about the document or to have ignored it.

The performance process starts with strategy and gaining commitment to it before you even think about translating the strategy into a set of performance measures. The previous chapter looks in detail at how you can challenge your strategy and ensure it is working through the use of performance measures. The point here is to emphasise that in creating a set of measures and displaying them around the company, you are saying these activities are important because you are measuring them. Creating a set of performance measures closely aligned to the strategy is an effective way of communicating that strategy right across the organisation. It makes the strategy live and it shows people how they fit into achieving it.

There is also a 'health warning'. If your performance measures do not reflect your strategy, your people are most likely to follow the measures and not the strategy. Therefore you must ensure that the measures always reflect the strategy and that when you update the strategy, the measures are also updated to reflect the change in direction. Updating your measures is a very effective way of communicating a new strategic direction throughout the business.

11.7   CHALLENGING STRATEGY

When you build a success map you rely on the team's understanding of the business and the collective experience and assumptions about how the business works. Sometimes these are correct, but often when assumptions are tested using the data collected for the performance measure you find something has been missed. That is an opportunity to learn.

As we said in Chapter 10, the classic case is presented in the *Harvard Business Review* and relates to Sears, Roebuck and Company. In the mid 1990s they looked at the impact of employee satisfaction on customer satisfaction, and on how their customer satisfaction had an impact on their sales revenues and financial performance. However, unlike many companies who made this link, they collected the data from around stores right across the country and tested the hypothesis. This meant they could predict the impact of a five unit increase in employee satisfaction on customer impression and financial performance.

The link between employee and customer satisfaction in retailing appears obvious, because many employees are in direct face-to-face contact with customers. Interestingly it holds true in other businesses as well. Clive Jeanes (formerly MD of Milliken in Europe) used to explain that, in his capital intensive business, there was about an 18 months delay between a fall in customer satisfaction and a downturn in financial performance. He also found a relationship between employee satisfaction and customer satisfaction, although the relationship was weaker – there was a 12 month delay in this case.

Gallup (as discussed in Chapter 12) have shown a relationship between employee satisfaction and attributes of business performance across a wide range of businesses in the UK and USA, but we would argue that you should use your own data to test your own success map. We explained how you test the links in your success map in Chapter 10. Remember, if you talk about a strategy, people will test your commitment to that strategy, as you can see from the example below.

The CEO of one of the UK high street banks outlined his strategy at a shareholders' meeting. His basic message was that happy employees make happy customers, which in turn creates good financial performance. The first question from the floor was from an analyst who wanted to know how well the bank was placed on the *Sunday Times* list of best employers. Unfortunately, the CEO did not know about the best employer list or that the company did not appear. It was reported that he exploded angerally after the meeting, but the moral of the story is that people will test your commitment to your strategy, so it has to be much more than a set of words.

We have described how you need to review the targets, the measures, the set of measures and the strategy itself. In the next section we will touch on some of the barriers to doing this.

11.8   OVERCOMING BARRIERS TO UPDATING YOUR SYSTEM

The reward system (discussed in more detail in Chapter 7) can be a major hindrance to updating your measurement process. While linking incentives and bonuses to your measurement system focuses minds and can stimulate improvements in performance, it can also make the measures difficult to change. Increasing targets from one year to the next will be met with resistance because this means the target is harder to reach and it may result in staff playing games with the target, just achieving the required figure so the bonus is paid, but not overachieving in case the target is raised significantly the next year. If this happens right across the company, it will cause significant performance issues. Changing the measures included in the bonus system will naturally cause concern among staff as they have become accustomed to the status quo. New measures will take them out of their comfort zone and will mean they have to put extra time and effort into what they are doing. You may meet resistance, which you will have to manage.

Functional comparisons can also cause problems when attempting to update measures. This is particularly true in larger companies when there can be a conflict between main board directors with functional responsibility and local business unit managers. The problem is that these directors may use their own measures of success to compare the performance of different parts of the business. In operations, plant utilisation is regularly used as a measure, but if the local business unit is competing on flexibility, plant utilisation may well not be the most important measure to use. This conflict between head office and local priorities can result in measures not being changed or, worse, two conflicting sets of measures being used at the same time.

One very obvious but sometimes overlooked problem in updating measures is the practical issue of IT systems and their capability to do what you want. It is likely that updating the measure will require changes to the data capture or calculations. It is fine to agree a change but you also need to ensure it can be done. In one company we know, an on-time delivery measure was delayed for several months while the company waited for the next release of the software needed to calculate it.

One very common reason why measurement processes are not updated is quite simply lack of management time. There is always pressure on management time, and reviewing the measurement system can be overlooked, delayed and even forgotten. It is one of those jobs that appears less important than dealing with immediate issues, but it is part of the longer term development of the business and so it is important. It may not affect your performance adversely in the shorter term but it probably will as time goes on. For that reason, as with all the tasks that are seen as 'essential but not urgent', regular updating meetings should become part of the process itself.

We will now present an example of how Faccenda managed the cycle of development and measurement over several years, keeping the two aligned while developing their ability to deploy their evolving strategy.

11.8.1 Faccenda

In this section we present a case example covering one company's journey through four cycles of strategy development. Starting from their initial attempt at identifying a clear business strategy and a balanced scorecard, Faccenda developed their approach through their annual planning and budgeting cycle, creating focus and an executable success map.

Faccenda Group is a successful, privately owned UK business and has been a leading supplier of fresh chicken products into the UK market for over 40 years. Established by Robin Faccenda in 1962, the company is a fully integrated business employing over 1,800 people across the UK in hatcheries, farms, feed mills and processing plants. Faccenda have an impressive range of customers and boast an excellent track record of strong customer relations and high quality service, but as market consolidation has produced bigger competitors and large customers demanding high levels of service, the business has recognised the need to develop its strategic and business processes to ensure it remains a successful business with a long term future.

We will start by describing a little of the company's history in developing their strategy and scorecard. Then we will move on to describe how they created a realistic and implementable strategy reflecting the future needs of the business and will look at the key elements that made this possible. Finally, we will reflect on the learning process and what the company has gained from taking this approach.

The development cycles

Faccenda began their current programme of strategy development, performance measurement and strategy implementation back in October 2007 when the senior team reviewed their value propositions. As a direct result of this review, they decided the company had to be a leader at the 'value' end of the market and that they must be committed to operational excellence. The 'value leader' proposition required Faccenda to provide the best value for a specific quality and service level. This drove the company to reconsider where they should compete and, just as importantly, the markets they should ignore. This they termed 'what's in our box'. The company decided to focus on the core poultry market producing standard chicken, which requires consistency in quality and excellent customer service levels, while staying out of the further processing and premium sectors (e.g. organic). The senior team realised at the end of this strategic review that although consistency and service levels were good, the company was not competitive on costs. This led to a restructuring process and the rationalisation of the factory operations to focus on large scale plants with good long term economies of scale.

Between October 2008 and February 2009 a success map was created capturing the new strategy and reflecting the customer value propositions. Over the next twelve months, a scorecard was implemented. However, this scorecard was not comprehensive. It was implemented from the bottom up so it reflected current business operational excellence requirements rather than the longer term strategic goals. Furthermore, the strategy map and the scorecard were not truly linked because the strategy map had not been developed into a set of deliverable strategic objectives. The result was a good operational scorecard that delivered the consistency, service levels and price position the company needed to reach, but it did not give sufficient emphasis to actions the company would need to take to secure its long term future.

In May 2010, the strategy was reviewed and refined. This time the lessons had been learned and the executive realised that there were no shortcuts. While the overall strategy remained similar with just a few refinements, a far clearer approach was taken to describing the future shape and scale of the business over the next five years. The resulting strategy map was defined in such a way that it could be translated into projects, objectives and measures with a clear link to the strategy. It was this commitment to thoroughness and clear thinking and the willingness to engage the senior management team in the process that made the difference. This latest round of planning took three months to complete, but created the level of detail necessary for the strategy to be implemented.

Articulating a strategy that can be implemented

The strategy to achieve 'value leadership' was depicted in ten major categories in the success map. As Andrew Brodie, Faccenda's HR Director, commented, 'It's like looking down on to the top floor of a one hundred storey high sky scraper. All you can see is the roof, but there are all the floors below that need to be created if the strategy is going to be executed. This was a huge step forward from our first strategy map, which, following this analogy, was more of a bungalow.'

For each of the top level objectives, the senior team worked through what the objective meant, how it was to be delivered and then itemised the list of actions that needed to be taken to make the change from where the company was presently to the future state. Creating a long list of actions and projects like this for each objective meant that there was overlap and some confusion. This was resolved by developing groupings of strategic actions. The team took the original list of actions and created their own grouping before coming together as a team to debate the final list. As a result, the ten top level scorecard objectives were translated into six groupings. Now came the time for them to communicate their deliberations to a wider audience.

Translating strategy into action

The results from the strategy mapping process and groupings were presented to the senior management team at an off-site meeting, so everyone was aware of what was being planned.

The next stage was to create six teams to put the strategy into action. These were the 'strategy delivery teams'. They comprised a few senior managers and were each led by a director. Their role was to transform the list of actions in their particular grouping into a project plan with clear deliverables, priorities, resources and budget requirements. The result was a programme covering the next 12 to 18 months, with the remaining activities and projects being kept for the next planning cycle. The plan was then reviewed by the board and agreed for execution, starting in May 2011.

This planning process had a number of important benefits:

1. The strategy now became inextricably linked to the implementation plan for the next 12 months. Figure 11.2 shows how this link was documented for all to see.
2. By translating the ten business functional objectives into strategy implementation groupings, barriers between those functions were broken down because the resulting programmes were cross-departmental and spanned boundaries.
3. The plan was holistic in that it represented all the improvement and development work planned for the company for the next period. This meant that workloads could be assessed, bottlenecks identified and realistic decisions could be made about what was to be done.
4. It created a clear distinction between the operational scorecard and the executive scorecard. Operations still had to deliver the high levels of efficiency, service and consistency required by the customer, but the executive now had a scorecard that could be used to track the execution of the strategy. Developing the company's capabilities to remain the category leader as the market developed was a clear goal. Instead of breathing down the necks of the operations managers, the board had a specific role in developing the future, which was targeted and measurable.
5. Finally, there was a much wider understanding of what the organisation needed to achieve.

Strategic Objective		Execution		
Top Line	Sub-Objective	Measure	Target	Deliverable
We will be recognised as a sustainable 'Employer Of Choice' and a 'Great Place to Work' by our customers and employees and in the local community	Achieving recognised external benchmarks (e.g. ETI/IIP) through rigorous assessment and continuous improvement			Simplified terms and conditions of employment together with improved benefits offer including some flexibility and good quality working environment
	Meeting internal standards as measured through employee satisfaction audit score, turnover & absence KPIs and safety indices.			Achieve a clear, planned communication framework both internally with employees and externally with customers, suppliers, local population and recruitment agencies.
				Structured training at all levels of employment which is accredited and formally recognised where possible
				Creation of a strong, recognised and positive employee brand that is recognised by key stakeholders
	Develop reputation as a great place to work with local community			Implementation of an effective safety management system and culture
				Consistent rigorous process for identifying talent and development needs

Figure 11.2   Linking strategy, measures and targets with execution plans at Faccenda

As Andrew Brodie put it: 'Our executive scorecard just used to be the sum of our operating scorecards. In practice, scorecards at different levels shouldn't be perfectly aligned. If they are, one of them is probably obsolete. The operating scorecard has to be very clear about what has to be achieved today and tomorrow, whereas the executive scorecard should reflect what we need to change to continue to survive and be successful well into the future.' Andrew Brodie believes a good measure of the worth of your scorecard is the answer to the question 'How many people in the organisation can talk convincingly about your strategy?' In this regard he believes the company probably moved from two such people to 15. A large number of people know there is a strategy and a considerable number can understand it, but the test is how many are confident enough to present it and take detailed questions on it. Andrew Brodie also believes the process created a more united executive team, focused and confident in their ability to lead the business in the next few years.

It was estimated that a whole month of all the executives' time at Faccenda had been dedicated to the success mapping and strategy execution process in the last year. 'It's not rocket science,' according to Andrew Brodie, 'but there are no short cuts. You have to work through the whole process of breaking down your objectives into projects and then recombining them again to create a comprehensive programme of work. That's quite hard to do and it's easy to get lost in the process, but you must do it to get the clarity you need.'

The 2011 strategy review cycle will start again in May, but it will be a lighter version this year. The senior team will reflect again on their strategy and will probably tweak their implementation plan. However, they need to keep the cycle going because a full review will be needed in 2012 to refocus the company again on its priorities.

Factors needed for success

There were two prerequisites for success. Firstly, there has to be sponsorship from the CEO or MD. 'They don't have to do all the work, but they are the driver behind the project and they make sure it keeps moving forward,' commented Andrew Brodie. 'Secondly, someone has to be capable of structuring the process. Ideally, this should be someone internally who has the appropriate knowledge and skills, although an external consultant can help facilitate the process. The more that is done in house by the senior team the greater the commitment, so use consultants and support staff sparingly.'

In this case there were also two critical factors the senior team needed to understand and agree. Firstly, they had to decide where the company would compete, where it was going to gain competitive advantage and where the business needed to be in five years' time. There was a realisation that if there was no clarity about the priorities and focus for the long term, the company could sleepwalk into crisis. Twenty years ago there were many significant companies in this sector; now there are only five and with similar consolidation in the major supermarkets, there is still competitive pressure to consolidate the industry further.

The second factor they came to understand was just how important it was to ensure the strategy was implemented throughout the entire organisation of the business. Faccenda has an extremely long and complex supply chain, from farmers raising the chickens to the supermarket shelves. The process cannot be turned on and off at the flick of a switch. There are lots of interrelated steps across functions and each of these has to be right. People must work together as a team to survive in this business. The recognition of how important it was to create an integrated team culture in the business had important consequences for design of the organisation, for internal communications and even for the reward system.

Reflection

The senior management team at Faccenda identified five key insights after reflecting on what they had achieved:

1. You have to be students of your business, understand where you are in the market, what your core competencies are and where you have or could have competitive advantage. Without this you are lost.
2. There is a reason why 75% of businesses fail to execute their strategy effectively; it requires a great deal of commitment to detail and there are no shortcuts.

You have to enjoy the journey as much as you want to reach the destination. Executing strategy is not achieved on an away day; it takes time and commitment over a prolonged period.

3. Developing a strategy and executing a process is not a one-off project. You should think of it as a cycle, just like continuous improvement, where you get better each time.

4. The key to success is to appreciate that strategy does not implement itself; it has to be planned, resourced and managed. In doing this, the establishment of a clear line of sight between the projects, their deliverables and the goals of the organisation is essential. A success map is only the very first step in doing this. Using Andrew Brodie's analogy, the success map is just the top floor of your skyscraper and you have to build the tower underneath it to be successful.

5. You cannot rely on an external consultancy to do this. The strength of this approach is the internal engagement, the 15 people who can explain the strategy and the 100 that can understand it, with both being real students of the business.

Finally, it takes a lot of executive time, but as the Managing Director put Andy Dawkins it: 'If the executive team isn't defining the direction of the business – what are they doing?'

Case conclusion

This case demonstrates the learning process that a company can go through if it is unswerving in its approach to strategy and performance measurement. The early insights of the first year in the cycle were important for understanding where the company was and the direction in which it wished to travel. Short term decisions and actions secured the future of the company by ensuring that it was operationally efficient and delivering to its customers. As the market developed, customer requirements continued to evolve and the senior team at Faccenda understood the need to develop their capabilities so they could continue to be successful. Moving from an operational scorecard to an executive scorecard that reflected these new capabilities was critical to their development and in doing so they created a programme that will drive the actions to make change happen.

As we said in Chapter 1, performance is comparative. You must balance current performance with requirements for the future and you need to look at different perspectives. This case shows how important understanding the customers' perspective is for Faccenda's development. It shows how the company focused on current performance to reposition itself, but how that did not guarantee the future because it did not take account of the evolving market and changes in customer requirements. The steps the company is now taking ensure that it is moving in the right direction, but the executive is aware that all performance is comparative and they have to keep reviewing their strategy if they are to remain in front of their competitors.

11.9   SUMMARY

In this chapter we have focused on how important it is to keep your measures up to date. Most companies have a cycle of reviewing their performance, but you will need to introduce processes to ensure that your targets, measure definitions, sets of measures and strategies are regularly reviewed. These should not all be done at the same time, but we would recommend that each of these processes should have been reviewed at least once over the course of a year.

FURTHER READING

Al-Najjar, M. and Neely, A. (1998) 'Customer satisfaction drivers and the link to financial performance: case study', in *Performance Measurement – Theory and Practice Conference*, Cambridge.

Bourne, M. C. S., Mills, J. F., Wilcox, M., Neely, A. D. and Platts, K. W. (2000) 'Designing, implementing and updating performance measurement systems', *International Journal of Production and Operations Management*, **20**(7), 754–771.

Buckingham, M. and Coffman, C. (1999) *First Break All the Rules: What the World's Greatest Managers Do Differently*, Simon & Schuster, London.

Rucci, A. J., Kirn, S. P. and Quinn, R. T. (1998) 'The employee–customer profit chain at Sears', *Harvard Business Review*, **Jan./Feb.**, 82–97.

Measuring Performance of People

12.1 INTRODUCTION

People are the most important element in the performance of an organisation – whatever the size, whatever the sector. Good strategy and processes are essential, but it is people who are developing and implementing the strategy and devising and using the processes. No amount of measurement will help an organisation to be successful if the people are not engaged and motivated and working to the best of their abilities.

Later chapters deal with the management and leadership issues that create the environment for high performance. In this chapter we examine the essential elements for creating and maintaining high performing teams and individuals and how you measure them. Although measurement cannot create good performance it does give you a benchmark of where you are and how you are progressing, and the act of measuring focuses attention on the most important activities. Many aspects of individuals' performance are intangible and problems come to light when it is too late to do anything about them. At an organisational level, measurement can provide an early indicator of what is to come. At an individual level, people like to know how well they are doing and what they are achieving, and measurement is a tangible way of showing progress and motivating people.

12.2 ESSENTIAL ELEMENTS FOR HIGH PERFORMANCE

What makes employees perform well? You can divide the elements for good performance into two groups – the tangible and the intangible. Tangible elements include the basics of recruiting the right people in the first place, having the right tools for the job, having a good physical working environment and having an appropriate reward for the job. Intangible elements range from the easily definable such as working for a highly respected organisation to the highly personal such as feeling recognised and having a sense of achievement.

Good (or bad) leadership and line management have the most profound impact on the performance of people. Of course it makes sense to have good physical working conditions, but these will make less difference than good leadership. Soldiers have to work in dire conditions but good leaders ensure they continue to be loyal and motivated despite the physical environment (you can read more about this is the case studies at the end of the book).

Individual managers have a major impact on the performance of their teams but what about the impact of HR policies? How do these affect performance?

Recently, academics have been looking more closely at the impact of HR policies and management on performance. In one study at Cranfield School of Management, the researchers gathered data in ten case company organisations by asking managers to identify the HR policies and management practices that they believed improved performance in their businesses. In total they interviewed 62 people in small, medium and large companies in both manufacturing and service sectors with each interview lasting for approximately one hour.

Figure 12.1 shows the results of this research by size of company. The practices are divided into two groups – directing and engaging. Directing is defined as informing people what is required of them at work in terms of performance for the organisation to be successful. Engaging is defined as getting the individuals to commit to the organisation. There is evidence to show that directing and engaging deliver higher levels of performance than either engaging or directing on their own.

12.2.1 What is measurable?

Turning now to the performance of people rather than the effect of HR policies, the factors most commonly measured are: employee satisfaction and engagement, skills and experience, individual performance (through appraisal) and staff turnover (both numerically and qualitatively through exit interviews).

12.3   MEASURING EMPLOYEE SATISFACTION AND ENGAGEMENT

12.3.1 Why measure?

Do happy and satisfied employees make a difference to the performance of the organisation? The intuitive answer to this is 'yes' and there are many academic studies showing this to be the case. However, there are also many studies that fail to show the link. It is a complex area and perhaps it is too simplistic to make a direct link between cause and effect without taking into account hard-to-measure factors such as what is done with survey results, leadership and the effect of economic conditions prevailing at the time of the survey. Nevertheless, many organisations do measure employee satisfaction and find it to be a useful exercise.

Employee engagement is not the same as employee satisfaction. While satisfaction investigates the employees' perception of their employer, engagement looks at their commitment to achieving the organisation's goals. Buckingham and Coffman conducted a study to measure engagement, based on Gallup's survey and interview data from 105,680 employee responses across organisations in financial, health care and restaurant businesses and a wide range of people in government and education. They set a series of questions and analysed whether responses were significantly linked to

Small	Medium	Large
Directing • Performance focus – one page plan and feedback Engaging • Coaching sessions – personal improvement • Team happiness	Directing • Communicating objectives • Communicating performance Engaging • Motivating the team and people to work as a team	Directing • Performance agreements Engaging • People engagement, discretionary effort • If we look after our people, they will look after the business • The combination of motivated people and effective systems
Engaging • Management visibility • Recognition • Good line management	Directing • Progress management Engaging • People engagement, discretionary effort • Good people, mix of youth and experience • Recognition • Strong cross- functional working • Good line management	Directing • KPIs • Appraisals Engaging • Staff bonus
Directing • Well structured goals and targets so individuals know what is expected of them Engaging • Motivated people	Engaging • Good and predictable HR policies and practices • People encouraged, listened to and motivated • Fun-based culture	Directing • The performance management system Engaging • The management conferences • The change management process
		Directing • Individual goals Engaging • The pay and recognition system promotes performance • Executive team, openness and leadership • Good morale

Figure 12.1 Summary of what the managers in each company believed affected performance

a range of factors important for the success of the organisation. What they found is shown in Figure 12.2.

There are two key reasons for measuring satisfaction and engagement. The first is that it gives you a better picture of what your employees really think about your organisation and how committed they are to it. Through means of a confidential survey they are more likely to say what they think than, for example, in a formal appraisal. In an ideal world you would aim to create a culture where all employees feel they are able to express their views at any time. That is unlikely to happen in practice and in any case while the one-to-one approach is helpful to deal with individual concerns, a survey provides a result based on an amalgamation of views and allows formal measurement and objectivity.

The second reason is that in conducting a survey you are demonstrating to your employees that you value their opinions. The caveat is that you are also building up expectations that something will be done as a result of the findings of the survey. Employees in organisations that conduct regular surveys and fail to take action may suffer from survey fatigue and often become cynical, causing more harm than good.

It is worth mentioning here the concept of 'Employer Brand'. Good people generally want to work for organisations that are perceived to be 'good to work for' and the ability to attract and retain good employees provides a competitive edge. Therefore, building a brand as a good employer is an important – and sometimes less remembered – aspect of building competitiveness. To build your brand you need to know how your organisation is perceived by your employees and what they value. This enables you to develop an image you can sell to future recruits – and it also enables you to retain your existing valued employees.

12.3.2 Conducting the survey

Employee surveys can be conducted to investigate a particular issue of concern, but more typically a survey covering both satisfaction and engagement will be conducted on a regular cycle – perhaps every year or every two years. Such surveys normally cover aspects like employees' views of the organisation's leadership, views of line management, level of communication within the organisation, commitment to the organisation, whether employees understand their part in the organisation and understand its goals, whether they feel part of a team and how they feel about their working conditions, and, more recently, issues such as work–life balance. Doing surveys over a period of years will give you a trend and show the progress you are making.

It is important to consider in advance why you are undertaking the survey, what you hope to achieve and what your priorities are. Once your survey is in motion you cannot easily change it, so plan carefully to ensure you are likely to get the information you require. You also need to think in advance how you will communicate the results.

Question	Result significantly linked to:			
	Productivity	Profitability	Staff retention	Customer satisfaction
0. How satisfied am I with xxx as my employer?	▲	▲	▲	▲
1. Do I know what is expected of me at work?	▲	▲	▲	
2. Do I have the materials and equipment I need to do my job right?	▲		▲	
3. At work, do I have the opportunity to do what I do best every day?	▲	▲	▲	
4. In the last seven days, have I received recognition or praise for good work?	▲	▲		▲
5. Does my supervisor, or someone at work, seem to care about me as a person?	▲	▲	▲	▲
6. Is there someone at work who encourages my development?	▲	▲		
7. At work, do my opinions seem to count?	▲	▲	▲	
8. Does the mission/purpose of my company make me feel like my work is important?	▲			
9. Are my co-workers committed to doing quality work?	▲	▲		
10. Do I have a best friend at work?	▲			▲
11. In the last six months, have I talked to someone about my progress?	▲			▲
12. At work, do I have opportunities to learn and grow?		▲		

Figure 12.2 Buckingham and Coffman factors important for organisational success

For smaller organisations it makes sense to run a census – that is to survey everyone. Larger organisations often take a random sample, which is certainly cheaper and overcomes to some extent the problem of survey fatigue. If you are doing this, however, remember some people will feel disenfranchised. It is important to explain openly in advance what you are doing, why you are doing it and how you are doing it.

As this is such a critical area – and you can cause significant damage if you get it wrong – we recommend you use a qualified consultant to design and conduct your survey. This has many benefits. An external consultant will help you decide what your priorities are and will help you design an approach and a questionnaire to meet your needs. Defining priorities is important, not only to clarify your thinking but also to ensure your questionnaire is of a manageable length. Having too many questions is a major problem as people will begin to lose patience and either not answer or not consider their answers sufficiently, giving you a distorted result. An external consultant will also have expertise in designing unambiguous questions, which is critical. You may ask for views about senior management, for example, when the term 'senior management' will be interpreted in different ways at different levels in the organisation, making your results virtually meaningless. Many a survey has been tarnished by those devising the questions having one idea in mind and those answering them having a wide variety of others! It is essential to test your questions in advance with a small group of volunteers to check they interpret them in the same way as you.

Another mistake is to make assumptions underlying the wording of your question. Let us say you pose the statement, 'The senior managers (and you have defined who they are) are visible within the organisation', and ask people to agree or otherwise on a rating scale. You may find that visibility of leaders in one part of the organisation is much higher than it is in others. Is that good or bad? Perhaps employees in that area feel they are the target of too much attention, that they are not trusted and find it awkward when senior managers approach their desks only to make polite conversation. You have assumed in asking the question that visibility of senior managers is a good thing. It may be better to ask whether the level of visibility of senior managers is appropriate.

Finally, give thought to the timing of the survey. Asking your employees in the accounts department to complete a survey at year end is not the best time and you are likely to alienate them rather than make them feel valued.

12.3.3 Analysing and reporting on the findings

Having results from several years' surveys in your own organisation enables you to measure progress, which is an excellent idea, but it is easy to be too internally focused. You may think you are doing well but you will not know how you compare with similar organisations. There is much merit in being able to benchmark with others in the same line of business and working with an external consultant or being part of a forum with others in the same sector will help establish external comparisons. Returning to the idea of 'employer brand', remember your employees can go elsewhere to work so benchmarking where you stand against others is a useful exercise.

Also, it is essential to consider the results of your survey in context and not to jump to conclusions. Perhaps there are good reasons why employees are feeling less satisfied. At times of recession people feel more insecure; they are under more pressure to deliver results and may also have higher workloads as colleagues who leave are not replaced. Some organisations convene small groups of employees to consider the findings and add their views to the interpretation of results. This usually creates valuable new insights.

In your analysis check the level of responses overall and by department as this will give a first level of indication about how seriously the survey was taken. Also analyse differences between different parts of the organisation and feed that information back to local management.

Communicating the results in an open manner is essential. It is easy to dwell on negative findings and sometimes to be defensive about them, but it is just as important to celebrate successes and improvements as it is to highlight areas for improvement. That said, there is no use in covering over problems because your employees will be aware of them anyway. The most constructive approach is to involve them in finding solutions.

12.4   PERFORMANCE APPRAISALS

The previous section dealt with surveys of the workforce as a whole. We now turn to measuring the performance of individuals. The thinking and practice in performance appraisal has progressed enormously from the days in which each employee entered the manager's office with great apprehension at the end of the year to find out what he or she thought about them, what their 'grading' was and probably also what this meant for their next year's pay. Now the focus is much more on helping employees to commit to and achieve their objectives and on discussing *how* objectives are achieved. In years gone by the discussion concentrated on outputs of a job, whether an objective or goal had been reached. Now the appraisal will probably include a discussion of behavioural aspects of a person's performance. Has the individual upheld the values of the organisation, for example. Have they worked well as part of a team? It is recognised that these aspects of performance are important as very few people work in isolation and how we conduct ourselves has an impact on others in the organisation. You may, for example, have someone in the team who reaches their objectives by thwarting others in achieving theirs, to the detriment of the organisation as a whole. The traditional performance appraisal has thus evolved into a more all-encompassing process. Many organisations do not even use the term 'performance appraisal' now, preferring names such as 'personal development review' or 'delivering shared agreement'.

Whatever they call it, the majority of organisations have some sort of formal review process that encompasses the agreement of objectives, the setting of standards and review of progress in the achievement of objectives. Around this core are discussions about training and development needs, career aspirations and an opportunity to discuss individual concerns and intentions. Research has shown that regular one-to-one meetings have more positive impact on performance than the once a year 'assessment' and the current thinking is about moving away from the very rigid pattern of formal subordinate/manager type appraisals to more regular informal meetings underpinned by a framework that provides a process for managers and employees to follow. However, the appraisal is not just about the individual; the organisation can also gain useful information, for example in succession planning and overall training and development requirements.

12.4.1 How do you set objectives?

In visiting businesses it is surprising how much 'activity on the ground' differs from the agreed strategy of the business. It is essential that strategy and action are aligned. Objectives should be cascaded from the top level strategic objectives through various departments and layers of the organisation.

Results are not, however, achieved just by activity. Many managers fall into the trap of setting a measure for activity rather than an expectation of results. To take a simple example, a salesperson would be performing as required if they conducted 100 sales meetings against an objective that said 'conduct 100 sales meetings', even though they had achieved no sales. If you set a target of £500k sales and the sales person achieved that figure, it would be far more beneficial for the business even if they were lucky enough to receive one £500k order!

There is no doubt that having a clear standard to achieve focuses the mind. For the high jumper the bar is clear to see. For the runner the time to beat is engraved on the mind. Having an imaginary bar or just trying to run faster would not have the same effect. The whole objective/target setting process, although essential to foster high performance, can become a time-consuming negotiation exercise, with employees seeking easier to achieve goals and managers trying to impose impossible to achieve targets. Setting standards involves judgement and also reaching agreement on what is fair. Stretch objectives and targets are good in that they encourage high performance, but if they are too stretching they will be demotivating as the individual believes them to be unattainable. So, how do you set realistic targets?

Past performance is one guide but it does not always predict what they will be able to achieve given better conditions and motivation. Knowledge of your employees' capabilities is essential. Getting to know them well and talking to them openly about what needs to be done and how it can be achieved is essential. This does mean that targets set across a team may vary and you will have to find ways of offsetting a lower target in one area with a higher target in another. If targets are perceived as being unequal or if one individual is seen as having an easier time without good cause, then you will cause friction. If you have an open and trusting culture in your organisation, the fact that you are playing to the strengths of individuals rather than imposing a blanket target on all should be well understood.

It is helpful to quantify objectives wherever possible because this gives a common understanding of the standard to be reached. However, it is not always possible and it is better not to attach a number unless it really does make sense. Often it is sufficient for the individual to supply evidence that they have achieved their objective. Even when you have a numerical goal, you need to use judgement as to whether an individual has performed well because so much can change between setting the standard and the end of the appraisal period. The key is to gain a common understanding of what is to be achieved and record that understanding as unambiguously as possible with both the manager and the individual putting their signature to the form. In this way there can be no wriggling out of it.

Most organisations set their objectives and targets in advance for the year and this does make sense because in constantly changing your target you lose credibility. However, there are times when targets do need to change. As we have seen recently, economic conditions can change rapidly. You may have no control over the external environment but you do have control over your response to it. You may need to adapt your strategy, in which case you *must* also change your employees' objectives and your measurement of progress so they are in alignment. People will put their effort into whatever is being measured, so if you do not change what they are being measured on to bring it in line with your strategy, they will continue to put their effort into the same things and you will not be able to change your course.

12.4.2 How do you assess performance?

We will focus here on how you measure performance rather than on how you conduct and use an appraisal interview or how you may link it to reward, because that is part of the management rather than the measurement process. Most performance appraisal forms have some sort of rating scale with three, four or five levels. It is important that these levels are labelled with descriptors so everyone has an understanding of what '3' means, for example. Obviously the more levels you have, the finer the level of distinction between the performance of each individual. However, this also makes it harder for managers to allocate a rating and some ratings on the scale may not be used.

Applying a rating to an individual's performance is something many managers find hard to do and indeed errors are many and varied. Typical mistakes include the tendency to make a quick decision on first impressions and to stick to it, or to take one area of a person's work in which they excel and assume they are performing at the same level in every other aspect of their work. There is also a 'recency' effect, where events that have just happened take on more importance than is justified and past events that may have been much better indicators of performance are forgotten. Most of us are naturally drawn to people who are similar to ourselves and this is no different in an appraisal situation, where individuals tend to give a higher rating to people they identify with. Other errors include generalising and putting people into categories rather than looking at them as individuals, allowing problems that have occurred well in the past to continue to dominate your view of someone's perform-ance and always rating people in the middle of the scale because it appears to be the easy option.

All this goes to show how important is it to prepare and reflect on individual per-formance. Understanding the types of pitfalls is helpful, but making an appraisal is not an exact science and it is ultimately a matter of judgement. It may be some com-fort to know that research suggests that discussing performance and what to do about it is more valuable than formally assessing it.

12.4.3 360 degree feedback

The 360 degree appraisal is becoming more popular. This is the process where views are sought on an individual, not only by their manager but also by their colleagues, people who work with them and even external contacts such as customers. The advantage is that it has a wider scope than the traditional appraisal (which it should supplement rather than supplant) and it also gives an element of empowerment to employees. However, it also has some disadvantages and many organisations have dropped the process. The main reasons for discarding it are because the organisation is not sufficiently 'open' (it will not work where there is mistrust between employees and the organisation or where there is a strict hierarchical structure) and because it has been used inappropriately. While it can be useful to determine training and devel-opment needs it should in no way be connected to bonus and pay.

The idea of a 360 degree appraisal can cause great amounts of mistrust and anxiety and is often resisted by employees. As a result many organisations decide to intro-duce it initially at senior levels to demonstrate its benefits. The typical approach is to select participants who interact with the appraisee and give them a short question-naire, which must be completed anonymously. Results are collated and presented to the appraisee in a constructive manner.

While there are benefits to 360 degree feedback, it is not a process to be entered into lightly. Dangers can ensue such as undermining a manager's authority and cre-ating a breakdown in working relationships. We usually know our immediate line managers and when we receive negative feedback from them we interpret it in the light of what we know about them. It is always hard to receive negative feedback and particularly hard when it is from an anonymous source. There is also the danger in smaller organisations that the manager will spend too much time trying to guess who has said what and may not guess correctly. The key is to ensure the person giving the feedback is highly skilled at doing so.

12.5   HR PERFORMANCE MEASURES

There are four elements you should track on a regular basis as part of your performance measurement system. These are: absence, staff turnover and internal and external appointments.

12.5.1 Absence

Let us deal with absence first. There are two facets to absence – tracking an individual's attendance and monitoring the overall climate of the organisation. Absence reflects to some extent the demographics of your workforce and the nature of the working environment. The parts of organisations that involve heavy manual labour, for example, will normally have higher absence rates. This is to be expected. However, absence is also affected by staff morale and management style. If there is a higher level in one part of the organisation and no clear reason why, then it is sometimes the result of the management of those people.

The information on absence collected by most organisations includes dates, reason for absence and whether the absence is certified by a doctor. In order to analyse the data you will need to record it in a usable format, remembering it is sensitive and paying heed to data protection requirements. If you are not going to use information then do not bother to collect it.

The most commonly used measure for absence of individuals or groups of employees is calculated as follows:

$$\frac{\text{Total absence in hours or days during a period} \times 100}{\text{Total contracted hours or days in that period}}$$

While it is useful to collect general 'time lost' information, you need more detail on the type of absence in order to understand what is happening in your organisation. Frequent, short absences are often more disruptive than one-off longer absences and *may* be an indicator of poor morale or an underlying problem with work, particularly if they are always on a Monday or Friday. The Bradford factor, developed in the 1980s, is a measure combining frequency of absence with duration. It is measured by $B = S^2 \times D$, where B = the Bradford factor, S = the number of spells of absence by an individual over a period of time and D = the total number of days of absence in the same period. It is a useful measure but should not be taken in isolation as it points only to short term absences. Also, it is dangerous to assume that frequent short term absences are not genuine.

Like the results of most measures of performance, they are more meaningful when you know how you compare with other similar organisations, and there are several ways in which you can benchmark your results, including sectoral bodies such as Local Government and The Chartered Institute of Personnel and Development, at www.cipd.co.uk.

12.5.2 Staff turnover

Staff turnover can be another indicator of morale but it is also highly influenced by the type of people you are employing and by the economic environment. If you are employing many young graduates you would expect them to move on to other organisations to further their careers. Accountancy firms, for example, recruit and train some of the brightest graduates and understand that in good times they will lose a fair number of them as they move on to work in other businesses. In bad times, however, few people will risk moving to a new job even if they are unhappy where they are because it may prove to be less secure. If you are running a smaller business and you are recruiting bright young individuals, you will have to accept when you recruit them that they will leave if there is no opportunity for them to develop. You will have to factor this in to your decision and decide how they will benefit your organisation if they are only with you for, say, 18 months to two years.

Staff turnover is not necessarily a bad thing. Bringing in new people with new ideas is essential if the organisation is not to become stale. However, there is a balance and too much turnover can affect morale and ultimately the overall performance of the organisation, as you will have too many people who know too little about the business.

Keeping an eye on numbers of people leaving is important, but you also need to know why they are going. This is why exit interviews are so important to find the root cause of departures. Most people are quite open about their reasons at this stage as they have nothing to lose and you may be able to glean useful information for building your employer brand.

12.5.3 Moving on internally

It is important to measure internal as well as external moves. There is no point in training and developing staff for the next stage in their career if they perceive the opportunities are not open to them at higher levels. However, as we suggested above, you do need to bring in new blood from time to time and ensure that there is true competition for important positions, so you bring in the best talent. Having a target for internal promotion does not really make sense because you will find unsuitable people are promoted just to achieve the right number. It is better to have a range rather than a target.

12.6 ACTING ON RESULTS

There are numerous factors to measure in terms of people and numerous ways of measuring them. Setting up review processes, reporting results to managers and focusing management effort can improve performance significantly. Just by measuring, you are in effect stating to staff that this is an important issue and making them aware that they are being monitored. However, the difficult part is often deciding what to do with the data you have. Through the information you collect from sources such as your employee surveys and your absence rates you can begin to build up a picture of what is happening in different areas. You may find, for example, that managers in one part of the organisation would benefit from further training or that workload in one area is excessive and you need to recruit.

The information you collect is supporting evidence, but the actions you take will be based on judgement and on knowing your people. If you have an individual who has problems at home and is absent frequently as a result, how will you manage them? You will need to consider how much slack and support you are going to give them to get through it. It is hard to make that decision without knowing the person and what they are likely to contribute to your organisation in the future and the effect their absences is having on other people in the team.

Survey results and quantitative and qualitative data are important for knowing where you stand as an organisation, but they are no substitute for understanding your employees as individuals.

FURTHER READING AND SOURCES OF INFORMATION

Buckingham, M. and Coffman, C. (1999) *First Break All the Rules: What the World's Greatest Managers Do Differently*, Simon & Schuster, London.
The Chartered Institute of Personnel and Development: www.cipd.co.uk

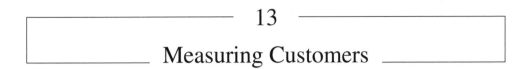

13

Measuring Customers

13.1 INTRODUCTION

Customers are the life blood of every business, so it is important to understand how they perceive you as a supplier. Whatever you do in your organisation will affect your customers. Their perception of your business and your goods and services will influence their actions, in particular their willingness to recommend you to others and their inclination to buy again. If new customers are drawn to you through the recommendations of existing customers and they come back and buy again, you will gain market share and a competitive advantage. In this chapter we investigate the link down this chain.

We will start by providing an understanding of what a customer satisfaction survey should be, defining some of the commonly used terms. We then move on to how you measure satisfaction, finishing with a case study of how a hotel chain used customer feedback to motivate staff and improve their performance.

13.2 WHAT ARE YOU MEASURING?

Customer satisfaction surveys abound. Most people will have completed one at some stage but we will take a closer look at what they are. A common description is:

> 'an unbiased sample of customer opinions about your organisation and the goods and services it provides'.

As with any survey, you need to be clear about what you want to achieve and how will you use the information you gain. Once you agree this you will be able to determine the sample size, type of survey and how frequently you measure. Then you will need to consider whether you are looking to establish trends, investigate a particular issue or check perceptions of a particular part of your organisation. Too often when we ask people to develop customer satisfaction measures they turn either to measures of service or customer complaints, neither of which are true measures of satisfaction.

Most organisations measure customer *service* and *perception*. The belief is that customer service influences customer perception, customer perception influences customer intention and customer intention influences customer loyalty, which in turn improves the financial results of the organisation (see Figure 13.1). Let us take a few moments to understand each element in a little more detail.

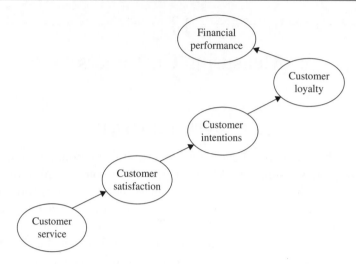

Figure 13.1   Customer measurement assumptions

Customer service refers to the measures you take inside an organisation to assess the level of service you provide to your customers. Such measures may include the length of time customers have to queue at a supermarket check-out, the number of items dispatched on next day delivery from a builders' merchant or the percentage of shipments arriving on time from a manufacturing company. We even met a police chief constable who had the percentage of police cars despatched to top category 999 calls arriving within five minutes.

Customer service measures are relatively easy to collect. They come from the internal systems within your organisation, essentially measuring the output of your processes. They tell you how well those processes are performing against the targets you have set. They do not necessarily reflect the view of the customer. This is an important point, as you will see from the Milliken example later.

Customer perception measures are based on asking your customer about their perceptions of the goods and services you have provided. You can ask about over-all perceptions or you can break down your survey into particular elements. If we take the example of a hotel, you could ask about the overall impression of the stay. You may break this down into the residential service, the restaurant and the bar services. You may drill down even deeper by asking detailed questions about the quality of res-taurant service, the choice on the menu, the quality of the food, the friendliness of the staff and the value for money. The more questions you ask, the greater the detail in the feedback, but beware, customers get tired of completing questionnaires, so there is a limit to the length and a limit to the number of times you can survey people. Always ask why you are asking the question and what you can do with the results.

Customer intention, as the name suggests, is about what customers are likely to do. Many customer surveys contain intention questions such as: 'What is the likelihood of you returning to buy this product or service again?' and 'Would you be prepared to recommend our organisation to your family and friends?' They provide a stronger indication of buying commitment than the other elements of the customer satisfaction survey and so are particularly useful questions with which to close.

In organisations we have worked with, there is often no statistically significant correlation between customer satisfaction and customer loyalty. However, there is usually a significant relationship between customer satisfaction and willingness to recommend and willingness to recommend and customer loyalty. Customer intention questions are not perfect, but they do start to make the link between satisfaction and actions.

Customer loyalty occurs when your customers come back to you and buy again. It is important because it is extremely expensive to keep finding new customers. Further, there may only be a limited number of customers in your market place, so losing a customer may block your access to a significant part of the revenues available.

However, customer loyalty is notoriously difficult to measure. How do you know that your customer has not come back with their next order? Airlines, for example, do not know when you have booked your next flight with a competitor and do not know whether this was because of convenience (the competitor flew to the destination they wanted to go to) or because you preferred what their competitor was offering. Many markets are like this, especially where there is a broad range of competitors to choose from. Watching the trend of your customers' spending from one period to another may provide some insight, especially if it is combined with regular intelligence from your sales team, but it will not be an accurate measure of loyalty.

Typical loyalty measures include:

- Share of customer spend – if you are able to establish what the total spend is – over a period of time
- Number of products taken regularly by the customer from your range
- Percentage of contracts renewed
- Frequency of re-purchase.

Customer value is not a measure of customer satisfaction but we include it here because it relates to measuring customers and is an important measure for the success of your business. If you do not have an idea of the value of a particular customer to your business you may find you are putting your resources into customers who are unlikely to deliver a return on your investment. So, what is customer value? Different companies have different approaches to working out the value of a customer. One way is to calculate the profitability of the customer's orders to your business. If you have an effective way of allocating costs – sales and account management costs in particular – this gives a good, if short term, estimate of their value.

Some companies are very good at doing this. Tesco, for example, looks at customer value from three perspectives:

- The current value: based on the customer's current level of spend with the store.
- The future value: based on an estimate of future potential spend with the store.
- Advocacy value: based on how much the individual influences the spending of others. (This is estimated through research showing how certain groups influence others. Mothers, for example, have been shown to be major influencers on their daughters' buying for new babies.)

They then allocate their promotional activity based on the value they assign to that customer and how they wish to influence them.

When considering customer value, do not forget future spending. One American fast food chain reputedly taught its staff to see teenage customers coming in to order food with an imaginary $50 000 note stuck to their forehead, as this was the value of all their future business.

13.2.1 Who do you survey?

When leaving our hotel after a week on the beach in the Caribbean, we were asked if we had had a good time. When we said 'yes', we were asked to complete the customer satisfaction survey. This is not uncommon. The National Trust recently found the most significant difference in visitor satisfaction results between different properties resulted from the way the survey was administered. A simple pre-selection question (how was your visit?) vastly improved the results. In business-to-business settings you should ideally go for a census (a survey of 100% of your customers), but beware, the customer contact list can be doctored to exclude customers who have had a recent problem. This is why companies, such as British Airways, use external agencies that specify the seat number of a survey recipient in advance, rather than leave the selection to the cabin crew.

You should also remember that you are only surveying existing customers. Customers who have left you during the year may well not be included and so you only see the more satisfied customers. You may wish to measure perceptions of the general population and this will give you insights into why some people buy from you and some do not, but clearly this is not a 'customer' survey. It all depends what you want to achieve.

The important thing about a customer survey is that it should be done as consistently as possible. This will enable you to track trends from one year to the next and identify your successes and failures.

13.2.2 Measuring customer satisfaction

Given that customer satisfaction is a perception measure, the only true way of measuring satisfaction is by asking the customer, 'How satisfied overall were you with the service you received?' However, although an overall customer satisfaction rating of 3.9 on a 5 point scale tells you something, it does not tell you enough to take meaningful action.

The overall satisfaction will be influenced by different elements of the experience. Continuing the hotel example, you may want to know how satisfied your guests were with the way they were greeted by the receptionist, whether they felt the person who dealt with them understood their requirements and so on. It is useful, not only to ask about overall satisfaction but also to ask about the satisfaction with the different elements of the service provided. In that way you know where improvements can be made. What you do not know is how important each of those factors is to your customers – and this is needed so you can prioritise those factors where you can make most difference.

In the example above, the initial greeting may have been well received but soon wore off when the receptionist failed to understand the customer's desire to have a room on a lower floor because he did not want to use the lift. The initial greeting may be important, but pales into insignificance in the customer's mind against his need to be allocated a specific type of room. You need to understand not only the performance of each element of the service but its relative importance. Some customer satisfaction surveys will attempt to capture importance and performance at the same time, but this does add to the list of questions being asked. In view of this, many organisations rely on focus groups to establish the relative importance beforehand and restrict the questions to satisfaction with performance.

By measuring both importance and performance you can create Figure 13.2 by plotting each service element against the two axes. The highlighted areas start to give you an indication of where to place your efforts, with high performance in areas of little importance to the customer suggesting overdelivery, while low performance on important elements being targeted for urgent action.

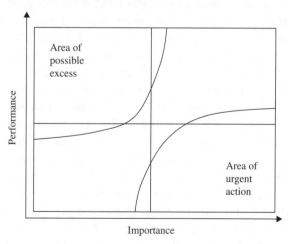

Figure 13.2   The importance/performance matrix

13.2.3 Linking service and satisfaction

Understanding the link between perception and what people in the organisation often call 'reality' is critical. Let us illustrate this with a case example.

Milliken manufactures industrial fibres and sells them to other businesses. They have been measuring customer satisfaction across all their companies for 25 years. Initially they attempted to measure satisfaction by using their staff to interview their customers, but found that the staff soon became defensive and so moved to having an annual survey conducted by a third party agency.

In the early years, Milliken spent considerable time and effort improving their on-time delivery. This rose to over 90% by the end of the year and they were impatiently waiting to see how the customer satisfaction survey reported on this element of their service. It was therefore a great surprise when the survey showed only a modest improvement in satisfaction with on-time delivery. Milliken went back to its customers and talked to them about this. The reply they received was that the goods left the factory on the day the customer requested delivery, but did not arrive until at least the next day. If the customers were overseas, the delivery took considerably longer. They were measuring customer services (i.e. their own internal measure) rather than their customers' perception.

Milliken therefore changed their internal performance measure from 'dispatched on time' to 'delivered on time'. Twelve months later and the next customer satisfaction survey showed again only a very modest improvement. The same questions were asked and the customers explained that although Milliken met their own delivery date, they were not meeting the requirement of the customer. Shorter lead times were required. Milliken then modified its internal system again, so that the date negotiated and agreed between the customer and Milliken was the date against which performance was measured. They also went on to develop their concept of the 'perfect order', delivered in full, on time, with no complaints and the correct paper work.

Improving on-time delivery of perfect orders was a significant task, but Milliken managed to get back to over 90% and, over time, managed 100% for long periods of time. In one instance, the Le Havre plant went some six and a half years without a late delivery to anybody. It was expected that this would really increase satisfaction with on-time delivery to record levels. However, they were disappointed, as although the annual survey did show a significant increase it did not show the extremely high levels of satisfaction they were expecting. When this was discussed with the customers again, it emerged that they simply were not aware of how good Milliken's on-time delivery was. As an experiment, Milliken asked its sales representatives to drop into the conversation on each visit how many weeks or months it had been since Milliken last missed a delivery date. This action did increase customer satisfaction.

This example demonstrates that the link between internal measures of service and customer satisfaction is not always as simple as it would at first seem. Customers do not perceive performance in the same way as the organisation does. It is therefore important to measure both satisfaction and service levels to understand the relationship better. Also, customer satisfaction can be manipulated by means other than improving performance and this too needs to be considered. Finally, customers act on perception and not on your measure of performance, so measuring and understanding customer perception is critical.

13.2.4 Linking satisfaction and loyalty

In the last section we emphasised the need for your organisation to track the link between customer service levels and their corresponding elements of customer satisfaction. However, we are only doing this because we believe that higher levels of customer satisfaction lead to customer loyalty and this is the first step in improving financial performance. It is also important to establish this link.

It is often said that customers who rate themselves very satisfied (on a normal five point Likert scale) are six times more likely to buy again than those who simply rate themselves as satisfied. However, in the studies we have seen, the link between customer satisfaction and customer loyalty are often not significant. The link appears to be indirect. Customer loyalty is often statistically correlated with willingness to recommend.

Evidence from studies done by others should give you some confidence that such a relationship exists, but we would urge you to test these relationships using your own satisfaction and loyalty data. We visited a major high street store chain some years ago who told us they believed the relationship to be 100 %. When we asked them why, they told us that the link had been demonstrated in US customer data and they had little interest in testing it again in their own stores. They were missing a trick, as such studies often produce surprises. Note the example of BA in Chapter 10, where delays in take-off resulted in higher perceptions of cabin crew service. The link often does not work as expected and when this happens you will have a real chance to learn something new about your business and your customers.

The link between service, satisfaction and loyalty is highly influenced by choice and competition, the subject of the next section.

13.2.5 Performance against the competition

Companies we work with are often surprised how loyal some customers are despite the poor level of service given. Similarly, others are shocked that seemingly satisfied customers have left. There is no automatic link between service, satisfaction and customer loyalty. Competition and customer choice have to be taken into account.

If you have a monopoly, customers have no choice but to buy from you. However, you can also create a near monopoly situation by making customers extremely reliant on you, becoming the de facto standard (e.g. Microsoft Office) or making the effort required to switch extremely high (this used to be the case with current account banking). One of the most extreme examples we were given was a Canadian state telephone service, where customers were trapped by the monopoly, but were so dissatisfied they took to driving past the offices and discharging their shotguns at the building in protest! In today's environment of instant communication it is easy for reputations to be damaged very quickly and that is just as true for monopolies as it is for others.

At the other extreme, very satisfied customers will switch on price. This may simply be an experiment to see if the competitor's value proposition is better than yours, in which case many will return. However, if competitors can deliver a very similar reliable product or service offered at a lower price, the business will be lost permanently. Therefore, it is useful not only to measure importance and performance but also to measure this against your competitors. Figure 13.3 shows how Milliken did this.

The left-hand axis shows the different elements of service in order of importance to the customer. It is interesting to note that in this business-to-business

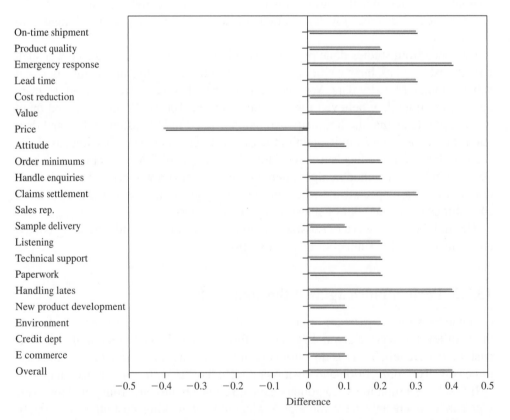

Figure 13.3   Milliken customer satisfaction survey (adapted from Jeans, 2004)

relationship, price is number seven in the order of importance. People are often surprised that price is not top of the list, particularly in business-to-business transactions. The importance of price varies depending on economic circumstances in the marketplace, but other considerations such as convenience are often seen as more important. The right-hand axis shows the perceived level of performance against Milliken's nearest competitor. Bars to the right of the central zero line show where perceived performance exceeds that of competitors and bars to the left show where perceived performance is below.

In this example, Milliken are producing a superior product and service offering but charging a premium price for doing so. The relationship between perception of value and price premium needs to be monitored. Although price is not necessarily the most important factor there is a limit to how much extra people will pay. Marks and Spencer were the classic example of a company who in the mid 1990s started to make excessive margins and found that customers responded by looking for alternatives. So be aware of the margins achieved in your industry. You will want to be better than average but if you are way ahead just question why that might be.

13.3   USING CUSTOMER FEEDBACK

In the last section we showed you how a business supplying other businesses used its customer satisfaction survey to obtain feedback and gain insights. We will now provide you with an example taken from the hospitality industry. In this example, the business is dealing mainly with individual customers.

13.3.1 Customer insight at Premier Inn

Premier Inn is part of the Whitbread Group. The first Travel Inn opened in 1987 and growth was rapid. Within ten years the company had 200 sites. By 2002 it was the largest hotel chain in the UK. It acquired Premier Lodge in 2004 and re-branded itself as Premier Inn in 2007; by the end of 2010 the company was running 590 hotels. The company has what it describes as 'Guest Obsession' and its goal is to 'deliver a world class guest experience in the hotel industry'. In this section we will describe how Premier Inn goes about this by focusing in particular on its measurement of guest satisfaction and the supporting systems and processes.

Premier Inn sees its role as balancing the requirements of three important stakeholders: its shareholders, its people and its customers. However, the different perspectives are interlinked. Premier Inn wants to become the most customer focused hospitality company in the world by making an everyday experience of staying in a hotel special. It aims to do this by delivering outstanding value and winning customer loyalty. Customer loyalty is a benefit for the shareholder because it results in better financial performance through customers returning. Customers return because they enjoy staying at the hotels. Their experience is highly dependent on the quality, training and motivation of Premier Inn' front line staff.

The guest satisfaction score is a key performance measure on the company's scorecard, but the process does not stop with measurement. At the company level, the insights from the guest survey are reviewed by the executive, they are passed to the guest research and operations teams for feedback, before actions are agreed on branding, standards and audit. At the hotel level, the results are available in near real-time as the intention is for site feedback to influence individual behaviour locally. Although the survey captures aspects of customer satisfaction, Premier Inn has a more demanding requirement. The most important score is the advocacy of whether guests are prepared to recommend Premier Inn.

The customer survey is web based and run for Premier Inn by OCR International, and guests are emailed within 24 hours of their check-out. The survey has a 35 % response rate with 98 % of those starting the survey completing it. This is partly due to the fact that the survey is limited to 40 tick box questions, but it is also helped by the supporting software. Guests do not have the usual irritation of surveys of telling the company where they stayed and when, as this is already captured in the system. The 40 questions are carefully selected from a complete list to keep the questionnaire short, so the guest does not get the same questions each time. Finally, regular guests are identified so they are not surveyed after every single visit. The questions are about basic aspects of product and service, brand and demographic, as well as the specific questions that form part of KPIs on topics relating to overall customer satisfaction and advocacy. Guests are also asked for their own written comments, and these are captured and are made accessible on-line to all staff. With 40 000 responses a month this is one of the biggest surveys of its kind in the world.

Feedback is compiled overnight giving daily results at company, regional and hotel level. Hotels can see their own performance and how this compares with the rest of the hotels in the group. They also have direct access to their verbatim comments and over half the hotels log on to the system every day to check up on the feedback and their scores.

Sites can use individual question responses to focus their improvement programmes. Simple questions about the 'cleanliness of the room' or 'team care' can be acted on within a few days. Therefore, all team members know their scores from recent feedback. Hotel teams meet on a regular basis to discuss the feedback and create guest action plans addressing tactical issues and team members singled out by guests for special praise are recognised.

Tools used to deliver performance

The guest satisfaction survey is just one of the tools used by Premier Inn to deliver the customer service. The survey provides feedback, but performance at Premier Inn does not happen by accident – it is planned and managed. The company has robust operating standards supported by high quality training material. The brand operating standards are audited and this information together with the guest survey is the main source of feedback. The whole approach is underpinned by the *Goodnight Guarantee*.

The brand operating standards are based on seeing the hotel experience through the eyes of the guest. They cover the service from when the booking is made, through to arrival, check-in, journey to the room, the bedroom itself, dinner, breakfast and check-out and finally to departure. The standards are split into *hardlines* and *guidelines*. *Hardlines* are things that must be covered and include standard items such as maintenance and repair, cleanliness, product, service and the management processes. *Guidelines* provide guidance on opportunities for staff to tailor the company's approach on how to 'wow' the guest.

The brand operating standards are underpinned by detailed instructions and training material. There are over 150 books covering every aspect of delivery. For example, there is a 6 page book covering the making of the bed complete with four photographs to illustrate exactly how it should be done. New recruits have an induction process and then are introduced to the business under the watchful eyes of a new starter champion who will be responsible for their training. Training is a key element of the brand operating audit and the progress of trainees is signed off in a managed process. Staff development continues beyond this with many opportunities for them to take NVQs and other training courses.

Mystery shoppers are used to audit what Premier Inn calls 'the customer journey'. It uses an external firm to do this to ensure they get unbiased feedback and that there is no favouritism between colleagues who know each other. Each audit is extremely detailed and comprises over 1000 questions. For example, it takes about 45 minutes just to audit one bedroom. Following the customer journey, the mystery shopper arrives incognito the night before and the results of the audit are announced the following day. Each hotel is audited a minimum of twice a year and there are serious consequences for a failed audit.

The *Goodnight Guarantee* may appear like a gimmick, but the intention is to empower staff to act and fix problems. The guarantee is advertised to all guests on arrival and any issues raised are measured, recorded and fixed. It forms one of the first inputs into the cycle of continuous improvement and is intended to underpin the consistency of the product and service offering right across the hotel chain. Guests are promised a good night or Premier Inn guarantees to refund their money.

Use of feedback

Besides feedback from audit and guests, there is a monthly steering committee meeting that reviews feedback from staff too. They are encouraged to share their ideas, and these are assessed for their impact on the guests and how they impact on the brand operating standards. Many of the suggestions from staff have been implemented, including blackout curtains in bedrooms and lighter jugs for orange juice at breakfast.

Guest reporting is treated with the same rigour as financial reporting in the business, with weekly and monthly cycles of reviewing audits, guest recommendations and complaints. These reporting cycles are supplemented by focus groups run every two months. Members of the Whitbread Hotels and Restaurants board attend these focus group meetings to keep in touch with guest feedback and sentiment. The output of the meetings may lead to further research and informs key decisions.

Many of the items identified at a local level can be addressed locally, but strategic decisions have to be made about elements of products and services to be rolled out across the hotel chain. Each suggestion is assessed for its likely impact on the guest and is prioritised based on an estimate of its effect on guest satisfaction. For example, guests were giving a lower than expected rating to in-room entertainment and so the reasons for this were investigated. It was agreed that making Freeview channels available in all rooms would make a dramatic difference and their rollout was prioritised. Similarly, Premier Inn is a 'value' brand so air conditioning was not offered as standard. When guest feedback was reviewed, this policy was revised and air conditioning was installed as standard in all city centre hotels.

In conclusion

Premier Inn does have the advantage of scale, enabling it to invest in its measurement of customer feedback, but they have shown clear commitment to listen to their guests and act accordingly. This has made them very successful, winning countless awards and managing a spectacular growth in their business. This case example shows how performance measurement of customer perceptions has been integrated into the wider performance management system, informing and shaping actions from local tactics to important strategic decisions about the product/service offering.

13.4   SUMMARY

In this chapter we have given examples of good practice of customer satisfaction measurement in both industrial and consumer markets. Measuring customer satisfaction is only the first step. Both companies in the examples have gone beyond measuring their customers' satisfaction by creating a process for acting on the feedback provided. Obtaining feedback from your customers is often an expensive process, so it is important that you maximise the benefits by acting on the insights obtained.

FURTHER READING

Jeans, C. (2004) 'Integrating customer satisfaction and performance measures', Chapter C2 in *The Handbook of Performance Measurement* (Bourne, M., editor), Third Edition, Gee Publishing, London.

Measuring Process Performance

14.1 INTRODUCTION

There are two different ways of looking at an organisation. The first is through the structure and hierarchy of reporting – formally mapped by the organisation chart. The second way is through its processes, the basic mechanisms by which the organisation delivers products and services to its customers. In this chapter we will look at the process perspective and show how a process framework can be integrated into the reporting hierarchy.

We will describe a framework for process measurement and explain how this enables alignment with both business and customer objectives. Firstly, we will describe a process framework and then move on to describe the elements of coordination and control. We will present two universal process measures that can be used to improve the performance of processes and will finish with an approach for integrating process performance into the organisation's top level scorecard or dashboard.

14.2 A PROCESS FRAMEWORK

Processes tend to be described in three elements, inputs, the process itself and outputs. However, there are four other elements that should be included. These are:

1. Outcomes: these are the direct and indirect consequences of the outputs from the process. In a prison, for example, you may have a process for educating prisoners. The output would be prisoners with qualifications. The outcome would be a lower rate of reoffending.
2. Resources: these are the people, equipment, systems, etc., that enable the process to function.
3. Coordination mechanisms: these are mechanisms that manage the process on a day-to-day basis, adjusting for changes. In a factory this may simply be the supervisor wandering around and watching what is happening and making changes where required.
4. Control mechanisms: these are the mechanisms that are used to set (and re-set) the targets, monitor performance and allocate resources.

Let us use an example to illustrate the framework.

14.2.1 Win order process – an example

In most companies this is one of the key processes – winning orders from customers. The inputs could be requests for quotations, the process could be translating the enquiries into acceptable quotations, the outputs could be orders won and the out-come could be the financial success of the business. The resources will include the sales representatives who visit, engage and negotiate with the customer, as well as the internal technical staff who interpret the requirements, create a solution and pro-vide the quotation. The coordination mechanisms will include all the conversations between the staff working on the enquiries with the day-to-day steering coming from the sales manager, who will juggle priorities and allocate technical staff to enquiries. At the most basic level, the control mechanism will be the monthly sales meeting when performance against targets is assessed and monitored. However, there will be higher level control mechanisms that monitor trends, produce forecasts for the next financial period, set short and longer term targets, establish strategy and reassess resources. These will take place through quarterly review meetings, annual strategy reviews and probably as a part of regular board meetings.

In coordinating this process, people need to be aware of the level of requests com-ing in, the number of quotations being processed, the staff available to deal with them, the number of quotations being made and the ratio of orders won to orders lost. These need to be adjusted in real-time on a day-to-day basis.

However, in controlling the process you have to take a wider perspective. You need to understand the factors affecting the enquiry level, so that the stream of inputs is better managed in the future. The efficiency and effectiveness of the process needs to be tracked, so appropriate levels of resourcing can be provided, the quality of the work is assessed and staff are motivated and directed in the right way. Winning orders may appear to be a successful outcome of the process, but if they are won at the wrong price, the future of the organisation can be put at risk. You can see from this that the link between outputs and outcomes is a significant element to control and manage.

14.3 PROCESS MEASUREMENT

When managing a process it is useful to distinguish between coordination and control. Coordination is the day-to-day management of adjusting to events, whereas control is the management in the longer term, taking on broad trends and adjusting the process in the light of performance. The use of the measures differs in these two circumstances.

For coordination, it is useful to have real-time measures and displays of work-loads. In the example above, these would include lists of enquiries received and not yet allocated, enquiries being handled by each of the technical staff giving an indica-tion of allocation of responsibility and workload, quotations submitted and a list of

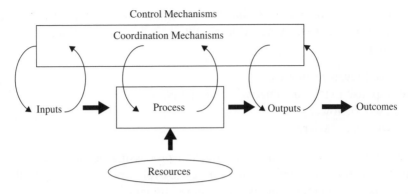

Figure 14.1   Key elements of the process

orders won. Making these visible shows up peaks in demand, bottlenecks and output produced, and they are often updated manually on display boards or on very simple IT systems. Good managers in these situations have a feel for performance as they are seeing the numbers and hearing the conversations all day every day. They are not looking to the formal measures to manage performance as these are usually too late. The formal measures are used to confirm that performance at the end of the week or month in question was as expected.

However, managers who focus solely on coordination are simply muddling through and miss the bigger picture. It is very important to manage from day to day, but it is as least as important to manage the performance (and improvement in performance) of the process over the longer term. In this context, key ratios will be important – the ratio of enquiries received to orders placed, the ratio of enquiries processed per member of staff and, importantly, the ratio of the projected profit margin to actual profit margin of the final order. These give early indications of emerging trends, which need to be understood and acted upon.

Figure 14.1 should be populated with key objectives, their associated performance measures and targets across the areas of inputs, process, outputs, outcomes and resources. The objectives, measures and targets should reflect the imperatives for the organisation and then the key elements of the process that deliver this performance. In this respect the objectives, measures and targets should be context specific.

14.4   KEY PROCESS MEASURES

There are two important process measures that can be applied in nearly any context and are useful for focusing performance improvement:

1. Cycle time
2. First pass yield.

The use of these two measures has been developed and refined by Thomas Group Inc., based on the underlying principle that speed is a good thing. If something is done faster:

- you need fewer resources;
- the response to the customer will be quicker;
- stock will be lower;
- you will learn faster.

The more a process is practised, the quicker processing becomes as those involved learn. The *raison d'être* behind shortening the cycle time is to intensify this learning effect, making the process quicker and more efficient.

However, speed is only beneficial when there is no waste; hence reducing cycle time is balanced by the measure of first time yield. In the next two sections we will explain how cycle time and first time yield can be measured and we will finish by discussing how the two measures can be used together to improve process performance.

14.4.1 Measuring cycle time

Thomas Group Inc. defined two types of cycle time – static cycle time and dynamic cycle time.

Static cycle time is a backward looking measure. It is the average time taken to complete a process. It is calculated by adding up the times taken for the process to be completed and dividing this by the number of times the cycle was observed. It can be used to measure the average time it takes to deal with a customer in a post office queue, the average length of time between an order being placed and the customer receiving it or the average length of time taken to make a car on a production line.

However, Thomas Group Inc. also created a forward looking measure they called dynamic cycle time. A dynamic cycle is the time required to process the work in progress. Dynamic cycle time is measured by counting, rather than observing the processes, so is a simpler measure to use in practice:

$$\text{Dynamic cycle time} = \frac{\text{Average work in progress}}{\text{Number of items processed in a period}}$$

Therefore, for a post office queue, at the beginning of the hour there could be 8 people in the queue, at the end of the hour 6, with 70 people being processed in the hour:

$$\text{Dynamic cycle time} = \frac{(8+6)/2}{70} = 7/70 = 1/10 \text{ of an hour or 6 minutes}$$

In a service situation, for example, this gives us the length of time at closing time required to process the average queue of customers still waiting to be served. In a manufacturing situation, it will tell you the number of days of production until you run out of work or, in a hospital, the number of days a patient must wait before they are treated.

Dynamic cycle time is very useful for measuring administrative operations. You can go to a desk and see the number of files pending at the beginning of the day, see the files closed during the day and the files still pending at the end of the day. From these three counts you have your dynamic cycle time.

14.4.2 Measuring first pass yield

First pass yield is measured by calculating the number of items that successfully pass through the process first time without any defects or re-work as a percentage of items processed:

$$\text{First pass yield} = \frac{\text{Items processed first time to specification}}{\text{Total number of items processed}}$$

In practice, this often has to be measured by:

$$\text{First pass yield} = \frac{\text{Total output} - \text{re-work} - \text{concessions} - \text{holds}}{\text{Total output} + \text{scrap} + \text{cancellations}}$$

In practice, first pass yield is often measured per activity (or subprocess). Thus, in a manufacturing plant, the first pass yield of each machining operation is measured independently. However, the calculation of the overall first pass yield can produce disturbing results because it is calculated by multiplying together the individual first pass yields from each machining operation.

Hence, a component that goes through a machining process comprising ten operations with the following individual first pass yields of 98%, 95%, 99%, 98%, 96%, 94%, 99%, 99%, 97% and 94% has a first pass yield of 73%. To put it more forcibly, over one-quarter of the production is scrap or re-work!

14.4.3 Improving process performance

The cycle time measures force the organisation to do the process faster, while the first pass yield measure forces the organisation to do it right first time. Both need to be improved together to improve performance.

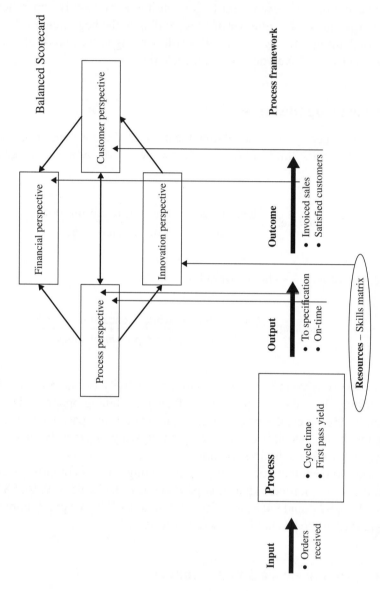

Figure 14.2   The integration of the Balanced Scorecard with a process framework

First time yield often gives you the first indication of where to improve. An analysis of the root causes of the scrap and re-work will identify the most frequently occurring problems, which should provide you with your priority list for action. Removing these problems will in themselves speed up processing before you even start to work directly on reducing the cycle time.

14.4.4 Integration of process measures

Processes need to be managed at a local level as a whole. They should be managed and reviewed on a regular basis by those who have the knowledge to make judgements and authority to take action. However, you cannot integrate all measures being used to coordinate and control a process into the Balanced Scorecard or top level dash board because the picture will become too confused.

The link between the process and the scorecard is usually made through the output and outcome measures (see Figure 14.2). In this way it is possible to link the delivery to the customer with reporting through the organisational hierarchy.

14.5   SUMMARY

In this chapter we have introduced you to the basic concepts of process measurement and explained how your measurement of process performance links into the organisational scorecard. Process performance measurement is extremely important. Your processes are the fundamental elements of the business that enable you to deliver what your customers need, so being able to measure the performance of your processes is a first step in an improvement programme. In Chapter 15 we build on this process measurement model to create a framework that also encapsulates the underpinning resources required for processes to perform effectively.

FURTHER READING

Brown, M. G. (1996) *Keeping the Score: Using the Right Metrics to Drive World Class Performance*, Quality Resources, New York, USA (for the process model, look at Chapter 8, pp. 95–103).

15

Measuring Competence and Resource Development

15.1 INTRODUCTION

SWOT analysis (strengths, weaknesses, opportunities and threats) is still one of the most widely used strategy tools. In our experience, most companies develop their strategy based on the opportunities and threats they perceive in the marketplace. The internal view, the strengths and weaknesses, is often ignored. If you are to develop a balanced strategy you need to embrace both views.

Resource-based theory of the firm has a long history, but more recently ideas such as 'core competences' have attracted considerable attention. However, many of these developments have been conceptual rather than practical and have been difficult to implement.

This chapter builds on the previous chapter about process measurement and presents a practical framework for examining the relationship between competence, resources and performance. We will start by defining the terms we are using and will go on to explain why it is so important to measure competence and resource development. Then we will present a framework for doing this and finally illustrate how this framework is used by way of a case study.

15.2 DEFINING TERMS

Different writers use different definitions for competences, capabilities and resources, so we will start by explaining what we mean by the terms.

15.2.1 What is a competence?

A *competence* is an ability to do something. When applied to businesses you could say:

A company has a strength or a high competence if it can outperform most competitors on a competitive factor that customers value.
A company has a weakness or a low competence if it underperforms most competitors on a competitive factor that customers value.

We are therefore using competence as a way of describing how well (or not) your firm performs its necessary activities. Competence is not an absolute but is measured on a range and comparing your competence against that of your competitors is a convenient approach.

A competence – the ability to do something – is underpinned by resources. Resources are the things an organisation needs to perform the tasks required of it.

15.2.2 What is a resource?

A *resource* is something your organisation can access to perform its activities. This may be because the resource is owned by the company, but resources include people and in this case the company only has temporary access while they are working for the business (either as employees or contractors). You can also describe resources as being either 'tangible' or 'intangible:

Tangible resources are the type of resources you can trip over. They include things like work in progress, stock plant, equipment, buildings and land. They also include patents and licences, debtors and even your employees. In general, you can touch and feel tangible resources as they physically exist.

Intangible resources are less easy to identify. The skills, experience and knowledge of your employees are intangible resources, as are those of your advisers, suppliers and distributors. These skills, knowledge and experience will be captured and embedded into your systems and databases as well as the personal and organisational networks within your organisation. Other attributes, such as your company's brands and reputation, are also intangible resources. Finally, your organisation's culture and values will be important resources as they will enable or prevent you from doing things. Your company's attitude to customers, quality and change will make a significant difference to how your people behave.

Although many of the tangible resources lie within your company's ownership, many of the intangible resources do not. These can be extremely important resources such as employee skills and experience, and they are only on loan to your company while the people work there. Therefore, some of the resources you have at your disposal today could be gone tomorrow.

A simple way of distinguishing between competences and resources is to remember that a *competence* is the ability to do something well (such as delivering new products to market quickly) and a *resource* is an object such as a machine, mineral deposit or patent.

15.3   WHY MEASURE RESOURCE AND COMPETENCE DEVELOPMENT?

The reasons for measuring resource and competence are fourfold:

1. It is important for balancing the short and long term development of your business.
2. It makes you focus on how the performance should be improved rather than simply on the target to be reached.

3. It will help you understand the key drivers of performance.
4. You need to develop measures of resources and capabilities to ensure that they are not simply ignored.

15.3.1 Short and long term

The competitive advantage of a business is not created overnight. Significant competences and resources take years to develop, but our management systems are not always geared up to work on those timescales.

For example, most performance measures tend to focus on short term results – what is to be achieved by the end of the month or the financial year. If these short term imperatives are not managed sensibly, they can conflict with building competitive advantage and even destroy the longer term processes of resource development. Therefore you need to be measuring and tracking key elements of your long term strategy as a balance against short-termism.

Here are some examples to illustrate this:

*   In larger firms, 'high flyers' tend to move up the organising quickly. During their tenure, performance improves in the area in which they are working. However, is this improvement sustainable? Has the 'high flyer' developed the people within that area or simply forced them to work harder in the short term? It is important to hold the managers responsible for both short term performance and longer term development of capability.
*   Return on capital employed (ROCE) is a key measure of overall business performance. However, increasing the returns is far harder to do than reducing the value of capital employed. The application of ROCE as a performance measure can promote behaviours that create short term improvements at the expense of longer term benefits. Delaying new investments will reduce the short term capital employed but will delay the creation of resources and competences that will deliver longer term success. One major oil company saved money for many years by drilling fewer new oil wells!
*   Company reputation in the marketplace can take many years to build but can be quickly damaged by short term actions. Service reliability may be reduced by stock reduction policies, quality reduced by a cost saving programme and flexibility through a productivity drive.

15.3.2 Improvement

There is increasing pressure on companies for continuous improvement. However, performance measurement focuses people on what has to be improved rather than how the improvement should be done. The only sustainable way of increasing the performance of an organisation is to improve the underlying resources and/or the way in which they are coordinated. Making improvements in this way will enable you to improve continually rather than hitting a brick wall when all the slack resource has been squeezed out of the system.

Here is an example of a company manufacturing measurement instruments for the process industry. One of their biggest problems was poor delivery reliability. As they had large customers working on substantial developments, late deliveries could cause the delay of a whole project. This was something their customers did not forget quickly and there were periods when repeat orders simply did not happen. The company survived as many of its competitors were as bad as it was, so eventually customers relented and came back, usually to be disappointed again!

The first attempt to improve was undertaken using 'high energy management'. Regular meetings were scheduled to track delivery performance on a daily basis, problems were highlighted and individuals were given the tasks of chasing up and reducing the delays. This had a significant impact and over a short period on-time deliveries rose to 100 %. However, it was not sustainable and performance slipped when the operations manager left. The second approach focused on the real causes of delays. The managers identified the suppliers who were causing the majority of the problems, worked with those it could and replaced those it could not. Rework was targeted, the causes identified and eliminated. Tooling issues were resolved so that products were produced by the correct methods. As on-time delivery improved, the culture started to change from 'how do we get round this problem?' to 'how do we ensure we never encounter this problem again?' As a result, the improvement became sustainable and the company started to flourish.

Figure 15.1 shows the different ways a target can be displayed. In most organisations the target is represented as a bar to jump over. The target is set at a fixed level and performance is increased to reach this target (the first box in the diagram). However, as your competitors are improving over time, there has to be continuous improvement for many targets and an upward sloping line showing how performance has to improve with time. This is shown in the second box. Many companies find they have improved but not fast enough to close the gap with their competitors, so either they increase the slope of the original line or they look to accelerate the rate at which they improve. This is shown in the third box.

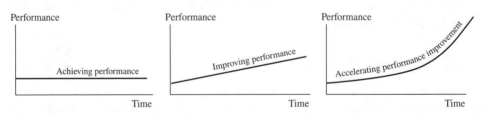

Figure 15.1   Improving performance

In reality, few companies ever achieve the third graph in Figure 15.1, but occasionally it happens when sustainable improvement is delivered through the development and improvement of resources.

15.3.3 Increasing understanding

One of the main roles of measurement is to facilitate learning – in this case understanding the key factors that drive improvement. Building a picture of how the improvement in resources delivers the improvements in performance:

- makes clear the relationship between performance and resources and helps to guide your actions;
- gives you an understanding of 'what' is to be developed and, more importantly, 'why';
- creates a picture that communicates the importance of the resources;
- allows you to track the implementation of resource-based improvement programmes.

15.3.4 Measurement

You often hear that if you cannot measure something you cannot manage it and that 'what gets measured gets done'. Now, although we do not subscribe to either of these statements, the reality is that not measuring resource and competence development gives a clear message that they are not as important as other objectives. The consequences will be:

- If you have no competence or resource measures, development will be ignored and only occur by chance.
- If performance is only measured in terms of outputs, resource development will be impaired.
- Your success in the longer term will be reduced.

Many performance measures are designed to squeeze out discretionary slack. Their *raison d'être* is to focus everyone on achieving measured performance. This leaves no time for experimentation or change. Your organisation cannot develop without the availability of slack resources to focus on the improvement and change required. Therefore, the poor or inappropriate use of performance measurement will destroy the activities that create new resources and competences.

In contrast, the *constructive* use of performance measures *will* help you build your resources, improving your competences and creating a sustainable future.

15.4   A FRAMEWORK FOR DISPLAYING THE RELATIONSHIP BETWEEN RESOURCES AND COMPETENCES

The framework comprises two halves:

1. Measures of resource development
2. Measures of process or competence performance.

Financial statements in company accounts provide a useful analogy. There are two principal components, the profit and loss account and the balance sheet. The profit and loss account is analogous to the performance while the resource development is analogous to the balance sheet. A successful company both performs well and has a strong balance sheet. Figure 15.2 illustrates how we are developing this approach to the measurement and management of competences and resources.

The framework used for process measurement (see also Chapter 14) is that described by Brown (see Figure 15.3). This framework creates an illustration of the relationships between the inputs, processing and outputs and outcomes. This should lead to a better understanding of how the process operates and provide an indication of how to improve performance.

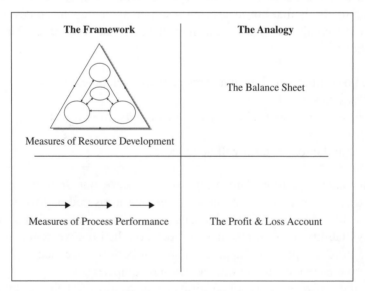

Figure 15.2   The competence and resource framework financial analogy

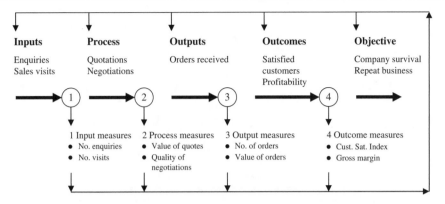

Figure 15.3   Macro process model (adapted from Brown, 1996)

This model effectively depicts current performance but has limited use in understanding how superior performance can be achieved. We have already said in Chapter 14 on measuring processes that the more you repeat a process the more you learn and the faster you repeat it the faster you learn.

15.4.1 A resource measurement framework

Figure 15.4 shows a resource development framework. The relationship between competence performance and its underpinning resources is not a simple linear one, so the depiction of the competence, resources and measures is less structured. In Figure 15.4 we represent the competence by the external triangle and the underpinning resources by the ovals inside.

Experience has shown us that it is useful to show the interaction between the main resources by means of arrows. The arrows are drawn to show how one resource influences another. Influences can be two-way or one-way. For example, in Figure 15.4, Resource 1 affects Resource 2 but not the reverse, and Resources 2 and 3 influence one another.

The description of the individual measures and how they relate to the resources is best captured in a table. The commentary is particularly useful as it describes explicitly the connection between the measure and the resource. Developing resource measures is a creative process, requiring you to understand how the existence of the resource underpins the competence. Assumptions are often made in arriving at appropriate measures. These assumptions need to be documented so that you remember the reasoning behind the use of that particular measure to track the development of the resource.

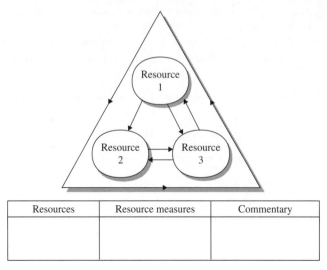

Resources	Resource measures	Commentary

Figure 15.4   The competence/resource measurement framework

15.4.2 An illustration

In this section, we shall demonstrate how the framework is used in practice using an example of a *recruitment competence*. This shows how resources interact to build a competence and how easily these resources can be destroyed.

This example is taken from GKRR plc, a major multinational engineering company who had developed a scheme for recruiting and developing high quality graduate engineers at group level.

GKRR plc

The main recruitment of graduate engineers was centralised in the group's R&D function, which recruited, employed and trained between 10 and 15 engineers a year. The training programme was centred on a series of projects, which each engineer undertook over the two to three year period they spent on the central R&D programme. These projects were primarily based in the operation companies around the group and each project was carefully selected and managed by a tutor.

The performance measures for the recruitment function focused on traditional measures in the form of a cause and effect diagram, which is currently the vogue for the Balanced Scorecard (see Figure 15.5).

However, conversations revealed that there was significantly more to the recruitment and training of the graduate engineers than had been captured by this approach.

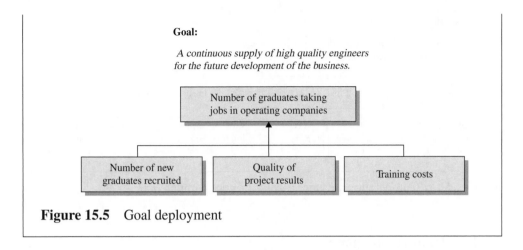

Figure 15.5   Goal deployment

It was agreed that the objective of the process was:

'To provide a continuous supply of high quality engineers for the future development of the business.'

15.4.3 Competence measures

Using the process framework the competence measures chosen were (see Figure 15.6):

Input
- Number of applicants
- Percentage of offers accepted
- Number employed

Process
- Variety of projects offered
- Percentage of projects successfully completed
- Cost per project

Output
- Value of business improvement achieved
- Number of graduates placed

Outcome
- Number of project alumni still employed by GKRR after 3 years
- Mean value of alumni seniority
- Mean time to reach level 3 manager position

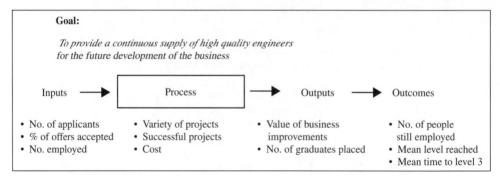

Figure 15.6   Competence measures – recruitment competence

15.4.4 Resource measures

Delving into the reasons why the recruitment competence performed so well revealed a more complex picture of the resources that underpinned it:

- Many companies in the UK had experienced difficulty in recruiting high quality graduate engineers. At GKRR, in contrast, central recruitment had been built up over the last 15 years and nobody in the company could remember when they last had a problem in this area.
- The company focused on the top four universities offering engineering in the UK, building up a track record of recruiting the best and developing relationships with the academic staff to help in this process. The staff were happy to assist, as they could see the quality of the training and development provided as well as the successful career paths of their previous students.
- The graduate engineers did not have to be found jobs within the group on completing the programme; they were often syphoned off during their second or third year when the operating companies were eager to place them directly into line management positions. The central R&D group had difficulty keeping many of their graduates until the end of their training.
- The projects were successful because they also brought benefits to the operating companies in which they took place. The graduates were still in demand despite the fact that operating companies had to pay for the projects. The projects were often used for spreading best practice around the group and as a result were usually highly successful in bringing rapid performance improvements.
- The engineers developed quickly during the 2 to 3 years in the development scheme. This was mainly attributed to the skill of the tutors in choosing the next project. Each project was chosen to stretch the graduate to the limit of their abilities, with support provided by the tutor to ensure that the graduate did not completely flounder. The managed progression and mentoring through simple to more complex projects greatly assisted the trainees' development.

- After 15 years of running the programme, there was a large group of alumni, with many in senior positions throughout the group.

The resources identified were:

- A very good in-house reputation
- Documented evidence of international projects and promotion
- The recruitment process
- The training process
- Long lived relationships with university staff
- The project group alumni
- The staff group.

These resources interacted and supported one another, for example:

- The evidence of international projects and promotion assisted recruitment but also helped build the relationship with the university staff.
- The relationship with the university staff enabled the company to recruit the best candidates, building their in-house reputation for quality people.
- The training process enabled the international projects to be undertaken with minimal risk of failure. It also helped build the reputation with the universities and the in-house reputation.
- The whole competence was further supported by the alumni, who had reached senior positions and who were now recruiting from the scheme.

These are illustrated by Figure 15.7.

Figure 15.7   Resources within the recruitment competence

The resource and competence measures chosen are summarised and represented in Figure 15.8.

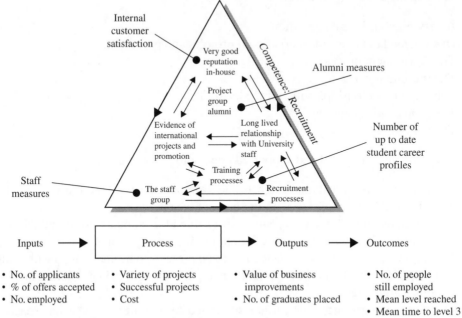

Inputs →	Process →	Outputs →	Outcomes

• No. of applicants
• % of offers accepted
• No. employed
	• Variety of projects
	• Successful projects
	• Cost
		• Value of business
		  improvements
		• No. of graduates placed
			• No. of people
			  still employed
			• Mean level reached
			• Mean time to level 3

Resources	Resource measures	Commentary
A very good in-house reputation	Internal customer satisfaction survey	Critical for new projects and ensuring the graduates first line positions
Documented evidence of international projects and promotion in the form of "student career profiles"	Number of up to date "student career profiles"	Seen as important by potential recruits and university contacts. Perception is important, hence the measure, but need to check for quality.
The training process	Staff experience (No. of tutors × length of service)	An essential ingredient in supporting stretching projects with low risk of failure. Difficult to measure quality here, but useful as an initial measure.
Long lived relationships with university staff	Staff relationships (No. of staff × length of relationship)	Important for recruiting the best and getting staff insights. Difficult to measure quality here, but useful as an initial measure
The project alumni group	Project alumni seniority score (No. of people × level in the organisation)	An indication of the potential support from the alumni

Figure 15.8   GKRR's resource and competence measures for graduate engineer recruitment

GKRR – a postscript

At the time of this analysis, moves to reduce central costs were underway. Two operating divisions decided that they could set up their own internal recruitment and development scheme, copying the scheme run by central R&D.

The problem was that the divisions did not have their own tutors to supervise the projects. They therefore had to rely on their own internal line management. They also had to use central R&D training for the short courses they provided.

Although the costs appeared lower (mainly because the line management time required to run the scheme was never fully costed) this approach began to undermine the resources built up over the previous 15 years. Firstly, it confused the university staff, who had always been ready to recommend the company in the past. Secondly, it reduced the quality of graduates taken, as the operating companies did not have the same reputation and these posts were seen as second class. Other effects are still awaited.

The case illustrates a number of important points that you need to consider when trying to develop and use competences and resources.

1. Competences and resources take years to build but can be destroyed almost over-night – in this case 15 years of work was overturned in 12 months. What was also apparent was that key members of senior management could not see it happening either.
2. Reducing cost is an important part of improving performance, but cost cutting has consequences in terms of changing competences and resources. Before you start changing things in sensitive areas, such as in the relationships between your company and your customers or in your relationship with current and future employees, you need to understand fully the nature and value of what is happening. Doing it more cheaply is easy, but it may destroy the thing that enables your business to survive.
3. We often believe that because something is going smoothly, it is easy to do. Sometimes you only find out how much skill is involved when someone leaves. Just because the activity never came to anyone's attention does not mean it is not a key competence.

15.5   CONCLUSION

In this chapter we have developed the process model further to capture the development of the resources that underpin the competence. Developing competence and resource-based measures for each process is a significant task, but it is worth doing for key processes that ensure you create and maintain competitive advantage. The very act of embarking on an assessment using this approach usually changes the way you think about your business. Doing this with your key processes will be extremely rewarding.

FURTHER READING

Brown, M. G. (1996) *Keeping the Score: Using the Right Metrics to Drive World Class Performance*, Quality Resources, New York, USA (for the process model, look at Chapter 8, pp. 95–103).

Mill, J. F., Platts, K. W, Bourne, M. C. S. and Richards, A. H. (2002) *Competing Through Competences: Achieving Sustainable Advantage Through the Strategic Management of Resources*, Cambridge University Press, Cambridge, UK.

16

Measuring Financial Performance

16.1 INTRODUCTION

There is a saying 'Revenue is vanity, profit is sanity, but cash is king!' In this chapter we are going to consider some of the key financial ratios used both internally and externally to measure business performance. However, before doing that we will give an overview of the importance of measuring financial performance.

The financial results of a business are the outcome of all the business activities over the last year and a reflection of many decisions taken in previous years. Retrospective they may be, but end of year results are important. Most businesses exist to make a return for their shareholders who have a keen interest in the performance of the companies in which they are investing. Financial analysts' and investors' views of the business will influence availability of funding. They will also influence the actions of customers and suppliers and they will even have an impact on personal bonuses, which in some organisations are substantial. Therefore, businesses take great care to manage the messages about their end of year results.

Given the importance of, and the focus on, financial results it is not surprising that, on occasions, the results are achieved through massaging. It is quite simple to cut out expenditure that falls this year but will not provide a return until next year, be it staff training, new product development, refurbishment of premises or advertising close to the year end. However, all of these actions have consequences. The training may not have an immediate effect, but it will have an impact on productivity over time and may also damage staff engagement, leading to a further reduction in performance. Cutting expenditure on new product development may also give huge short term financial benefits, but in twelve months' time if you are behind the curve and trying to compete with a better offering than your competitors your margins will be squeezed. Refurbishment is another effective short term profit booster. Your hotel rooms can survive another year without redecoration, the soft furnishings will do, but over time your premises will look tired and guest numbers will fall. Marketing experts tell us that you need to spend seven times what you failed to spend when you cut back, so what appears to be an excellent tactic for reaching the quarter or year end figures may well turn out to be an expensive decision in the longer term.

High profitability may be too good to be true. Marks and Spencer found itself in this position in the 1990s. Suppliers were squeezed and prices were increased to create spectacular sales margins. Costs were also contained by reducing the number of staff on the sales floor. The financial result was excellent but it was unsustainable. While profitability looked good, employee satisfaction was falling, customer satisfaction followed and within twelve months customers had deserted. It took several years for the company to recover.

If you are making significantly higher profits than your competitors, give a thought to why that is the case. Is it because you have:

1. A monopoly position (e.g. through regulation or very significant market share)?
2. Customers who are locked in to your product or process?
3. Access to resources that others cannot access (e.g. departure slots at a busy airport, gravel in a quarry) or at a price they cannot access?
4. A unique or superior product (through investment or patent protection)?

If not, you should ask yourself, 'How sustainable is my position?' 'Are we really operating better than everyone else or are we making money today by mortgaging the future?' Even the advantages listed above are not necessarily sustainable – monopolies do not last for ever, customers find ways to defect and competitors find ways to access resources and develop superior products. Therefore, it is always worth considering how you will maintain your position.

It is often said that 'cash is king'. If you run out of cash, the business will close, so you must ensure you never get close to that position. If you do, you will be forced to take unpalatable action. Some companies have been known to launch new products early, and before they are really ready, in order to have sufficient cash to run their payroll. Arie de Gheus makes the point in his book, *The Living Company*, that successful companies are conservative in financing. They have enough money in their pocket to control their timing.

Measuring financial performance is important as it is a measure of success. It is a little like 'keeping the score'. It is also a powerful and visible measure to the outside world that will have an impact on the future of your business. However, you must not treat it as the only measure of success, as it is only a short term lagging measure. Now this 'health warning' is over, we will look at how you can use financial measurement to provide key insights into your business and how it is being run.

The use of key ratios will enable you to highlight issues and identify trends while giving you a degree of comfort that the organisation is progressing satisfactorily – at least in the short term.

16.2   A SHAREHOLDER PERSPECTIVE

Shareholders, whether they are individuals or institutional investors, are interested in many things, but from an economic perspective they are interested in their wealth. With respect to the financial performance of your organisation they are particularly interested in the growth in value of the shares they hold and the flow of income from the dividends you pay.

A firm's profitability is not directly linked either to the share price or to dividend payments. Making a profit may allow you to make a larger dividend payment, but, technically, companies can still make a dividend payment from previous years' profits even if they have made a loss in the current year.

Similarly, higher profits do not always result in the share price increasing. The share price represents the perceived current value of all the future income streams, so if you increase your profit this year, the market will need to understand how sustainable this increase is into the future before the share price will increase.

Finally, there is one other element – risk. Shareholders want an appropriate return for the risks they are taking. That does not mean shareholders avoid risk; it simply means the higher the level of risk the shareholders perceive, the higher the levels of return they require. All these factors make the link between the share price and the reported profits at year end opaque.

Let us take some examples. A bank in a mature but growing market may find that it can grow its dividend payments slowly but progressively year on year. The rise in share price would reflect the stability of this growth and the shareholders' view about the long term certainty of the income stream. However, a quarry operation may be in a market with a similar stability, but unless it increases the size of its mineral reserves it will face a declining share price as every year represents a move closer to the exhaustion of the quarry. The same is true of oil companies and that is why the misrepresentation of oil reserves caused such a big issue for Shell. Dividend increases are not always the driver of share price growth. Many companies in fast moving markets, such as electronics or pharmaceuticals, may need all their cash to fuel their rapid growth. In this situation, the share price increase may by driven by the growth in sales and profitability, with the expectation of either dividends in the future or a premium on the share price when the company is bought out or the shares are sold.

However, you should beware of the risk trap. ICI produced commodity chemicals for many years. The company saw its profitability as being too low so, through a series of disposals and acquisitions, it moved out of commodity chemicals into more specialist chemicals. The company's profitability increased but so did shareholders' expectations as they saw the specialist chemical market as being more risky. Thus, although profits increased, the market sentiment did not as the company was still seen as delivering a level of profit lower than expected for the risks involved.

You can see from this that share price is a good indicator of how well the business is doing because, in the longer term, it reflects the underlying and fundamental performance of the business. However, in the shorter term, share price is influenced by performance and expectations. The Centre for Business Performance at Cranfield School of Management conducted a study into the impact of financial management on share price and the results have been summarised in Figure 16.1.

Besides the cost of planning and budgeting (which if not well managed can hit profitability), the main determinant of share price is the difference between expectation

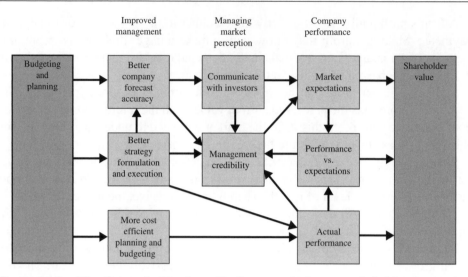

Figure 16.1   The Centre for Business Performance's framework linking budgeting and planning with shareholder value

and actual performance. Shareholders do not like surprises and studies have shown that issuing a profit warning can cut some 25% off the share price. The task for management is twofold. Firstly, they have to manage the expectations of the share-holders through communicating with them and, secondly, they have to be consistent in the delivery of performance. Management teams that understand their businesses well and that have well functioning financial and performance management systems can do this. These two activities, over time, create a confidence in the ability of the management team. The consistency of delivery reduces the risk to the shareholder, and so the share price will rise as a direct result.

Management teams have a significant role to play in influencing the company's share price. Economic outlook also has an obvious influence on share price and business performance. Managers are expected to understand their market and business well enough to predict the impact of normal economic trends. However, they cannot be expected to foresee one-off events, such as the 9/11 Twin Towers attack or the ash cloud that closed much of the northern European airspace after the explosion of a vol-cano in Iceland. Both of these events put considerable strain on many types of business. In these circumstances managers must communicate clearly the approach they are taking to cope with the unforeseen problems and the impact this will have on short and medium term performance. Stronger companies will take the financial hit and manage their way through the situation. Weaker companies may find themselves having to take short term actions to reduce costs that undermine their future competitiveness and profitability.

16.3   KEY SHAREHOLDER RATIOS

Most businesses will track their performance using financial ratios. Managers need to understand:

- how profitable they are, especially in relation to their peers and competitors;
- how liquid they are, whether they have the capacity to pay short term liabilities as they fall due without disrupting the business;
- if they are solvent, whether or not they have more assets than liabilities;
- how financially efficient they are, especially how well they use their capital;
- their capacity to repay loans that fall due.

There are standard ratios, but as a manager it is important to choose the ratio that gives you the information you need. Short term liabilities may look good for a company this year, but if there is a major debt repayment in 14 months' time, you will need to think carefully about how you define short term. Return on assets may look very good, but is this because the asset base is now fully depreciated and has no book value? You should bear this in mind while reading the following descriptions of ratios used by managers and analysts to track the performance of organisations.

Earnings per share
This tracks the earnings against the issued share capital and should show a growing trend over time (unless the shares are split):

$$\text{Earnings per share} = \frac{\text{Earnings after tax}}{\text{Number of shares issued}}$$

Dividend cover
This shows the number of times the dividend is covered by earnings and gives an indication of the level of variation in profitability that is needed to cause a change in dividend policy:

$$\text{Dividend cover} = \frac{\text{Earnings after tax}}{\text{Dividend payments}}$$

Interest cover
Similar ratios can be derived for interest cover to establish the level of variation in profitability that is needed before the company has an issue with making its interest

payments. In a highly geared company (a company with high levels of borrowing compared with its asset base), this may be an extremely important ratio:

$$\text{Interest cover} = \frac{\text{Operating profit}}{\text{Interest paid}}$$

where operating profit is the net profit before the deduction of interest and tax.

P/E ratio, or price/earnings ratio

This is the ratio of the company's share price to the earnings per share. A low price/earnings ratio reflects the market's expectations of slow growth and a share value based on current earnings. A high P/E ratio means that shareholders have high expectations for future growth and development. There is not a perfect P/E ratio, but companies can get an indication of how they are doing by comparing themselves to their peers in the same industry sector:

$$\text{P/E ratio} = \frac{\text{Share price in the market}}{\text{Earnings per share}}$$

Total shareholder return

This is the total return to the shareholder over a period (share price increase and dividend payments) per share divided by the initial share price. As such it gives a comprehensive indication to the shareholder of their returns, but it does not account for the risks the shareholder is taking.

Market value added

Market value added (MVA) is the difference between the market capitalisation (the share price multiplied by the number of shares issued) and the equity capital held in the balance sheet. This measure is seen as an indication of the value created in the company compared to the market valuation of the company as a whole and is an indicator of wealth creation.

Economic value added

Economic value added (or EVA™) is an interesting ratio that is both of interest to shareholders and management alike. EVA™ is defined as:

$$\text{EVA}^{\text{TM}} = \text{Net operating profit after tax} - \text{Capital} \times \text{Cost of capital})$$

The assumption underpinning EVA™ is that companies do not exist just to make a profit, they are tasked with a more demanding goal: that of creating a profit in excess of what would be normally expected for the level of risks being taken. Hence in the formula, the profit after tax is reduced by the normal level of profit that would be expected. This is calculated by multiplying the capital by the weighted average cost of the capital used in the business. As the weighted average cost of capital reflects the level of risk the company is perceived to be taking, the measure tells shareholders whether the company is creating or destroying value.

From a shareholder's perspective, they want to invest in businesses that are going to create returns in excess of what they would normally expect to receive for taking this level of risk.

From the management's perspective, they should only be investing in projects that create returns that are high enough to justify the investment of the new capital. This then becomes the guiding principle within the company and if there are not sufficient numbers of suitable projects, management should seriously consider returning the money to the shareholders either through dividend or repurchasing their own shares.

The major proponents of EVA™ are Stern Stewart & Co, who combine the measure with an incentive scheme that pays out based on increases in EVA™ over a three to five year time horizon (to ensure the improvement is sustainable and not simply generated within a single accounting year). Their books itemise the adjustments you have to make to the published accounts to calculate a company's EVA™. However, calculating EVA™ within your own company is a simpler task through your own management accounts.

16.4   ACCOUNTING RATIOS

Some definitions will be set out here before explaining accounting ratios.

Profit is defined as the difference between income and costs (profit = income − costs). However, profit can be measured at many levels so it is important to decide whether the profit is before or after items such as depreciation, interest and taxation when making any comparisons.

Contribution, on the other hand, is defined as contribution = profit − direct costs. Contribution gives an indication of whether, say, a product, service, market channel or customer makes a contribution towards the overheads of the business. There is a well known saying in banking that 80 % of the customers make 120% of the profits, which means that the other 20 % of customers have a negative contribution.

There is a wide range of accounting ratios used externally by both analysts and investors and internally by management accountants. These can be subdivided into profitability ratios and liquidity ratios. We discuss each briefly in turn.

16.4.1 Profitability ratios

$$\text{Gross profit margin} = (\text{Gross profit/Sales}) \times 100$$

where gross profit is defined as the profit before deducting overheads, which is a measure of the profitability of the core operation.

$$\text{Operating profit margin} = (\text{Operating profit/Sales}) \times 100$$

where operating profit is sometimes know as PBIT (profit before deducting interest and tax) or EBIT (earnings before deducting interest and tax). This is a measure of the extent to which profits are being earned as sales are made.

$$\text{Return on assets} = (\text{Net profit/Net assets employed}) \times 100$$

These can then be broken down into subratios such as

$$\text{Return on fixed capital} = (\text{Net profit/Fixed assets}) \times 100$$

$$\text{Return on working capital} = (\text{Net profit/Working capital}) \times 100$$

where working capital = stock + short term debtors + cash – short term creditors.

Taking a similar approach, Figure 16.2 shows the components of return on net assets. This diagram ties together pictorially a number of the key ratios discussed above and Figure 16.3 shows the actions you should consider taking if you wish to increase your return on net assets.

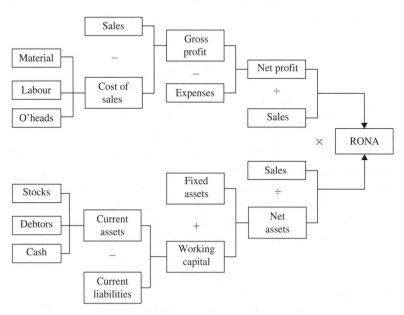

Figure 16.2   The composition of the return on net assets

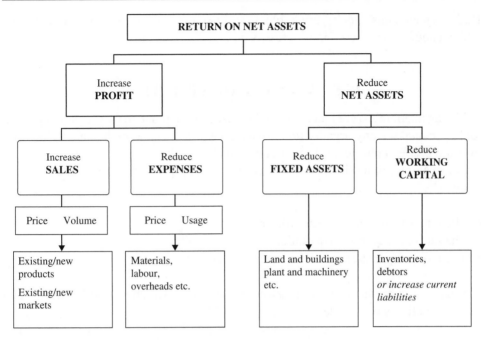

Figure 16.3   How to increase your return on net assets

16.4.2 Liquidity ratios

These are ratios of short term liquidity and tracked by credit rating agencies and suppliers alike. The two key ratios are:

$$\text{The current ratio} = \frac{\text{Current assets}}{\text{Current liabilities}}$$

where current implies short term – those payments falling due within 12 months. Current assets usually include stock, WIP, debtors and cash, and current liabilities include trade creditors, tax liabilities, bank overdrafts, etc.

$$\text{The acid test} = \frac{\text{Current assets} - \text{Inventory}}{\text{Current liabilities}}$$

This is a more stringent test as it assumes that in the short term inventory is not as liquid as other assets. Whether this is so in practice will depend on the industry.

Builders merchants' stock – brick, blocks, timber, etc. – is usually considered liquid, while manufacturing work in progress is not.

16.5   MANAGEMENT RATIOS

Management ratios are much less widely used but in practice they are an important tool for managing any organisation. Management ratios capture the underlying relationship between physical activities and financial results.

For example, in a sales pipeline, a company selling business to business should know:

- The ratio of sales calls to enquiries made
- The ratio of enquiries to quotations
- The ratio of quotations made to orders placed.

Similarly, in a business to consumer company, ratios which should be known and tracked are likely to include:

- The ratio of advertising spend to enquiries made
- The ratio of leaflets sent out to inbound call centre calls
- The ratio of inbound calls to quotations given
- The ratio of inbound calls to orders placed
- The ratio of search pop-ups to click-throughs
- The ratio of click-throughs to orders placed.

The idea behind each of these ratios is that you can predict – or at the very least estimate – the results of your activities. If your sales team visits customers, you expect them to generate a number of enquiries. For each enquiry, you expect to generate an average quotation value. For each quotation, you expect to win an average value of order. In this way you can look ahead at your sales presence, the pipeline of quotations and your expected order intake.

Using these ratios also helps to establish where you are getting the best return on your activity and thus where you should focus your resources. They can also be used to forecast changes in performance that may be expected if you invest in more resources. If the spend on pop-ups is increased, you would expect the click-throughs to follow, leading to more orders. However, the law of diminishing returns applies, so it is important to track changes in the ratios that occur after the investment has been made to ensure you are getting the returns you expected.

You can use these ratios in other ways as well. Is there a significant difference in the ratio of visits to enquiries between the good and bad sales representatives? If so, what is it that the good sales representatives are doing that the others are not doing? Is there a difference between different parts of the country and what does that mean? Is there a difference between different types of customers and different customer segments? These are all ratios that indicate how different behaviours, processes or customer groupings produce different results. We would strongly recommend you use these financial ratios in the budgeting process as they provide opportunities to learn.

In difficult times, organisations frequently make across-the-board savings by shaving a percentage off every budget. As a once-only initiative this is not usually too much of a problem, but if it is an annual occurrence the cost savings can become unsustainable. When costs are cut primarily at an accounting level, the link to the physical changes is often not made. If you cut £100 000 from the annual budget of a particular department, what will that mean? What will the department have to do to make the savings and what will the impact be? Rather than rushing through budget reductions, ask managers how the savings can be achieved and what the impact will be.

To take an example, let us consider a call centre that has been asked to reduce its costs by 10 %. Do they do this by reducing the number of staff? If the call centre manager knows the number of calls an hour the average call centre operative can handle, she can look at the impact of staff reductions on the number of calls handled and lost. Now you can see the direct financial consequences of reducing the staff numbers. If it is decided that the current volume of calls needs to be handled by fewer staff, the question turns to 'How should this be achieved?' It might be done through better staff training and reduced use of agency staff, who are expensive and slower. It might be done through improved software support making the processing faster, perhaps, or through partly automating the call handling process, directing calls to specialists or providing automated responses. Now we are talking about the physical changes that have to be made to improve productivity rather than making financial decisions in a vacuum without any consideration of the wider impact on the business.

One very effective way of using management ratios is to track them over time to trace the improvement in performance that has occurred through learning and through improvements in processes. Ideally these ratios will be linked to improvement initiatives and the time and money spent on these initiatives will be tied to the improvements in the management ratios. However, there is one word of warning: there is a limit to how far the ratios can be pushed. If you have a 100 % conversion ratio of enquiries to sales it probably means you are not being adventurous enough in the business you are chasing. Similarly, if you have no bad debts on the loans you give, are you restricting the lending you are making? A good manager is constantly monitoring and discussing these ratios, looking for the signals they give about how the business is performing, how the market is changing and what new opportunities may be out there. Of course, these ratios need to be seen in the wider picture represented by all the other KPIs in the business. An improvement in call centre productivity might give a short term cost saving, but if it is combined with a fall in customer satisfaction, you may find customers defecting in the longer term.

16.6   CONCLUSION

Financial performance is often seen as the key measure of business success. As you will have seen from this chapter, it is a very important measure, but it is backward looking. It tells you a great deal about the past – and it will help you to extrapolate what will happen in the future. However, it does not stand on its own. You need to understand the dynamics of the business. You need to understand the impact of one activity on another. You need to know how the business will be influenced by changes in technology, demographics and evolving customer needs. Strong financial performance is a measure of a healthy business and having financial strength gives the business the resources to change and adapt. However, the business will only be successful if the resources are used wisely.

FURTHER READING

Atrill, P. and McLaney, E. (2008) *Accounting and Finance for Non-specialists*, Sixth Edition, Pearson Education, Harlow, Essex, UK.

Rappaport, A. (1998) *Creating Shareholder Value: The New Standard for Business Performance*, The Free Press, New York, USA.

Stern, J. M., Shiely, J. S. and Ross, I. (2001) *The EVA Challenge: Implementing Value-Added Change in an Organization*, John Wiley & Sons, Inc., New York, USA.

17
Measuring Sustainability

17.1 INTRODUCTION

Sustainability and corporate responsibility are becoming too important for businesses to ignore. There are pressures from governments introducing legislation and 'green taxes' in order to protect the environment, consumers want to know the provenance of the goods they are buying and employees are becoming more concerned about the values of the organisations for which they work. On top of this, investors are increasingly concerned about an organisation's sustainability and environmental impact. Indeed, there is research to show that investors' wealth is harmed when businesses behave in a socially irresponsible way, as described by Frooman (1997). All these pressures are forcing businesses to consider the impact of their activities on the environment and on the communities in which they operate.

Measuring sustainability is not exactly like measuring customer satisfaction or employees. It is more complex and all-embracing. Of course you can and should measure practical initiatives such as reduction in energy usage, recycling and time devoted to community projects. These are relatively easy to measure and the act of measuring them demonstrates to employees how important they are. However, important though these factors are, sustainability is also about ensuring your organisation has a sustainable business model, and that is often more difficult to measure.

17.2 WHAT ARE 'SUSTAINABILITY' AND 'CORPORATE RESPONSIBILITY'?

'Corporate responsibility' describes the actions, activities and obligations of businesses in achieving sustainability. 'Sustainable business' is essentially about creating an enduring business model. To give an example at a very basic level, if your organisation is relying on scarce mineral resources it is unlikely to be in business when those resources run out. One could also argue that a business lending money to people who cannot afford to pay it back is also not likely to survive.

There is a common misconception that sustainability is just about the environment and climate change but that is not the case. Also, there is a debate about the extent to which businesses (or the people within them) take actions for altruistic reasons or for purely financial gain. We are not going to enter into that debate in this chapter other than to say acting responsibly and making a profit are not mutually exclusive.

One of the difficulties in considering sustainability is how it is defined and where you set the boundaries of your influence. In terms of geography, the operations of a business have an impact not only on the local community in which it is situated but also on the communities affected by its suppliers.

Coca Cola is a good example of the importance of considering local conditions. A ready supply of water is a major challenge for the company and they came under intense pressure for taking too much water to supply their plant in Kerala, India. This led to unrest in the local community and major protests and strikes. It also came to the attention of the media and eventually the government revoked the company's license to operate. Coca Cola went to the high court to have the decision overruled but a spokesman for the company did note that this episode had made a short term but significant impact on sales. For the company this meant a negative effect on their business; for the local people it meant loss of work and there were significant knock-on effects as a result. The company responded to the challenge of water supply, setting up wastewater treatment facilities at its bottling plants and offering training sessions to plant managers on the subject of water stress.

The example above shows the direct impact of a business on its local community and (whatever the rights and wrongs of that particular argument) it is relatively easy to see cause and effect. One of the difficulties in measuring sustainability is assessing what is to be encompassed. For example, about 80 % of energy needed to produce a can of beer is used in making the can. It would be easy for a drinks company to ignore this in assessing their environmental impact as they buy in the can. If you are a retail business, for example, where do you draw the line? Do you include emissions from your suppliers' lorries as they deliver your goods? Do you consider the impact your suppliers in Kenya have on their local community? Another difficulty is how you measure some of these more intangible effects. Your reputation as a business, for example, is crucial and while it is possible to measure impact on your reputation it is not always easy or clear.

Creating a sustainable business is complex as there are many factors involved and there are no hard and fast formulae for measuring progress. Decisions have to be made about what you are measuring and why. Judgement is required in balancing advantages and disadvantages of various courses of action. One way of deciding where to draw the line in considering the impact of the operations of your business is to consider whether they help or hinder the environment, whether they speed up or slow down the use of finite resources and whether they have a positive or negative impact on the wellbeing of the population. Despite the complexity of these issues, organisations of all types do measure aspects of their sustainability and it is important that they do so, because, 'what gets measured gets done'.

In this chapter we are outlining the importance of sustainability to the performance of a business and some of the simpler ways in which organisations can build sustainability into their strategic thinking and measure their progress. We are not looking at external reporting, however. If this is of interest there are references to further sources of information at the end of the chapter.

17.3   WHAT ARE THE BENEFITS?

Some people believe building a sustainable business is highly costly and the trick is simply to avoid any legal pitfalls and to use the benefits of sustainability, such as good PR. This may seem cynical and perceptions are changing, but it is a view held by a sizeable number of people. It is unfortunate because taking sustainability to the core of the business can bring major benefits. There may be costs but in many cases these can be balanced against benefits, although these benefits may be accrued in the longer term. There is a well known example of the Suffolk brewer Adnams whose board courageously decided to take the more expensive option of investing in an environmentally friendly distribution centre. This paid off faster than expected when energy prices rose substantially, so sustainability can be a mechanism for creating a competitive edge. (You can find out more about Adnams' approach to sustainability in the vignette at the end of this book.) According to a survey from IBM by Pohle and Hittner, of 250 global executives, 68 % believe that having a corporate responsibility strategy in place gives them a competitive advantage to their top line.

Looking in more detail at the benefits, they can be divided into five broad categories: reputation and marketing, people, innovation, culture and finance.

17.3.1 Reputation and marketing

We have already seen the effect on Coca Cola of problems faced in Kerala and there are many other examples. BP suffered enormously as a result of the damage to its reputation following the Gulf Coast oil spill in 2010. It is not only the major corporations, however, that need to pay attention to this. Take the example of small local firms of chartered accountants. Many of their clients will come from referrals and from relationships they have built up with people in their local communities.

In terms of marketing, consumers are becoming increasingly concerned about how the products they buy are produced. Green and Black's chocolate, for example, created a successful brand based on organic chocolate produced ethically and sold at a premium. Free range eggs and chickens are now almost universally stocked by supermarkets because consumers want to buy them.

17.3.2 Innovation

Grayson and Hodges (2004) suggest that commitment to higher standards of performance stimulates the search for newer and better ways of doing things. Adnams, the brewers, redesigned their beer bottles to reduce their weight and the amount of materials used. This also resulted in a reduction in distribution costs.

The quest for sustainability has also led to innovation in markets. Carbon Trading is a market-based mechanism designed to mitigate the increase of CO_2 in the atmosphere. Carbon trading markets bring together buyers and sellers of carbon credits operating with standardised rules for trading.

17.3.3 People

Being an attractive employer has distinct benefits in enabling you to choose the people you want and generating commitment and enthusiasm from your employees. The John Lewis Partnership created a distinct brand as an employer around their principle of 'employer of distinction' by treating all their employees (partners, as they call them) as individuals with respect, honesty and fairness.

Unilever, in its website under graduate recruitment states: '...we all work to the highest standards of professional excellence and integrity. Our reputation as one of the world's most admired employers is hard-earned. We've achieved it by offering opportunities for our people to pursue their goals, both professionally and personally. Because we operate a truly global business, we recognise the importance of diversity; of understanding individual ways of working, and how they can complement each other to deliver outstanding results. Our commitment to developing strong local businesses is what makes us unique – that's why we call ourselves the "multi-local multinational".' Sustainability is one of four tabs at the top of the graduate recruitment page along with 'about us', 'our brands' and 'innovation', and under the sustainability tab performance highlights are listed including 'community', 'safety', 'hygiene and well being' and 'nutrition'. Unilever obviously sees this as an important strand of their business.

17.3.4 Culture and dealing with change

We live in a world of 'discontinuous' change where what happens in one part of the world can have a major impact elsewhere. Floods or earthquakes in the southern hemisphere can affect markets and businesses in Europe and the US. Just think about the impact on businesses from the 9/11 terrorism attack. We know there will be change but we do not know what that change will be, so businesses need to be able to use the strength of their brand and the expertise and skill of their people to build an organisation that can adapt quickly to changing circumstances. They need to be 'fleet of foot'.

Adnams, has worked hard at doing this and at creating competitive advantage from it. They work on a model with four fields: values, stakeholders, leadership and brand. The area of intersection between these fields is where their sustainable competitive advantage lies, something that is very difficult for the competition to copy.

In the Adnams model, 'values' are about *how* things are done. A sales manager may be hitting targets but if problems are created in doing this those need to be addressed. 'Stakeholders' are about engaging with, for example, the local community. It is important to influence decisions and make views heard. 'Brand' is about bringing the values to life. 'Leadership' is about creating an appropriate culture and climate within the organisation. Adnams works on the principle that people need to know themselves first and use 360 degree feedback to measure adherence to values, respect, thoughts and ideas *(the how)* as well as traditional measurements of budget, profit, ROI and KPIs *(the what)*.

17.3.5 Financial benefits

Financial benefits include the obvious one – saving money. Being sustainable generally involves using less of something. Toyota, for example, eliminated waste to landfill and halved their water usage per car, saving them money. Acting in a responsible way can also have financial benefits – paying heed to health and safety issues results in reducing the number of accidents and thus to reducing costs arising from them.

Financial benefit is not confined to cost cutting and saving; it also includes being attractive to investors. Research by Ernst and Young's Centre for Business Innovation has shown that about one third of inputs to investors' decisions are based on nonfinancial information including environmental and social issues. Indeed, sustainability stock indexes have been developed that provide guidance for investors. Launched back in 1999, the Dow Jones Sustainability Index tracks the financial performance of the leading sustainability-driven companies worldwide with the aim of providing asset managers with reliable and objective benchmarks to manage sustainability portfolios.

17.4 BUILDING SUSTAINABILITY INTO YOUR BUSINESS

We have looked at the benefits of sustainability and have touched on the difficulty in defining and measuring it. The following is a simple process that can be used to build sustainability into the strategy and plans for your business (see Figure 17.1).

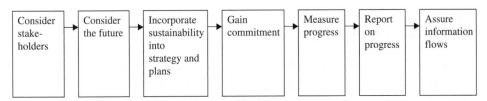

Figure 17.1   A process for building sustainability into strategy

17.4.1 Stage One: Who are the stakeholders?

Your stakeholders are those people that affect or are affected by your organisation. These include customers, employees, government, investors, NGOs, regulators and the local community, among others. Because each organisation has a huge range of stakeholders, it is important to identify those with the most significant relationship with your company.
  Think about:

- Which stakeholders rely on your organisation for their own success, such as employees, investors, suppliers and those that are most significantly affected by what you do. For companies that pollute, for example, this might be the local community within which they operate.
- Those stakeholders who are capable of affecting business performance the most, for example competitors or customers.

17.4.2 Stage Two: Consider the future

When you have identified your stakeholders and their key concerns the next step is to use this information to develop and implement an organisational strategy around these issues.

Outputs
At this stage you should be looking at the possible outputs of your business in five or ten years:

- Will people want what you are selling/the service you are providing?
- Will what you are doing be constrained legally?
- Will what you are doing be socially acceptable?
- Will what you are doing still be the leading technology or approach?
- What will your customers *really want*? For example, for a car manufacturer, does the customer want a car or a means of getting from A to B?
- Is there another way of looking at what you do? This will help you think about new opportunities that might be open to you. For example, by thinking of your company as being providers of heat and light rather than electricity and gas you are opening your mind to new ways of providing those services.

Inputs
You should also be thinking about the inputs of your business:

- What are the key resources your business relies upon? These include things like raw materials, energy and fuel as well as people, investors and money.
- What will affect their availability and price in the future?

- What effect would this have on my cost base?
- What type of people will you be looking for in your workforce?
- What will people be looking for in an employer?
- How can you develop your employees and make your company an attractive place to work?

17.4.3 Stage Three: Incorporate sustainability into your strategy

- Ensure your plans for sustainability are totally aligned with existing organisational strategies and that top managers are involved.
- Could embracing sustainability within your strategy help build reputation with key stakeholder groups? For instance, a brewer provided blankets made from recycled materials to keep their customers warm when sitting outside rather than patio heaters. This helped reinforce their brand as the blankets were printed with their logo and included a message about sustainability.
- Are there any opportunities to gain access to new markets? For example, offering a new environmentally friendly product.
- Could sustainability provide solutions to current business problems? For example, reducing waste sent to landfill reduces costs and helps the environment.
- Could it be an opportunity to build internal company competencies? For example, businesses that allow their employees to become involved in community projects are offering those people the opportunity to gain leadership and team working experience, which they otherwise may not have.

17.4.4 Stage Four: Gain commitment internally

You will need to gain commitment for your plans to be successful in implementing your strategy. Involving a representative group of staff from your business at the outset will help. You may also want to include people from other stakeholder groups (such as your suppliers) in your scenario planning stage, if there are no confidentiality issues.

One of the great difficulties with sustainability is building it into the fabric and the culture of the business. Too often it is seen as a separate entity, which runs alongside the main operation of the company. In larger organisations there is often a person such as 'Head of Corporate Responsibility', whose job it is to oversee and record what is happening, but this person may have no real responsibility. To help overcome this problem and indicate that sustainability and corporate responsibility are part of the mainstream business, involve at least one person from the senior management team.

17.4.5 Stage Five: Measure progress

The process of implementing your strategy is continuous and it needs to be monitored continually to ensure it is on track and still appropriate.

To track process you need to design appropriate performance measures, such as key performance indicators (KPIs). Choose a few key measures that reflect what you need to achieve and that will help you track progress towards reaching your sustainability goals. They can be used to measure the implementation of policies and management of material issues. Businesses use all types of measures from health and safety to diversity, energy usage and so on, but the key is to focus on measuring what is important for your circumstances and not to measure anything just for the sake of it. Including measures of sustainability in regular performance reviews will communicate how important this is to your employees.

KPIs should be:

- Measurable;
- consistently measured across the company;
- collected and reviewed on a regular basis so they can feed into the management process while not being too onerous;
- limited to those that really matter, otherwise the system will become unwieldy;
- performance compared to baseline or starting point as a reference;
- assured internally or externally;
- understandable and meaningful;
- expressed in terms relevant to the audience;
- connected to future performance targets;
- worthwhile – with the benefits of measuring outweighing the costs;
- able to be acted upon;
- owned by an individual or team.

You may like to use a performance measure record sheet like the one shown in Figure 17.2 to help you design and monitor your measurement system.

It is essential that you identify the issues that are likely to have a major impact on the business and have a high probability of occurring. Plot the key issues you have identified on the table shown in Figure 17.3 and develop plans and measures for the issues that appear in the top right-hand box (Action zone).

17.4.6 Stage Six: Report on progress

Reporting appropriately is essential to focus effort on implementing improvements and to maintain commitment. Some key pointers for doing this are:

- Include sustainability KPIs in your regular management reporting pack.
- Ensure sustainability projects and performance are reviewed as part of your monthly management meeting.

Measure	Volume of waste sent to landfill
Purpose	To avoid landfill charges and environmental impact
Relates to	Waste reduction
Targets	2000 kg reduction by end 2009, zero in 2010
Formula	kg sent to landfill
Frequency	Measure weekly, review monthly
Who measures	Quality controller
Source of data	Purchase order system
Who acts on the data?	Bill Owens, site general manager
What do they do?	Identify sources of waste, systematically reduce and remove
Notes and comments	

Figure 17.2   Example of a measure of sustainable performance

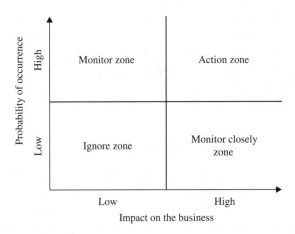

Figure 17.3   Prioritising your actions

- Post the sustainability KPIs with your other KPIs on the notice boards, intranet or other prominent place.
- Include sustainability issues in your staff briefings.

One benefit of reporting and reviewing the measures is to encourage debate about the performance and how it can be improved.

17.4.7 Stage Seven: Assurance that information flows

If you are using your sustainability and corporate responsibility information for any external purpose, you should consider having it assured. Assurance is about making sure that the information reported is accurate and meets the user's needs. It may be provided by stakeholder views, statements from consultancies or opinions from accounting organisations (audit reports).

Independent assurance of information should include the following:

- Clear, specific information on both the scope of the exercise undertaken as well as the areas not reviewed or assessed.
- Level of assurance – whether the practitioner is providing reasonable assurance (by giving a positively worded opinion, such as the information is accurate in accordance with what the management says) or limited assurance (nothing indicates that the information is inaccurate or incomplete on the report prepared by the company).
- Criteria used to assess the information – for example, whether the report has been assessed against a recognised standard such as the Global Reporting Initiative (GRI is a network of experts worldwide whose vision is that disclosure on economic, environmental and social performance become as commonplace and comparable as financial reporting, and as important to organisational success. www .globalreportingworldwide.org) reporting guidance or any other publicly available criteria, which could include the company's own criteria.
- Work performed – an assessment of underlying processes, systems, reporting procedures and performance.
- An opinion or conclusion.

17.5   CONCLUSION

Sustainability and corporate responsibility are becoming increasingly important for businesses and provide both opportunities to improve corporate performance and threats to damage it. The question of how you measure and report internally and externally on these complex issues is not an easy one to answer. New ideas and practices are emerging all the time. In this chapter we have outlined a basic process for building thinking about sustainability into your strategic planning and for deciding what you need to measure. You can adapt this for your own circumstances. This is a fast moving subject and one that businesses cannot afford to ignore.

FURTHER READING AND SOURCES OF INFORMATION

ICAEW	www.icaew.com/sustainability
Business in the Community	www.bitc.org.uk
The Carbon Trust	www.carbontrust.co.uk

Akkinson, N. (2010) "Social Enterprise and Social Development," MST Dissertation, University of Cambridge.

Frooman, J. (1997) 'Socially irresponsible and illegal behaviour and shareholder wealth', *Business and Society*, **36**, 221–249.

Grayson, D. and Hodges, A. (2004) *Corporate Social Opportunity, 7 Steps to Make Corporate Social Responsibility Work for Your Business*, Greenleaf Publishing, Sheffield, UK.

Pohle, G. and Hittner, J. (2008) *Attaining Sustainable Growth Through Corporate Social Responsibility*, IBM Institute for Business Value.

Creating a Culture of High Performance

18.1 INTRODUCTION

Good corporate performance is achieved by knowing what you are aiming for, being as certain as you can that the actions you are taking are going to lead to where you want to be and ensuring those actions are carried out at the right level. While it is not easy, all these steps can be worked out analytically with an added element of good judgement. You can use the tools described in the earlier chapters to create a model performance measurement system but what you will not be able to do with the tools on their own is to create higher levels of performance over the longer term.

In Chapter 1 we referred to the work of James Collins and Jerry Porras. Theirs is not the only work conducted into corporate performance over sustained periods of time. Arie de Geus, Corporate Planning Director at Royal Dutch Shell, explored the idea in his book *The Living Company: Habits for Survival in a Turbulent Business Environment*, in which he shows that organisations which are successful in the long term regard themselves as 'living work communities' rather than purely economic machines. These 'living' companies were sensitive to the world around them, they had a sense of cohesion and corporate identity and, interestingly, they also had a management syle tolerant of some experimentation and eccentricity with decentralised structures and delegated authority.

Contrary to what many people believe, there are usually plenty of ideas for improvement in organisations. The difficulty is implementing them – getting things done and getting them done to a satisfactory level. That is because you have to rely on other people and people are people and not robots – you cannot exactly programme them to do what you want. The trick is to get the right people in the right roles, to get them involved, to gain their commitment and to motivate them to use their skills and knowledge. Yet leading and managing people are two of the hardest tasks.

We have already described some of the management and leadership factors and have made references to organisational culture. In this chapter we explore these issues in a little more detail.

18.2 CREATING THE RIGHT ENVIRONMENT

Good performance comprises many elements, the most important of which is having good people. However, other factors play an important part. If you sow good seed on stony ground your yield will be less than if you plant it in fertile, well prepared soil. The same is true of business. It is important to create an environment for success. Quite what that environment will look like will depend on circumstances, but it should be 'appropriate'. Rather like the seed and the soil – some seeds prefer more water or more heat to germinate – you will have to decide what is most important for your business. However, there are elements common to most organisations which we will outline here.

Any organisation must have good processes if it is to have success in the long term. While there is evidence that good performance is achieved despite bad processes because people find ways around the problems, how much more could be achieved if individuals could do what they needed to do without spending time circumnavigating bureaucracy? Bad processes slow down efficiency and, quite simply, they annoy people. We have looked in some detail at processes and how you measure them in Chapter 8 so we will not go into detail here. The key is to examine your systems and processes and to check they add sufficient value to warrant time and effort adhering to them.

The second element in creating the right environment is to ensure people have the tools they need. Rather like having the right processes, good people will find a way around not having the right tools for their job. How much better it would be to ensure that they have the right tools at the outset. (Tools can be anything from being able to select the appropriate groups of people from a customer database for marketing purposes to having the correct IT equipment.) Needs change over time, so make sure you are still up to date with what is required.

Even a physical environment can make a difference to performance. One company we visited deliberately arranged their space so employees could meet in small coffee areas and chat. They were actively encouraged to talk to each other and the reason for this was that their business depended on generating new ideas. Another very successful marketing and design company located their business in a large loft and furnished it with comfortable armchairs and startling pictures. They felt people were unlikely to come up with innovative ideas sitting at a desk in a traditional office setting.

The third element is more intangible and is about creating the right culture, which is the subject of the next section.

18.3   CREATING THE RIGHT CULTURE

There is no doubt that some cultures encourage people to perform well and others do not, but there is no single formula that works everywhere. An informal and democratic type of culture works well in a hi-tech company, for example, whereas in the army you need more hierarchy and discipline.

So what is culture? While it is largely intangible and felt rather than seen or touched, it can still be strong and ingrained, having been built up over many years. Culture is about 'the way things are done here'. It is about the organisation's values and behaviour. At its best it can be a good source of competitive advantage because it is not something your competitors can easily or quickly copy. If you have a culture of innovation and flexibility you have a distinct advantage. At its worst it can act as a wet blanket smothering any spark of creativity or innovation. We can all think of organisations with a strong blame culture where there are so many checking processes to ensure everything is right (and mistakes still occur) that everyone spends their time checking rather than working on new ideas. In these organisations no one wants to take a risk. The bureaucratic processes get in the way of the real work and demonstrate lack of trust. It is strange to reflect that some companies trust their employees to handle major customers who keep the finances ticking but not to handle relatively small amounts of cash without time-consuming checking systems.

An organisation's culture is not only how it is perceived internally; it is how it is seen outside the organisation as well. It can affect your 'brand' as an employer and whether you are seen as a good organisation to work for; it can affect the way your suppliers, customers and investors perceive and act towards you. It is therefore well worth reviewing what the culture of your organisation is and the image it portrays.

The example of Semco in Brazil is a good one. For many years, the CEO, Ricardo Semler, gave his employees amazing freedom, allowing them to set their own hours of work and even their own wages. They became very loyal to the business, which achieved substantial and sustained growth in a very difficult economy and increased in profitability. This does not mean to say that bad performance was tolerated, however. In the case of Semco the transparency led to peer pressure to perform well. It was not a cosy environment in which to hide if you were not prepared to work hard. The company's reputation for being a good place to work meant that when there were vacancies they were able to choose the very best people. This helped to ensure their continued success.

Changing the culture of an organisation is not a quick fix. It evolves. As a leader you cannot just say 'from now on we'll be innovative' and expect everything to change. Culture is about the way people behave and it takes a long time to change habits. Some management teams begin the process in tandem with re-branding by considering how the organisation is perceived, what it stands for and what its underlying values are. Through a process of deciding what is good and needs to be developed and what needs to be dropped, they distil the values of the organisation into a set of messages. In the case of re-branding, these values may also be symbolised by logos, house style and so on, which not only project the image to the outside world but signal a new beginning to employees.

18.3.1 ICAEW (The Institute of Chartered Accountants in England and Wales)

ICAEW is a good example of how this can be done. The Institute of Chartered Accountants in England and Wales started life over 130 years ago and has continually evolved over that time to become a world leader of the accountancy and finance profession, with more than 136, 000 members worldwide. It offers a well established qualification, ACA, and a portfolio of training and development programmes to support chartered accountants throughout their careers. In addition, ICAEW has many other activities, some focused around 'working in the public interest', a requirement of its Royal Charter, and others ranging from 'capacity building', helping governments and institutes to develop their financial systems, to research into technical accounting and financial and economic issues.

With such a wide remit and a diverse membership it has sometimes been difficult to create a consistent view of what the organisation was about. It also meant staff tended to work industriously in their own departments, but sometimes at the expense of sharing information and working collaboratively with their colleagues elsewhere. Not surprisingly this led to a fragmented view of the organisation. ICAEW recognised that it was important to do something about this situation, to create a more consistent, coherent view of the organisation, and so it began to evolve its brand. This involved working with an external agency to help it to understand the role and values of the organisation. ICAEW then developed a set of messages to create clear and consistent communications about what it stood for and to convey its values both to employees and to external audiences worldwide. ICAEW's booklet for new employees states: 'Our brand story helps us understand our role and purpose as an organisation. It captures what we want to be known for, guides us towards our goals and connects us with our members and the people we want to inspire and influence.'

Once the messages – the purpose and values – had been developed a new visual image was created, but without losing the heritage of the organisation. The new image was applied not only to promotional material but also to internal communications and premises. On the launch day for the new brand all staff were sent a letter from the chief executive, a brochure about the new brand and some gifts with the new logo, heralding a new start. Great attention was paid to internal communication as well as to communication externally. The term 'One ICAEW' was used to mean working together, sharing information and working as a joined-up organisation. As much as possible was done to make each employee feel part of a vibrant and growing organisation. The chief executive's message was 'Whatever your role is in the organisation, you will play an important part in helping us to enhance our brand – it guides the way we work, what we say and how we behave.'

This exercise is on-going – the values must be constantly present – and new employees need to understand what the organisation stands for and what its values are. So far it appears to be working well as surveys show ICAEW's profile is increasing and it has been recognised as one of the UK's Business Superbrands.

18.4   RECRUITING THE RIGHT PEOPLE

The next element required to create a high performing organisation is having the right people. This also links to culture. In any culture change programme there will be a group of people who are at the forefront, who are the champions of change. There will be a bigger group, the majority, who will eventually adapt to the changes and there will be another group who will never change. The latter will have to be managed out of the organisation – some will leave of their own accord because they do not like their new environment.

Some years ago there was a need for universities to earn more of their income from commercial operations. In one particular university it had been decided that the conference department, which had been largely there to raise the profile of the establishment, should become a commercial operation and generate much needed funds. A new general manager was recruited to make this change. The conference department comprised only 10 people and the new general manager was horrified that three of these people, who had been loyal and long-serving staff, left within the first six months of her tenure. Much later, when the new operation had been established and began to bring in money, she realised the departure of these people had been essential to allow the necessary changes to take place.

When a vacancy does arise, particularly at a senior level, it's a wonderful opportunity to speed up the process of change. However, it is important to get it right. Recruiting someone with appropriate skills and experience is only the start – they should also be a good 'fit' with the organisation and with its culture. Many recruiters look primarily at skills and experience and this can be a mistake. Skills can be learnt and knowledge acquired. Experience is more difficult, but there are ways of 'fast-tracking' and immersing someone in the role to build their experience. Attitude, however, is difficult to change.

Also bear in mind the team of which the individual will be a part. You are probably aware of Dr Meredith Belbin's 'team roles' associated with a particular type of personality (implementers, shapers, plants, completer/finishers, evaluators and so on). A team comprising only plants (people who come up with original ideas) with no implementers could be a real problem. Therefore, bear in mind the types of people on your team and try to find a new recruit who complements them.

The following is a good example of the problems recruiting like-minded people can cause. A subsidiary of a successful engineering group developed water treatment solutions for the oil industry. The majority of the company's employees were research engineers, recruited for their innovative thinking and ability to solve tricky problems. They thrived on challenging projects. Alas, the company had a poor record of profitability, despite the highly qualified and motivated team. The new American owners of the company wanted to put this right and recruited a market analyst to help identify potential new business. After a few months she began to realise what the problem was. The engineers gave far less attention to any project proposal for which they had already designed a solution because they were less interested in it and thus the success rate was lower. Yet these were the projects likely to be more profitable because less time would be involved.

18.5   WHAT MOTIVATES?

Having the right people in place is only the start – you need to make sure you retain those people and ensure they still contribute to their full potential. There is no doubt that an organisation packed with highly motivated and enthusiastic employees will have an edge over its competitors. You may be able to select people likely to be motivated by the job you are offering or the values of the organisation in which they will be working, but how do you maintain that motivation?

Maslow's hierarchy of needs may seem 'old hat' now but it is still a useful framework. It is amazing how quickly one's perceptions as an employee change when the business environment becomes more uncertain. Before the recent recession there were far more complaints about lower than expected bonuses or meanness in allocation of company cars. Now the talk is more likely to be about keeping one's job! We have moved from 'esteem' – the need for respect and feeling of worth – to 'security' – the need for money to pay the mortgage. Different factors will assume more or less importance according to the context. Offering a measure of stability at a time of turbulence may become more highly valued, so do not assume that the same factors will always motivate someone.

Individuals place different values on different factors and sometimes even the factors we think are important to ourselves prove not really to be so important when put to the test. If we are not always honest to ourselves about what motivates us, what hope is there for a leader trying to motivate a group of individuals? The only way to motivate an individual is to get to know them and find out what is important for them.

It is worth a moment to recap on the work of the other motivation guru, Frederick Herzberg, who divided sources of motivation into 'motivators' and 'hygiene factors'. Hygiene factors include factors such as working conditions, company policy, salary and personal relationships. Motivators include recognition, progression, achievement, responsibility and the work itself. Hygiene factors do not actually motivate but if they are not dealt with they cause annoyance and affect performance adversely. Therefore, if you perceive you are being paid fairly you will be satisfied; if you are paid above the average it will not necessarily motivate you.

One interesting point to consider is the relationship between the organisation and the employee. If you are an owner, partner or director then your organisation is probably part of your DNA. This is also true for some long standing employees. For many other employees doing a good job it is a matter of personal pride. Of course, they want to receive a fair salary for their work and a bonus is always welcome. However, they do not see that their every action necessarily has a price tag for the employer attached to it. Paying someone to do a job is part of a contract between employer and employee. It is purely a transaction. Rewarding someone financially can also be part of a contract – a contractual bonus perhaps based on achieving a certain target. How you thank someone for extra effort involves judgement and knowing the individual.

It can take the form of a financial reward or it can be some other token of appreciation. Either way, it must be sincere.

One organisation we know has a fairly elaborate system of reward and recognition, which was introduced as part of a re-branding and culture change process. A rather 'well heeled' friend who works for this organisation was delighted to receive a bottle of champagne from her boss, given as a spontaneous gesture because she had worked long hours, completely unprompted, to help out a colleague. She was further delighted to receive a certificate resplendent in the new corporate colours and a note from the Managing Director thanking her for her contribution. In fact, she put the certificate on display in her office. Her delight was slightly tarnished, however, by the £25 gift voucher enclosed with the certificate, having noted from the intranet that 'recognition vouchers to the value of £25, £50, £75 and £100 were available to staff who went beyond the call of duty'. Was her effort worth only the lowest amount? The bottle of champagne, which probably cost little more than £25, was more valuable to her. Putting a financial value on her kindness in helping a colleague felt somehow like a transaction and left a jarring note.

Formalised reward and recognition systems can work well but they need to be applied appropriately, with due consideration given to the individual, and alongside informal systems. The question of 'fairness' always comes in, but it is not unreasonable to trust managers with a pot of money to spend on spontaneous tokens of appreciation when they see fit.

18.6   DEALING WITH UNDERPERFORMERS

We have discussed how you motivate people and reward them for their good work. Let us turn now to how you deal with underperformers. This is one of the most dreaded tasks for most managers and one that tends to be delayed for as long as possible, making the situation worse.

Once you become aware that someone is underperforming it is important to help them put their performance back on track in as fair a way as possible. However, it is also true to say that you can waste a great deal of time on people who are not performing and probably never will, when it would be more productive to spend that time developing people who are more likely to perform better. Research has shown that 17–19 % of people are actively 'engaged', 60–62 % are 'fairly engaged' and 19–23 % are 'actively disengaged'. Which group takes up most of our time? It is usually the 'actively disengaged' when, in fact, we are likely to have more success working with the 'fairly engaged' group, where it takes less effort to make them more productive.

Suppose you are becoming concerned about the performance of one of your direct reports. What do you do? Obviously, your approach will depend on the circumstances. If it is a question of a few silly mistakes, let them know you are aware of what has happened, but if problems persist then you will need to meet to discuss what is going wrong. One of the difficulties in these meetings is trying to get people to admit their performance is not up to standard and set the stage for an honest discussion. For this reason it is important to ensure that standards of performance are agreed and understood at the beginning of the year and also to gather clear evidence of where the individual is falling below those standards.

One thing is clear. If you do not manage underperformers you will be doing a disservice to the rest of your team and you will undermine your own authority as a leader.

18.7   UNDERSTANDING YOUR INFLUENCE

One of the most common reasons for poor performance and for dissatisfaction among employees is weak line management. Good leadership and line management have a major impact on the performance of people and can overcome other obstacles. Think about soldiers who have to work in dire conditions – good leaders ensure they continue to be loyal and motivated despite their physical environment.

Newly appointed managers are generally more conscious of their influence on the people working for them. When you have been in a management role for some time and you become a leader, it is easy to forget the extent to which the way you behave will affect others. If you have ever worked for a boss who is perhaps nearing retirement and counting the days to departure, you will know how difficult it is to work with someone who is not motivated themselves. It is a useful exercise to reflect sometimes on what motivates you. Look to a time when you were 'firing on all cylinders' and full of excitement about what you were doing. What was it that fired you up? Can you recreate it? If you are always negative how will you motivate other people? Be enthusiastic when you can. Remember Martin Luther King said, 'I have a dream.' He didn't say, 'I have a nightmare!' (used by Ed Milliband at the 2010 CBI Conference).

When you are under pressure to achieve targets it is easy to forget about your relationship with your team because you are so task-focused. However, you will not be successful if you are so preoccupied with getting the job done that you forget you are not the only one doing the work. If the only time you ring someone up is when you have a problem or are angry about something, think how they will feel each time you call.

There is much discussion about management style. In a study conducted by Cranfield for *Investors in People* the researchers observed that role model leaders created a management style that pervaded throughout the organisation. Employees recognised the style from the role models and gave a consistent description of their attributes. It appeared that informally this became the 'way of doing things round here'.

In fact, there is no 'correct' style and it is best not to try to be something you are not; otherwise people will not trust you because you will not appear to be sincere. The key is to remain true to who you are but to adapt your own style to circumstances and individuals, and in that way you can feel more comfortable and maintain some consistency of approach. That does not mean to say that you should, for example, avoid conflict if you do not relish it (as many people do not). You will inevitably have to deal with situations you do not like but you should feel free to deal with them in a way that leaves you feeling as comfortable as you can with your actions. Remember nobody is liked by everybody. It is more important to be respected and trusted than liked.

There is often a difficult balance to be struck between being 'one of the team' and being the leader of that team. How you position yourself will depend on the culture of your organisation – some organisations are very flat in structure with virtually no hierarchy, whereas others have clear levels of seniority. Just remember it is more difficult to deal with poor performers if they happen to be your friends!

18.8   DIRECTION SETTING AND ENGAGEMENT

There is no doubt that people today are looking for more say in the way they work and in the running of the organisations in which they work. If you ask managers what they would rather have, an organisation where people are highly engaged or an organisation where people know exactly what has to be achieved, you get an interesting response. One group will typically argue that motivation and engagement underpins everything, while the other group will claim such an organisation would be totally unfocused. In contrast the other group will argue that direction setting is everything while their critics will claim that this only leads to the type of behaviour that is focused solely on achieving personal results, creating a silo mentality and an inability to see new opportunities.

Research does, indeed, show that higher levels of employee engagement lead to higher performance and there is no compelling evidence that companies that deploy performance measurement tools such as the Balanced Scorecard as a way of directing performance do better then those that do not. Simply having a Balanced Scorecard is not sufficient to improve the organisation's performance. However, that does not mean the Balanced Scorecard is not effective or that direction setting is not important. What really matters is how direction setting tools are developed and used. If the process of designing and implementing them is done properly, they can be useful in themselves to create engagement and commitment. An organisation with either a high engagement or a high direction setting is not likely to perform to the best of its capability. Both are necessary (see Figure 18.1).

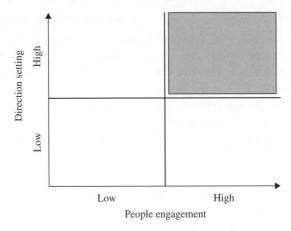

Figure 18.1   Factors that contribute to organisational performance

18.9   COMMUNICATION

It is worth highlighting poor communication here as it is often cited as a problem in employee satisfaction surveys. This usually leads to the setting up of more formal communication channels – staff newsletters and briefings, a new improved intranet, email alerts from the chief executive. While most of these are good ideas, communication is a two-way process and it is not just about telling people something; it's also about listening to them.

Autoglass, the UK-based windscreen repair service, for example, run a regular managing director's forum where they invite a cross-section of staff from around the country to meet the managing director. Those attending are asked to write down on post-it notes the issues they want to discuss and an HR facilitator groups these into themes. The managing director then takes each theme in turn and talks about it. By doing it in this way real concerns are raised anonymously and from the number of post-it notes the managing director can see the level of interest or concern about any particular issue.

Some organisations use 'skip-level' meetings, where on a regular basis managers meet the staff, reporting to the level of managers below them. This allows a better sounding of what is going on.

At BI, an incentive and reward consultancy based in Newport Pagnell, employees' roles are changed for a day. This means that the managing director could end up manning the reception and a receptionist visiting customers. Of course, this has to be managed carefully, but it is a good way of opening people's eyes to the roles of others. This approach helps create what is known as 'cross-understanding' and it is being used increasingly because it is becoming even more important to have a holistic view of the organisation. It particularly helps senior managers to keep in touch with what is happening lower down in the organisation.

It is not just about 'the organisation' communicating with 'the employees'; it is also about line managers communicating with individuals in their teams. In order to communicate effectively you need to know how each member of your team likes to receive messages. Some people prefer email, others a phone call. Some like to hear the facts and figures straight away, others want more of the context. Of course, you cannot always telephone or visit the offices of each of your direct reports – it would be impractical – but a little 'personalisation' on occasion helps to build relationships.

Being 'in the loop' is part of communicating. It is about knowing what is happening in the organisation at an informal level. Office politics are notorious and usually unavoidable. While you do not necessarily want to become involved it is important to know what is going on because it could undermine the success of a particular individual or project. Make sure you are switched into the various networks.

All this may seem basic but it is essential.

18.10   CONCLUSION

Performance comes from two elements. Firstly, people need direction so they know what the organisation is trying to do and how they contribute to the organisation's success. Secondly, they need to be engaged and motivated, so that they take ownership of their work. The appropriate use of performance measurement tools such as the success map goes a long way to providing the former, but it is leadership and management style that creates the culture of engagement.

Many writers on performance refer to 'driving' performance. Our belief is different. Performance comes from motivated people and through leadership, using performance measurement to guide and direct their energies towards achieving success and the goals of the organisation.

In the next chapter (Chapter 19) ten leaders describe how they create high performance in their organisations.

FURTHER READING

Bourne, M. and Franco-Santos, M. (2010) *Investors in People, Managerial Capabilities and Performance*, IIP/Cranfield Report., Cranfield University, UK.

Bourne, M., Franco-Santos, M., Pavlov, A., Lucianetti, L., Martinez, V. and Mura, M. (2008) *The Impact of Investors in People on People Management Practices and Firm Performance*, IIP/Cranfield Report, Cranfield University, UK.

de Geus, A. (1997) *The Living Company: Growth Learning and Longevity in Business*, Nicholas Brealey Publishing, London.

Hertzberg, F., Mausner, B. and Snyderman (1959) *The Motivation to Work*, Second Edition, John Wiley & Sons, Ltd, Chichester.

Holbeche, L. (2005) *The High Performance Organization: Creating Dynamic Stability and Sustainable Success*, Elsevier Butterworth-Heinemann, Oxford, UK.

Leadership Vignettes

19.1 INTRODUCTION

In the previous chapters we have demonstrated the benefits of implementing a performance measurement and management system, outlined the various approaches you can take and given you some tools to help ensure that your system is effective. In this chapter we want to enlarge on one of the underlying themes of the book – that you can have the most efficient processes and still fail in the longer term if the leadership and culture within your organisation is not conducive to encouraging good performance.

There is no single right or wrong way to lead; it will depend on the circumstances. However, there are some common characteristics. The following vignettes are drawn from discussions with leaders operating in very different sectors who kindly gave their time to discuss their views on leadership with us. They have each been chosen because of their track record, as they all have demonstrated their ability to deliver consistently high levels of performance over many years. They are all either at, or have been at, Chief Executive level and the examples are taken from both companies and charities. A number have done both, delivering successfully in the private sector before moving to third sector appointments.

19.2 PAUL WOODWARD – CHIEF EXECUTIVE, SUE RYDER CARE

Paul Woodward is the Chief Executive of the charity Sue Ryder Care, which supports people with specialist palliative, end of life and long term neurological care needs. Each year they provide 4 million hours of care to people living with such conditions as cancer, multiple sclerosis, Huntington's disease, Parkinson's disease, motor neurone disease, stroke and brain injury.

Paul joined Sue Ryder Care from the pharmaceutical company Schering AG, where he was the UK CEO and Member of the European Board. The change in culture was enormous, moving from a well resourced global organisation with well established processes to a charity with 3,400 staff and 10,000 volunteers, and income from a variety of sources including primary care trusts, local authorities and fund raising through many different activities and 500 shops.

Paul quickly realised the need for change. While perceived as being successful, he knew the charity was not performing as well as it could; in fact it was losing money.

There was a need for greater focus and a more commercial approach – something that would be quite difficult to implement in the current culture. Like most organisations, there were practices that had remained unchallenged for many years and were there simply because 'things had always been done like that'. In many cases, Paul could see what should be changed (more effective financial processes, for example) but appreciated that some of these changes would be difficult for the current team to swallow. He needed to get commitment from the majority of staff and to get their own ideas in order for change to take root.

Paul Woodward firmly believes that the performance of an organisation depends on having a good team. As chief executive he sees his role as 'acting as an enabler to make things happen'. He says you must create a compelling case for change to make your team want to come on the journey with you. The keys to this are plenty of communication and plenty of involvement. The more people you involve the greater the likelihood of success.

With this in mind, Paul embarked on a series of two hour interviews with key people across the depth and breadth of the organisation, asking them for five things they wanted to keep and three things they wanted to change. He also asked them what they were looking for from their chief executive and what advice they would give him. Most people came up with about ten things they wanted to change and three they would like to keep. Paul reported on his findings at a staff conference after just three months in the post and also revealed information about the current financial performance, which shocked many people – they had been losing money for 8 years, drawing down on reserves. They just had not appreciated how bad the situation had become and how important it was to change. Of course, there were some who would not accept plans for change and those people left the organisation. However, as the plans had come about largely through discussion with a significant number of people in the organisation, there was less resistance to his direction of travel. He had created a compelling case for change. The majority of employees were dedicated and could now see change was essential.

Since then, the changes have been many and varied. Many people moving to a chief executive's role in a charity would reduce their expectations of the type of people they would be able to recruit to top roles. True to his view that you need to build a good team, Paul recruited the very best new members to his top team, paying them commercial salaries. He has no doubt this has paid dividends and has resulted in better performance overall, achieving their first surplus in 10 years in 2009/10, at the same time as increasing hours of care.

Among the most interesting developments were the changes to the retail operation. Unprofitable shops were closed – there are now 370 – and there was a focus on modernising their image. Stock levels were reduced and each shop adapted to suit local needs; different things were available in different shops and in some cases large format shops were introduced. The retail presence was no longer just seen as a means of raising funds; it became an intervention hub. Shops became an integral part of the process of raising the profile and image of the charity.

In his work at Sue Ryder, Paul drew on his experience at Schering, obviously a very different organisation. It was there that that he first implemented a Balanced Scorecard and used success maps to communicate the goals of the organisation from the board-room to the warehouse floor. In fact, the success map was shown on the company's intranet for all to see. At Sue Ryder they are in the process of implementing 'People Perform', a computer-based performance management system that visibly links each individual's objectives to the strategic goals of the organisation.

Paul is a believer in setting bold targets that force people to think hard about how they are to be achieved. Setting appropriate targets made people focus on what mattered and also on the link between what they were doing and other people's work. At Schering staff clearly understood the impact of their part in a complex process such as the registration of a new product. The measurement system made sure that staff completed their part of a project, say before going on holiday. This meant the registration process could progress on time rather than be delayed for two weeks while they were away. Each person's performance contributes cumulatively to the overall performance and this could have a major impact on peak year sales income. Performance related pay was not simply related directly to financial performance but based on activities and issues over which individuals had control.

In both roles Paul's principles have remained the same:

- Build the best team you can.
- Communicate and involve people.
- Set clear bold targets and expectations of results.
- Be brave and make decisions based on what you believe to be right – do not take second best because it is easier to implement.

19.3   PY GERBEAU – CHIEF EXECUTIVE, X-LEISURE

Pierre-Yves Gerbeau, better known as PY, is Chief Executive of X-Leisure, the retail, leisure and attractions business. He is an unorthodox leader who believes in inspiring people all the time, which seems to work as he has a very dedicated and loyal team and considerable success in what he does.

PY's background combines what you would expect of a successful business man – an MBA from a top school, with some highly unusual experience working with a team of rubbish collectors at the back of a dustbin lorry, being a delivery man and then accountant in his parent's business. He began his career as a professional sportsman and captained the French ice hockey team, representing France in the Olympics. At that time, he was very much in demand and his phone rang all the time. When he had an accident, however, all this changed. The phones were quiet and he knew he had to find another challenge. So he set up his own business in Paris, a management consultancy, using lessons from sport to help management teams deal with performance. After this he went on to join EuroDisney and was then brought in to reverse the fortunes of the Millennium Dome before becoming Chief Executive of X-Leisure. He has learnt from each of these roles and firmly believes leadership is something you learn through experience rather than something you are taught.

The culture at X-Leisure appears relaxed – there are very few 'suits' on view, working times are flexible and it has been known for the staff (including PY) to play rugby in the office, on one occasion breaking a computer to the annoyance of his Finance Director! However, if something needs doing, everyone 'falls in'. If investors are coming and suits are appropriate then people will dress accordingly. There is no culture of poor performance here despite the unorthodox and relaxed style. Robust processes and KPIs are very much in existence, with KPIs concentrating on business performance. People are focused on achieving results and, wherever it is possible, departments have become profit centres. Front line staff have access to £3,000 in cash in each area to use as they see fit in order to improve the business. This is one indicator of how strongly the boss trusts them to have a positive financial impact on the business.

PY is passionate about his team and this comes across clearly when talking to him. He drops into the conversation: 'X is amazing', 'X is the best', 'X is really brilliant' with great energy and enthusiasm . Although he has strong opinions he knows he cannot be successful without other people and nurtures what he calls 'positive viruses' – people who can carry the business forward. He says: 'Be humble. You can't rely on your own knowledge – you need to accept other people may know more than you and be self-confident enough to accept it.' His advice is to surround yourself with good people whom you can trust.

In terms of leadership style, he points out that the old way of 'leadership by terror' is dying out. It will not work with Generation Y because they do not want to obey rules. They constantly challenge and ask why. The leader's role is to influence and not to dictate. He also believes it is no longer possible to have a different 'work' persona. You cannot be inaccessible – you have to be the same in the office as you would be at home and this has the added benefit of people getting to know the real 'you'. If you are in a bad mood one day, they will pick up on that and accept it. Above all, it is important not to take yourself too seriously – a sense of humour gets you everywhere.

Good leadership is part of the DNA of the organisation and PY expects it from his team. He frequently visits different parts of the business unannounced and takes the opportunity to speak to people at every level. He admits this can be disconcerting for managers when junior people come into his office or when he approaches them for a chat. However, he believes you can find out a great deal about the quality of the leadership in an organisation by talking to the junior people. If you talk to the junior person who is sulking in the corner you can learn a lot.

PY believes in moving people around. They move desks every quarter – at a cost of about £70k per year. In one instance when two people were at loggerheads, PY put them in the same office so they had little choice but to speak to each other. It helped solve the problem. On occasions they also change roles because people embroiled in the day to day do not see what is in front of them. For example, it is good for an IT person to spend some time in sales to understand what it is like, what the problems are and what sales people really need from IT as opposed to what they are given. Everyone in the business spends one week a year doing something very different.

The structure of the organisation is very flat and there is no relying on job titles. PY recognises that job titles are sometimes important externally because people outside the organisation want to know who they are dealing with, but internally there is no bowing and scraping to more senior people. He does have one rather curious business card, which has the letters MFIC where the job title would normally be!

X-Leisure is in the entertainment business and the organisation itself has a 'fun' culture. There are leadership contests – which PY has never won – and there is also an award for the biggest failure, which he has won three times. You have to keep the award on your desk for a whole year to remind yourself what you have done. This is not as bad as it sounds because the business is 100 % about innovation (8 % of turnover is spent on R&D). According to PY, 'change' is just part of the world now; it has become a constant. You are aiming to be a cruise ship but you have to act like a speedboat and you cannot do this without (a) taking risks and (b) ensuring your underlying processes are in place to provide underpinning. As an individual, if you have not made any mistakes, you probably have not taken any risks and are probably not being sufficiently innovative. You can win the biggest failure award for not taking any risks. Of course, if you make too many mistakes and do not learn from the mistakes you have made, that is clearly a problem.

PY is a genial and friendly host but he is not afraid to make difficult and sometimes painful decisions. People have to fit into the organisation and it is not necessarily a structure or culture that would suit everyone. If someone does not fit in or is not performing well then they go, even if he has known them for a long time. He is also careful about ensuring people are in the right role, giving the example of a very popular ski instructor who was promoted only to find he was not suited to his new responsibilities. He made a great ski instructor but did not enjoy the new management tasks. Above all, PY will not tolerate sceptics, believing they can poison the organisation. When recruiting he looks for a certain attitude rather than for skills that can be taught. Management is not about popularity, he says, it is about being firm, fair and consistent.

19.4   RICHARD BOOT OBE – IRC GLOBAL EXECUTIVE SEARCH PARTNERS

Having spent many years at KPMG as a partner and finally as Head of Corporate Finance, Midlands, Richard is currently a board member at IRC Global Executive Search Partners. He also chairs and holds directorships of various companies associated with staffing and recruitment, including Board Evaluation Limited, a new company set up to help companies create more effective Boards and Leadership teams.

He has a great deal of experience in understanding what makes a successful company tick and what makes a successful leader. He sees this not only through his own direct experience of the businesses in which he has worked but also through the eyes of potential investors.

'Well structured organisations are good,' he says. 'But you need electricity in the business and the electricity is provided by the leadership. Typically the voltage comes from one person, although you can have a small group of people with enthusiasm.' Positive energy is important as is sense of direction. While decisions should not be made without open and fair debate, negativity is damaging. He quotes Clive Woodward, the former English Rugby Union coach, who said the best way of sorting out a team was to get rid of those creating negative energy.

To some extent it is good to have a 'benign dictatorship' within the business but, of course, there are dangers when the leadership becomes too powerful and remains unchallenged. If a leader is surrounded by 'yes men' it is a recipe for disaster. Enron, for example, had a flawed strategy and a flawed culture promulgated by a flawed leadership that remained unchallenged for some time. Checks and balances are important to help avoid this problem, but it is interesting to note that the major company failures in the US had all passed the 'tick box' approach to corporate governance. However, in the main he believes most leaders are well intentioned and are open to healthy debate and discussion.

What can work extremely well is a collegiate approach. KPMG changed its structure from being a 'partnership type' partnership to being a 'corporate type' partnership with an executive board and this has worked effectively. Partners were happy to give up some of their rights to that executive board because they perceived it as being more effective. In a sense it cut out some of the 'noise'. It has obviously been a successful move as it has resulted in the firm being successful through difficult times and it has moved forward strategically.

In his experience of seeing businesses from the outside, Richard has seen many examples of bad leadership. This is often true with entrepreneurs who have grown businesses in their own image and are then unwilling to take advice, for example, from nonexecutive directors. They are bold enough to create a business but not brave enough to use external help. Succession planning is also an issue for these businesses. They need a plan. Big plcs will typically have a plan but small businesses do not have a large enough talent pool and so cannot rely on an internal 'market'.

Richard believes you need drive and a little bit of 'positive tension' to get things done. Any business is complex. It is easy to become bogged down in that complexity and you need forward momentum and energy to progress. He uses the analogy of a sailing boat. If a sailing boat is going slowly it is difficult to turn it around. The faster it moves the quicker it is to turn.

Richard has seen bright people fail in their leadership because they have implemented too many initiatives and this has, in itself, created unnecessary complexity and negative energy. Linked to this, you need focus. He believes some people have an immense propensity for discussing things ad nauseam, for creating noise that hinders rather than helps progress. Once a course of action has been agreed it should be maintained. Forward momentum is critical lest you go very quickly backwards!

Thinking about personal traits, good leaders do not have to be tub thumping rabble rousers but they do have to be good at spotting ideas and recruiting good people. They have to be determined and dogged and want to achieve something for themselves and for their organisations, but without being autocratic.

Leaders also have to be 'in tune' with their organisations and be good communicators. They must be close enough to create rapport but not too close to damage their authority. Charisma helps. Richard speaks about his first senior partner at KPMG, John Adcock. 'You knew when he was in the building,' he says. 'You knew he had arrived. He had charisma. People were fond of him and were loyal although he could be quite brisk at times. You had your quarter of an hour with him and you knew when your time was up. But, he had a vision. He had a clear purpose and you knew where you stood.'

'People are good at managing customers, suppliers and staff but they're not good at management of the management group and yet it is the management group that is the driver of corporate success. And that,' Richard says, 'is what leadership at the corporate level is about.'

19.5   DAVID CHILD

David Child is an achiever, exceeding the sales and profit targets in his last company for each year over a period of seven years. He is a leader who is driven to achieve results but who knows he can only do this through other people.

One of his greatest achievements was to persuade Lloyds Development Capital to part with £42m to acquire a controlling share in 1st – The Exchange, from the giant outsourcing company Vertex, in a rare private equity deal. Within Vertex, David was Managing Director of 1st – The Exchange, which provides software to small and medium sized financial advisers, and was also responsible for their life and pensions outsourcing business.

The buy-out meant a huge change for David. He had to move from being MD of a divisional unit within Vertex, a company of around 10,000 people, to being MD of a smaller business with about 400 staff – but in a much higher profile role. Everything had to change. The entire management team had to 'up' their game. They needed to understand *how* they had to change as individuals, how they dealt with each other and how they interacted with the layer of management below them. It was also important to make sure members of the senior team complemented each other and understood the unique skillsets that they brought to the table. He did not want to fall into the trap of having too many people with the same personality type/skillset on his board.

Faced with this challenge, David decided to introduce coaching for the senior team from an external company. This approach worked well. It became apparent that, on occasions, some board members had either purposely or accidentally been undermining other directors. The coaching process allowed them to explore why in a group environment and to set up a code of conduct to prevent it from happening in the future.

Having considered the composition and conduct of the senior team, David turned his attention to how they would take the company to the next level. It was already highly profitable but they needed to build on what they were doing. They also needed to signal to all employees that 'things were different'. As part of this drive they set up a formal reward system. The reward mechanism was split into three areas:

1. Revenue growth
2. Profit
3. Personal objectives (nonfinancial).

Senior people could only achieve bonuses relating to their personal objectives if both financial targets were hit. The scheme described above was only applied to the Executive Board Directors and senior managers, a number of whom also had shares so there was a real financial incentive to deliver – essential in a private equity backed business. All employees were included in a bonus scheme of some type although it became less complex further down the organisation.

The bonus was not the only scheme used to motivate people in the short term. There was also an informal scheme where a provision was put aside for, say, allowing employees to take their partners out for a good meal if they had been working long hours or had been away from home for a considerable period. This was discretionary and ad hoc. The staff were also made aware that the new company would be able to take its own decisions, whereas under the previous regime the parent company often had other priorities. This meant decision making could now be faster, which was advantageous for all. These new bonus schemes helped to communicate the change in ownership and mind-set, although in practice the day-to-day work of the staff had not changed that much.

One of David's strong beliefs is that a leader should be honest and open. In addition, a leader must always 'be present', giving their full attention to the people they are with. Even actions a leader may consider harmless, such as using their Blackberry in a meeting or switching off after their presentation, have an impact.

David is keenly aware of the shadow cast by a leader, citing a report from McKinsey stating that being a leader is like being a high status primate. People watch their leaders constantly and often follow their example when they are absent. Anthropologists who study primates report that members of baboon troops typically glance at the dominant male every 20–30 seconds. As a leader you are a role model.

David says his early experience as a bank official at the Bank of England gave him a good grounding in the discipline of a formal organisation and how to conduct oneself. Of course you have to adapt your style to suit the culture of the organisation – the culture of a software business is totally different from that of a bank – but there are underlying disciplines and principles.

One of these principles is about commanding respect by using your emotional intelligence. Be aware of your influence on others. Consider their perspective and think about how you would like to be treated if you were in their shoes. Seek to understand before being understood. Do not make knee-jerk reactions – listen to the facts and make a balanced decision. As a leader you sometimes have to be brutal in your decision making but always ensure you are compassionate in the execution. This is especially relevant with failing staff. Make sure you give credit to people who did the work and do not take it for yourself. Ensure people feel they can take risks without intimidation. It does not matter if some things do not work – if everything goes right first time you are probably not driving the business hard enough.

As the leader you have to take ultimate responsibility for what happens even if it was not of your own making and this is tough. Shortly after David joined Vertex he discovered a bad decision had been made concerning a customer. It was too late to overturn that decision so he had to grit his teeth and take responsibility for it although it was not his fault. It took three years of rebuilding trust and relationships before the damage was repaired, but he did it and people understood the importance of acknowledging mistakes.

Being a leader is hard and, while being aware that you are ultimately accountable for what happens, you must have the confidence to do what you feel is right. David gives the example of a particular decision to sell one of the business assets. There were plenty of analytics to support it but it did not feel 'right' to him. He was not convinced so he went against the recommendation and was ultimately proved right.

It is hugely important to trust the people you are working with. Before recruiting senior people David checks their track records very carefully and explores informal routes to find out more about them. Having done the checking he also listens to his instincts. If you feel a sales person will not live up to the job, they probably will not.

David is clearly someone who is very focused on achieving targets but he is acutely aware that this can only be achieved through good leadership. He ensures he has the right people, ensures they work well together and that they are aligned and motivated to achieve results.

19.6   BARONESS SALLY GREENGROSS

Baroness Greengross has spent much of her life supporting the needs of older people. She is currently chief executive of the International Longevity Centre – United

Kingdom, as well as chairing a number of parliamentary groups on various aspects of ageing. She spent many years with Age concern and was Director General for fourteen years, steering the charity through difficult times and seizing new opportunities to make it a success. Ageing and care for the elderly has not always been a high profile area – discussions about topics such as dementia and dying are difficult and often avoided, although inevitably they face all of us at some point. Yet Baroness Greengross has managed not only to improve the charity's financial performance through commercial enterprise but also to raise the profile of needs of the elderly and influence policy at the highest levels. So how has she done it?

Understanding your own strengths and weaknesses is essential. If you know what you can and cannot do, you can bring the right people in at the right time. In her case, Baroness Greengross – a very modest person – admits her 'butterfly mind', excellent for spotting opportunities and lending energy to her thinking, is probably not the best for, say, project managing a big event. Therefore, when it came to planning the very high profile millennium debate on ageing, which was led by Age concern, she delegated the task to her colleague Charles Carter, whose military experience came to the fore.

The understanding of strengths and weaknesses applies not only to individuals but also to organisations. Baroness Greengross knew that the charity Help the Aged was more adept at fundraising, so competing with them head-on to raise funds was not a good idea. However, with her 'butterfly mind' and her business background she spotted commercial opportunities in selling low value contents insurance to the many people who needed it. The brand name 'Age concern' was reassuring for the purchasers of such insurance and the business flourished. Age concern Enterprises grew mainly through the insurance business, which expanded to cover travel, home and pets rather than through the traditional charity shop route.

The insurance opportunity arose through a meeting with someone from Lloyds, who helped the charity to get started with what is, in effect, a major social enterprise, all profits going to the charity, and this highlights another important aspect of developing business performance – making the right contacts. Knowing who is important to your organisation and making links with them.

The tension that exists between head office and subsidiary businesses will have resonance for many people in business. There is a fine balance between ensuring all parts of the organisation are working to achieve the same goals with some coherence and stifling local innovation. Head office teams sometimes feel local teams are self-interested and have little regard for requirements from HQ. Local teams often feel demands from head office are excessive and people working there live in an ivory tower. In charities this can be even more acute than in business and there is the added difficulty of managing volunteers and dealing with emotion. In Age concern there was an umbrella organisation at the centre with local groups of various sizes operating independently. Sally Greengross managed the relationship by making sure the local groups always had some incentive. She would go out and speak to them, address their AGMs, ensure letters always went out in the name of the local group. Bigger groups were incentivised by setting up their own local enterprise with their own board.

Part of the development of the charity was to move it from simply looking at the day-to-day care of elderly people (important though this is) to look to the future needs and the influencing of policy. They needed to get to the stage where they could measure their performance through their impact on policy in critical areas. This was not universally liked. To use her own words, Baroness Greengross had to 'battle and persevere and develop a thick skin'. She shows a quiet determination and is prepared to debate subjects where people hold diametrically opposing views to her own.

Although probably not a stereotype for a leader, Sally Greengross is an excellent role model. Her success in developing Age concern was the result of bringing in the right people, understanding strengths and weaknesses and spotting the opportunities. Her vision of how the organisation needed to change and her energy and enthusiasm for her subject helped ensure success.

19.7   CHARLES CARTER

Charles is Director, Regions, at Institute of Chartered Accountants in England and Wales, responsible for setting up and ensuring the smooth running of ICAEW's regions worldwide. In this interview Charles draws on his military career, which helped form his views on leadership.

Good leadership and sound management are very different things. A good leader will inspire during both smooth and difficult times; he will be imaginative, will not flap when difficult issues have to be resolved and will always be a welcome part of his team. This last statement is the clue to what makes a leader and what better place to see this in action than the British army.

For centuries officers have trained at Sandhurst, looked upon by the rest of the world as the 'the place to train'. There, potential officers are taught the skills of their intended profession but at the heart of everything they learn is leadership. Leadership is simple to understand through the actions of good leaders. It is not about being overtly courageous, it is not about sound administration and it is not about forcing people to do things they do not want to do. It is about excellent 'people skills'; soldiers simply expect their leaders to make the best decisions in difficult times, to be able to show that they will be part of the solution and to always be trusted.

Often good leaders will not be liked and they may even be harsh, but they will always be fair. Field Marshal Montgomery, on the eve of El Alamain, was confronted by one of his commanding officers saying that what was required of him and his soldiers would lead to heavy casualties. Montgomery explained the rationale and need for such a course of action – the following day the Regiment was virtually annihilated. Sound leadership led to those men understanding what they had to do even to the ultimate sacrifice of themselves.

Another element is the forming of recognisable groups that can be akin to families. Within businesses good departments will ensure they provide the 'best' service for the good of the wider organisation. The example of the tank regiment at Alamain shows that the power of the regimental family spirit was so strong that all adversities can be overcome. We see it today on the battlefields of Afghanistan; the sad reporting of the loss of soldiers stating their Regiments rather than 'the Army' is for a simple reason – it shows an affiliation to a 'family regiment' as the most important part of a recognisable team.

So what skills does a leader have in his rucksack? He is compassionate and understanding, is not afraid of undertaking the task he is asking others to do, he will know how to draw out the best from others, delegating as low as possible, he will not get upset about mistakes (we all learn from them) and he will know that any plan does not stand the first shot of battle so clear thinking under pressure is necessary. Of course, he will be a sound manager, but a good manager alone does not make a great leader.

19.8   NIGEL BOND – CEO, DOMINO PRINTING SCIENCES

Domino Printing Sciences plc was founded in 1978 and has established a global reputation for the continual development and manufacture of its total coding and printing technologies. Domino products are used for a wide range of purposes, from printing on delicate and permeable items such as eggs to printing on plastic cards and glass bottles.

The Cambridge-based company has a global network of 25 subsidiary offices and more than 200 distributors, with manufacturing plants in the UK, China, Germany, India, Sweden and the USA. It employs about 2,200 people and now has a turnover of about £300m, selling to over 120 countries.

Nigel Bond, who is a chartered accountant, joined Domino in 1987 as its financial controller, becoming CEO in 1997 after a period of five years on the board. There is no doubt that during this time Domino has grown to be a highly successful company, achieving record sales in 2010 and recently winning the accolade, Company of the Year, in the PLC awards. So how has this been achieved?

The company has two critical aims:

1. To provide leading edge technical products
2. To provide excellent services.

Linked to this, they aim to be a good company to work for and a good company to do business with (they have had an ethics policy in place for the past 20 years).

These are clear and seemingly simple aims. Nigel believes in simplicity and clarity. In 1997 the company set out what they call the 'Domino Effect'. This shows the goals, objectives, strategies and values of the company in a pictorial way and is to be found on the company's intranet and in the receptions of all the plants around the world. Not only does it show each employee what the company is trying to achieve and what their role is ultimately about but it also helps to bind people together wherever they happen to be.

The 'Domino Effect' has four categories:

Objectives
- Satisfied loyal customers
- Market share leadership in specific sectors and geographies
- Industry leading products
- Service excellence and brand recognition growth in sales, profits and cash generation
- Unfaltering growth in earnings per share

Things we must always do well
- Understand customers and convert their needs into marketable, profitable products and services.
- Develop and acquire new products, ensuring rapid and successful introduction.
- Build an efficient global business organisation and a strongly supportive international network.
- Communicate a clear and consistent message to customers, investors, colleagues and communities.
- Understand all elements of business performance and driving improvement in financial results.
- Devolve responsibility with authority to make decisions.
- Perform with maximum effectiveness and efficiency through good development and training.

Practices we seek to make habits
- Set clear goals and constantly challenge our own performance; never accept things cannot be improved and higher standards achieved.
- Communicate openly, honestly and consistently.
- Take every opportunity to meet better the needs of our customers.
- Learn from our mistakes, using data, analysis and problem solving tools to improve our decisions.
- Appoint and develop people to the benefit of them and the company, matching talents to the job to be done.
- Care for our people, their aspirations, needs and desires.
- Recognise individual and team achievement by rewarding and celebrating success.

Our values
- Seek to listen and understand first.
- Are honest with ourselves and with others.
- Ensure there is total clarity and focus on what we do.
- Create positive energy through our enthusiasm and through urgency in action.
- Work as a team and have fun doing so.
- Live our Quality Policy.
- Constantly fuel our ambition to be the best in all we do.

Being clear about targets and goals is essential. If operational excellence is what is to be achieved, every employee will understand that the targets are relating to that. In Nigel's view too many companies have too many metrics, many of which conflict. To avoid that problem occuring in Domino, every member of the senior team has a clear understanding of the goals of the other team members.

Domino is populated by accountants. Clearly you need a mix of skills, but financial know-how is very important to the business. You must have a plan to know where you are going and you must know where you sit in the market. The budget, which is the short term encapsulation of the long term plan, reflects what you want to achieve.

People are important. Nigel believes in having a good strong team, from senior management downwards. The senior team, he says, must be 'intelligent and aligned'. He looks for team players and will not tolerate prima donnas who may agree something at an executive meeting and then go away and do something else. Honesty is important. At executive meetings there is open discussion, opinions are aired, but decisions have to be made and, once they are, subsequent actions must be in line with those decisions.

There is one golden rule, according to Nigel. You are only as good as the people you work with so make sure, when you do have the opportunity to bring in new talent, that you bring in the right person. Do not compromise. It is better to wait than to appoint someone who does not fit. One good person is worth six average people. He gives the example of a new production engineering manager brought in from the car industry who completely transformed the efficiency of the factory to a whole new level.

Ideally, you should try to recruit someone who is better than you are. It can feel threatening to do that, but it is the leader's job to make sure you do not feel threatened. Quite apart from the immediate advantage gained from bringing in good people with useful experience, it is essential for succession planning.

Cultural diversity is viewed as a huge strength and is much valued in the company. Having so many people from different countries is helpful in developing strategies. It helps with choices and agreeing what should be done.

When you are recruiting, look for someone who fits with the culture and standards of the company. Senior people help create the culture so it is especially important to get it right. Domino, for example, is an action-oriented company, so someone who wants to sit in an 'ivory tower' would not fit. Nigel also looks for people who want to remain with the company. The nine people on their senior team have 135 years of experience between them and the senior teams in India and China have remained constant since they were set up in 1995. This does not mean that the team should stagnate and new talent has been brought in through various acquisitions.

Nigel describes himself as being a very 'hands-on' leader. He likes to know what is going on in the business and tests this out in informal ways, chatting to people on the factory floor about what is happening. This is not because he does not trust his management team, quite the contrary; it is because he wants to keep in touch with people and make sure agreements have been interpreted in the right way.

As CEO it could be tempting to think you have all the answers. This is a mistake, according to Nigel. 'Know what you are good at and what you are not good at, and find people in the team who have those skills,' he says.

Energy and drive are essential characteristics for a leader. You have to be energetic and drive things through and Nigel says he 'pushes people hard'. However, he does not expect them to accept absolutely everything; he expects them to tell him when the limit has been reached. Domino respects the fact that people have a life outside work, that they need holidays and a good night's rest.

There is a good example of the importance of being energetic and 'pushing things through' and also of being positive, which is another trait Nigel believes to be important. In 2008 during the recession, the company had to make redundancies. This was very painful but it was essential. As the CEO it was Nigel's job to impart the bad news. However, at the same time he wanted to give people hope of better times ahead, of something to aspire to. He told them Domino would emerge from the recession as a much better company. He was adamant that by 10 a.m. on Monday 22 November 2010, the company would launch a brand new range of products at the Paris trade show. Many people said this was an impossible task, but they achieved it, and the virtual tour of the Domino stand and products is on the website for all to see. Perhaps most importantly, it is there for all the employees to see what they have achieved.

Recognition is important and Domino has a number of team-based bonus schemes for performance that is measureable. However, it is not just about money and incentives. As an employee it is also about feeling part of an exciting company and sharing in the success. Giving praise where praise is due is essential. Nigel says openly that he has not always been happy with the performance of engineering. However, it is primarily engineering that has delivered the new product range and he openly praises their achievement in front of the rest of the company.

Good performance is rarely the result of one person's effort so, in his view, senior managers should never say 'I did this' or 'I did that'. In talking to his teams about collecting the best company award Nigel told them: 'I had the privilege of representing you at....'

In terms of his own personal style, Nigel is a listener, believing listening to be a much underrated skill. 'You must listen before you react,' he says. 'You can tell someone isn't listening when they cut other people off in the middle of a conversation.' He is also approachable and has an open door policy where any employee can come and talk to him. Unlike some CEOs who say this but do not put it into practice, employees at Domino do take advantage of the opportunity to talk to him. He believes in being as open as possible with people, and not covering issues with a shroud of confidentialty. 'Employees have to trust their leaders,' he says. He is also someone who likes to deal with things and get them done. If you do not tackle something it can fester and you are only cheating yourself.

Returning to the idea of simplicity, Nigel believes in applying common sense. 'You must do the best you can and if you do that you shouldn't beat yourself up about things,' he says.

19.9   MARK LEVER – CEO, NATIONAL AUTISTIC SOCIETY

Mark trained as a chartered accountant at Kidsons (now Baker Tilley), reaching his goal to become a partner by the age of 32. However, he is perhaps not the archetypal chartered accountant, as he became particularly interested in HR and training and took responsibility nationally for training in his firm.

Having achieved his goal to become a partner at a young age he felt ready for another challenge. When he was headhunted to set up a training centre for the Women's Royal Voluntary Service (WRVS), which offers a range of practical services to help and support older people, he decided to accept, despite the fact that working for a charity had never entered into his career plans. The success of the training project led Mark to stay on with WRVS and they offered him an important role running its operations with the opportunity of undertaking an Executive MBA at Cranfield. Within a relatively short period of time Mark became the organisation's Chief Executive.

Within WRVS there were shops, meals on wheels services and a number of other social projects, with 70 % being funded by the government. This government funding meant there had never been any major concern about money within the organisation, but when it was reduced significantly, it became imperative for the organisation to develop a more business-like approach to its operations to ensure survival. This meant embarking on a major cultural change.

Mark realised that the change programme would be tough and that it would cause a great deal of uncertainty within the organisation. In his training days he knew what level of knowledge the trainees needed to acquire by the end of the day; he knew what they needed to achieve and the goal was clear. In this case the future was uncertain and there were no easy recipes for success. He had to shape both the destination and the route. His approach was to share the context and get the people to collaborate with him.

To explain what was happening, he went on a series of roadshows around the country. There were plenty of questions and some very angry staff and volunteers who could not imagine a situation without government funding. Mark had to be straight with them and answered all their questions even if they did not like the answers. Managing in uncertainty means you are sometimes discussing the strategy and plans with people who are not part of your future and this is hard. Although it was painful, most people appreciated the straight talking, but it was a major shock, as people so passionate about what they were doing had never even contemplated the thought that WRVS would not survive. Mark admits this was an emotional time for him and sapping of energy. In the short term people still disagree with you and sometimes hate you, but in the long term you hope that people will respect the decisions you have taken. You hope that once they have received the message and taken time to process it they will better understand the rationale.

After defining the context, it is all about collaboration. Others have to be involved to help you shape the destination and how you get there. At Cranfield, Mark came across the 'culture web', which is about aligning your organisation's culture with strategy. This helped him as it captures what your current culture looks like and helps you define what you would like it to be. The trick is to adapt your approach as you go and get others involved in helping create what that culture should look like.

After sharing the context in the first round of roadshows, Mark went back for another round asking. 'How can we....?' By then the drip, drip of the message had started to sink in and people were more constructive in their responses, coming forward with useful ideas. It was hard bringing about such a major change and it took three years. It altered the way Mark thought about change and brought him to the view that developing strategy and culture were essential first stages before considering structure and recruitment.

After 13 years with WRVS with six as CEO, Mark decided to move on, agreeing with his family to build his own consultancy. However, within six weeks a headhunter approached him about being the CEO of the National Autistic Society (NAS). In doing his due diligence on the job Mark found a report that highlighted a number of challenges for the NAS. Despite being the largest organisation in the sector it was not seen as the leading organisation. Eventually, the challenge of undertaking another cultural change and the question: 'How can such a large organisation not be valued by its sector?' won the day and he became CEO in 2008.

One of Mark's first challenges was to develop trust in the organisation and, indeed, in the sector. Initially he went to visit those organisations that had a less than positive relationship with the NAS. These were organisations where trust and confidence in the NAS needed to be rebuilt. It was clear after the initial meetings that more would need to be done to regain the trust and confidence of most of these organisations. Quite by chance he had an opportunity to signal very clearly that things were changing. Along with his campaigning and policy colleagues he managed to persuade MP Cheryl Gillan to put forward a private members' bill to put obligations on local authorities and health bodies to recognise the needs of adults with autism and promote services for them. The selection of private members' bills is largely a matter of luck and when, against the odds, the autism bill was selected, Mark brought into play the coalition of charities he had created to support the initiative. Part of the work included managing the media. All along he emphasised to the media how the coalition worked together to move the legislation forward with various charities sending out their own press releases and sharing in the publicity. The bill became an act and later when the Department of Health wanted a National Chair for the External Reference Group to support the development of a national strategy for adults with autism Mark was proposed by a representative of the charities in the sector. In leading that group, Mark ensured other charities were involved by asking them to put forward representatives to chair subgroups.

Change was not only needed in terms of external relationships. The organisation itself needed to move forward. Mark started by taking stock, understanding what the NAS should be for. He immersed himself in the sector, and went out to speak and listen to people at all levels to help develop a sensible strategy. What he found was a very autocratic culture where people felt they had no real say in new developments. He had to tease ideas out of people because they felt strategy was *his* job, not theirs. One of the big issues was the existence of siloed structures. He also came to the view that all the charities in the sector were competing for a larger share of the 'funding' cake, but the fundamental issue was that the 'cake' just was not big enough in the first place. This was a sector that was woefully underresourced. It was clear that the sector required someone to take a step back and take on a capacity building role. This role, Mark believed, should be the role of the NAS.

Mark built three planks into his strategy:

1. Creating a more strongly networked autism community.
2. Establishing a Centre for Autism that acts as a hub for collaboration and capacity building within the sector as a whole.
3. Demonstrating innovation and best practice within our own services.

The third plank was important, as Mark put it: 'If we are not actively demonstrating a commitment to excellence and innovation, how can we purport to lead the sector? We would be open to criticism.' NAS are now on the journey towards this, but it has not been easy. The senior management team has been completely restructured with a number of senior personnel changes. It is vital that the leadership team have the appetite and motivation to change and, above all, can see that major change is necessary and possible. By benchmarking internally you could already see the spread, the variability in service quality and the opportunity. The NAS was organised regionally with each region developing and growing in different ways.

Mark changed the structure to create national leads to ensure consistency of approach across the organisation. Those people that could see the opportunity for improvement and, importantly, could see how to effect it were retained, but unfortunately a number left the organisation.

A key change in the structure was the introduction of a joint Chief Operating Office and Deputy Chief Executive. The focus of the role would be to provide leadership and direction to all operations.

The new person would have to be quick and nimble – someone who had the mindset of doing things differently. Headhunters found someone in a regional charity who was young and enthusiastic and fitted the bill. The first stage in the change programme was to look at the finances, particularly as there was pressure on local authority funding. A key part of the plan was to reduce costs by 15 % over a three year period. A review of all costs associated with people, technology and property was a useful way of understanding the working of the organisation and identifying opportunities for change.

Mark went on a 30 day roadshow asking people working in the front line of services how they would improve things. The response was huge and positive. There were so many ideas. Then he created the plan using these ideas and shared it with people showing how he had listened to them.

Through his experience Mark has developed a number of pieces of advice:

1. Communicate the context; explain the issues facing the organisation. People have one piece of the jigsaw and they need to see the whole picture.
2. Go out and listen well. Speak to a wide range of people throughout levels in the organisation and allow what you hear to shape your thoughts.
3. Synthesise what you hear into a plan of what we need to achieve.
4. Collaborate. Seek involvement by asking the question 'How do we get there?'
5. Develop the strategy and culture and then the structure.
6. Leave people with a very clear brief in terms of *what* has to be achieved, but not the *how*, working with staff throughout the organisation will help shape this.

The trick is to feel your way through the uncertainty with your team but leave the organisation with some key pillars. He always relates his plans back to the three planks of the strategy: networking in the sector, capacity building and having the best services NAS can possibly have. He highlights a maximum of three issues and explains how they will be approached and what he has been hearing on the ground. However, as he says, you are always on a journey, constantly learning as you go.

19.10   MIKE OPHIELD

Mike is an engineer by background, but throughout his career he has alternated between being head of sales and marketing and holding the CEO's job. In the 1990s he was Sales Director and then Managing Director of Ai Qualitek Ltd, a small instrument manufacturer providing products and systems primarily for the automotive industry. In 2002, the company was bought by Roper Industries and, as part of the deal, Mike moved to the USA to take the Vice President Sales and Marketing Role for Uson, Roper's instrument business. This was initially an 18 month contract, but he stayed 7 years, becoming President of Uson in 2004. During this period, the company achieved double digit year-on-year growth in both sales volume and profitability. Mike's current job is Vice President of Sales and Marketing for Diba Industries Inc., a company producing specialised components and complete fluid transfer assemblies for IVD, life science and scientific instruments, running a global sales operation out of Danbury in Connecticut, USA.

Mike's early exposure to the Balanced Scorecard was at Ai Qualitek when he decided to seek help from the team at Cambridge University to help him implement the process effectively. His primary aim was to give the workforce an understanding of the organisation's objectives and what it was trying to achieve, and his main concern was to put together a package of measures that would be meaningful.

Mike and his team learnt a great deal from the process. He says one of the most satisfying outcomes was using measures to stimulate debate, to discover what was behind the measures and thus to know where to concentrate for the greatest improvement.

His experience of implementing the Balanced Scorecard over many years has shown him that measures must be visible, they must not be too diverse or too many in number and they should be linked. Mike also points out that the measures must be useful for the business. It is easy to think something is important when it is not. He also believes too many measures are inward looking, not focused on what is happening outside the organisation.

For Mike, 'boundary spanning measures' are the ones that are the most useful. These are measures that capture results of many different functions working together. Very few measures of business performance are the responsibility of only one department or function.

On-time delivery is a good example of this. It is one of the most powerful measures because it touches every part of the business from sales to manufacturing and to despatch. He says: 'We are not using on-time delivery as a punitive measure, it is a measure for discussion and understanding. It touches on how we won the order, how pushed the salesman was on giving away lead-time, how fast the order was processed, loaded into the MRP system, manufactured, tested and delivered. You have a graph and a trend, but it is the understanding that matters and what you do about it. People need to understand their part of it, their role in delivering performance.'

Mike's belief is that business objectives are different to individual objectives. The business objectives should form part of your organisational scorecard and you should cascade these down to create functional level objectives too, but they are not broken down further to create individual objectives. Business objectives are what the business needs to achieve and individual managers and directors are tasked with helping achieve them, but individual objectives are separate. They consist of the actions and projects individuals need to complete to support the achievement of the business goals.

Mike has introduced what he calls the 'RAP' meeting, which he holds every four weeks with his direct reports. 'RAP' stands for 'report, analyse, plan'. He introduced these meetings in response to his concerns about traditional annual appraisals. Everyone can remember what happened in the last month, they have some knowledge of what happened in the last quarter, but have forgotten what happened in the last year. Therefore appraisals are heavily weighted to the closing months of the year. In his RAPs he talks about the tasks for the last 30 days, what is planned and what has been achieved. Achievement is broken down into fully, partially, not at all and no longer applicable. The business in which Mike works is very dynamic. He says: 'Quite often things change during the year and with the normal appraisal system what was asked for at the beginning of the year wasn't relevant at the end. You start with a set of goals and then people are re-assigned to deal with other priorities as they arise.' Despite this volatility, he contends that you should not change your scorecard on a monthly or quarterly basis as it becomes too confusing. You can change individual objectives to keep pace with events. However, the most important thing is that he sits down with each member of his senior team to discuss what is expected both ways – what the individual is going to achieve in the next thirty days and what is required from Mike in support.

The appraisals then become the sum of the 12 snapshots from the RAPs and you get a fuller picture of performance over the year. Mike bases salary increases on performance but he is careful to focus on continuous improvement and monitoring performance through the year rather than leaving it to the end. He says: 'Sales performance is too late. You must have measures of the activity that make up that sales performance. If someone has to reach the target of 10m dollars gross margin, this requires a certain number of visits and number of quotations and a certain level of conversion. As there is usually growth in the target, it will mean identifying new customers and winning new business. You will see those who are good at identifying new customers, good at closing and you will help them understand what they are good at and what they need to improve. You will also establish what support they need in their development.'

Mike believes there are problems with scorecard measures for some functions. If you have an engineering project over three to four years, you cannot wait three to four years to measure the outcome. You need to use the RAPs to measure progress and to have individual objectives. This also gives consistency throughout the organisation and overcomes the comments frequently heard in organisations that 'only sales are measured' or 'only operations are measured'.

Mike believes integrity is paramount. He says: 'As a Chief Exec you have to believe in the business and its goals. If it doesn't fit with your values you have a choice. It may be time to move on. People know when you believe in what you are delivering.

If you don't, you have to look for something else to do.' It was this principle that led him to leave Uson after many successful years and to find his current role with Diba.

'Trust and integrity are very important for me and the company I work for,' he says, 'They are a key element of leadership. You have to have real conversations with people about performance and without trust and integrity you can't. Then the process becomes pointless; you lose the traction to move the business forwards.'

19.11 ANDY WOOD – CHIEF EXECUTIVE, ADNAMS PLC

Adnams plc is a medium sized regional brewery founded in 1872 in rural Suffolk by George and Ernest Adnams. (Although there is evidence of brewing on the site long before that – the earliest record dating back to 1396.) The company produces cask ale and pasteurised bottled beers and has very recently established the Copper House Distillery for the production of spirits. Apart from brewing, wholesaling and retailing of its products the company owns a number of pubs and hotels.

On the face of it Adnams is in a difficult place in the market. It is a mature market and the company faces the legislation and challenges facing all providers of alcohol, above all the need to act responsibly, a need with which Adnams is completely in tune. It operates in a competitive environment Brewer consolidation on a global scale at one end and many microbreweries at the other end, encouraged by the low barriers to entering the market. Nevertheless, the company has been a success. It has won several awards – one of which is Brewer of the Year for 2011. How has this been achieved?

The main contributors to success are the effectiveness and goodwill of the workforce, the culture of the organisation and the leadership. These combine to allow the company to build a major brand (with fewer than 500 employees) and to stretch that brand into new areas such as the distilling operation. The flexibility and agility of the Adnams, team allow them to move fast when economic and market conditions require it and this gives them an edge over their competitors.

Andy Wood is Adnams' Chief Executive. His approach to leadership is based firmly on understanding people as individuals. He wants to appreciate their motivations, understand their morale and understand what makes them tick. He believes it is important to see the world through their eyes. 'You can't have exactly the same KPIs for everyone,' he says. To an extent the KPIs will, of course, depend on organisational requirements; for example, someone working in distribution may have cost targets while someone in marketing will have customer service targets. However, beyond this you have to realise that there are different ways of achieving things. Indeed, Adnams allows plenty of autonomy and are very open to people taking responsibility for their part of the business. This can be challenging occasionally, Andy admits, because people do sometimes want to take the organisation in different directions.

The approach to strategic planning is both top-down and bottom-up. The board will go away once a year and will receive presentations on how people see the next three years. They consider what has been said in the light of shareholder requirements and the level of returns on investment they need and from this create a three year plan, which is updated annually. The strategic plan is communicated to every employee through small groups. Adnams' research has shown that the most trusted person is typically the immediate line manager and so it is this person who will lead the discussion with their direct reports. However, Andy does check informally that people further down the organisation fully understand their role in achieving the company's plans.

In terms of measurement, the board receives reports on four key areas for the business – customer service, staff morale and motivation, financial performance and impact on the wider world (environmental and social impact). Each leader will produce a report on progress in these areas and nonexecutive directors will look at these and challenge the executive team on the results.

There is no doubt that people are important to Adnams and Andy sees employees as the creators of business success. That is clear from the company's own website, which states: 'Continued investment in our brand and a clear business strategy will ensure we are prepared for the constantly changing marketplace. But this is only made possible by the expertise and passion of our people throughout the business.'

The company rewards the loyalty of its staff and there is a share incentive scheme for employees where a percentage of the profits are allocated in shares. The scheme has around 50% of employees holding on to shares for the long term.

Every two years a staff survey is conducted, the results of which are displayed not only internally but also externally on their website. In the most recent survey (2009) there was an 88% response rate with 91% of that 88% saying they were proud or very proud to work for the company and 84% saying they were very clear about what was required of them. So there is clearly a huge level of staff engagement. The staff see their work almost as a 'cause' and even have to be told to take a break on occasions. It is interesting to note that 10 years ago the company found it difficult to recruit people in this rural backwater tucked away on the east coast. For some it would have been seen as a graveyard for their career. However, all this has changed and the reputation as a good employer has enabled the company to choose from the very best people.

Talent spotting and talent nurturing is important in Andy Wood's view. The company deliberately works with top universities such as Imperial College, Cranfield and the Ukrainian Economic Association to make links with bright young people. Anyone who is brought in, however, must fit with the organisation's culture. They do not want what Andy calls 'pseudo-political challenges'. They look for openness. In order to ensure this happens the company has a well crafted recruitment process and makes use of very sophisticated assessment centres. On the few occasions where people have not fitted in, the situation was dealt with in an adult way and they are moved out of the organisation – with some of them going on to flourish in jobs elsewhere. 'If you treat people as adults,' Andy says, 'they will behave as adults.'

Andy is a believer in developing people's potential and where possible recruitment is from within. One excellent example of this is the person currently responsible for the brewing, credit control and customer service functions – who sits just below board level and who started work with the company as a cleaner. In 2007 she became the East of England Business Woman of the Year. Adnams spotted her potential and encouraged her back into learning. They also supported her in becoming a magistrate because they recognised this would help her critical thinking. Talent is not always found where you would expect.

Leadership is a vital skill in nurturing and getting the best from this talent. The company uses 360 degree feedback and each of the executive directors is measured on their adherence to agreed behaviours such as approachability. The results are openly published for named individuals.

You can see from this that Adnams has a clear view on how they wish to operate. They do not shy away from stating very clearly their values:

Sustainability
We work for the long term, looking beyond immediate success to a sustainable future.

Diversity
We encourage diversity of choice, experience and employment opportunity.

Fulfilment
We want fulfilled customers and employees, whose lives are enriched by their involvement with Adnams.

Quality
We want to create the best products and offer the best service, and are always looking for ways to improve.

Environment
We aim to manage our impact positively on the social, natural and built environment.

Integrity
We deal with people openly and honestly, building strong, supportive relationships.

Commitment
We expect commitment to these values and aim to translate them into everyday realities.

Community
We value our place in the community and work to enhance the quality of local life.

Pride
We take pride in all that we do, aiming to be a beacon to inspire others.

Therefore, in Adnams good performance is very clearly the result of having a committed workforce and some very clear values.

20
Bringing It All Together

20.1 INTRODUCTION

In this final chapter, we will bring together the content of the book by discussing three elements: performance measurement, performance management and performance leadership.

20.2 PERFORMANCE MEASUREMENT

You need to track three elements of performance with your measurement system:

1. You need to monitor the performance of your underlying processes. You should do this to follow how well they are performing and how well your customers perceive the products and services you are delivering. Doing this should enable you to manage your current performance on a day-to-day basis, sensing and responding where appropriate.
2. You need to monitor your environment. You should do this so you are aware of changes that are happening and so you can plan your strategy with these changes in mind. Tracking the environment should help ensure that you are not taken by surprise by unfolding events. You should also be comparing your performance with others, so your comparative performance is known and understood.
3. You need to monitor the implementation of your strategy. People often become carried away by delivering their short term goals, so it is essential that you not only create a long term strategy but also track the progress of its implementation.

What we are proposing is that you need to measure your performance today, track changes that could affect your business in the future and monitor the implementation of your strategy (your path from today to tomorrow). Figure 20.1 shows a simple representation of these three elements.

Having established what you should measure, let us now return to the five roles of measurement we discussed in Chapter 1. From measuring the current performance of processes, tracking the environment and monitoring your strategy implementation, you should be able to *establish your position*. The success mapping processes we have covered will enable you to *communicate your direction*. The difference between where you are and where you want to be will *influence behaviour*. You also need to ensure that your measurement system *stimulates action* as and where appropriate. Finally, all these activities must *facilitate learning* in the organisation so that

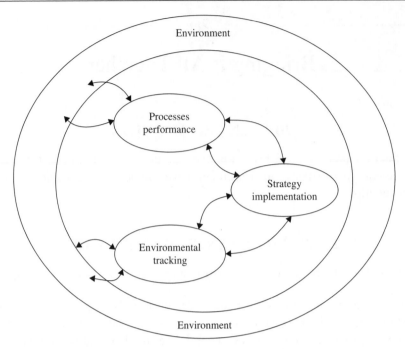

Figure 20.1 What you should measure

you reflect and respond to everything that your performance measurement system is telling you. We have captured this diagrammatically in Figure 20.2.

20.3 PERFORMANCE MANAGEMENT

As we have explained throughout the book, performance measurement does not in itself improve the performance of your organisation. Performance measurement is simply a tool that you should use for communicating where you want to go and getting feedback about your progress. It will focus people's attention on what is important, but to make sustainable improvements in performance you need to change the way the organisation operates.

Managers become involved in a wide range of organisational activities. With regard to performance, they need to ensure that people in the organisation follow the plan, do, study, act cycle (see Figure 20.3).

The starting point for performance is planning. You need to plan to achieve your goals. Processes have to be created, resources marshalled and people influenced to engage in the endeavour with a clear sense of direction. The second step is the execution of the plan when the people and processes are deployed and the processes run. The results from this need to be studied, to understand what is working

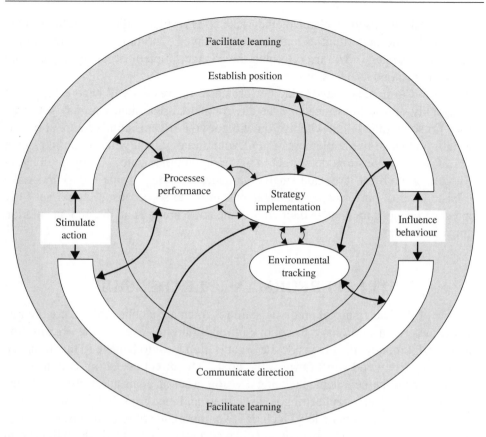

Figure 20.2   The five roles of measurement

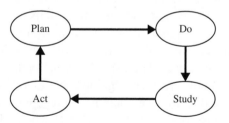

Figure 20.3   The Deming cycle

and delivering what you planned and what is not. Only after careful study should changes be made to update the process and ultimately the plan.

We propose that you should do your performance management at three levels (see Figure 20.1 again). The first level is the traditional level of the process, planning delivery, executing, studying what happened, including the customer response and finally taking action to make improvements. The second level is the environmental scanning. This needs to be planned, undertaken, the results studied and actions taken to respond to the opportunities and threats perceived. The third level is the implementation of strategy. You need to plan the change, implement, study its path and effects and respond as necessary.

If you fail to manage day-to-day performance, the results will become apparent very quickly. If you fail to manage the environmental scanning, you may get away with it for some time but inevitably you will put your organisation's future at risk. If you fail to manage the implementation of your strategy, you will end up like some 70 % of organisations that do not get their strategy implemented. Company longevity is falling, both for large and small companies. Although some fail to undertake the basic level of performance management, most do so because they do not fully appreciate the need to manage their environmental scanning and the implementation of their strategy.

20.4   PERFORMANCE LEADERSHIP

The role of the leadership of an organisation is to create a believable future. People outside the organisation have to believe in this future to invest in the organisation and to lend it money. People inside the organisation have to believe in this future so that they will stay and work towards the goals. The direction setting is immensely important, with the key elements being a vision, a set of goals and priorities. Much of this book has been about setting goals, targets and measures, but you should note that *direction* at a leadership level includes two important softer elements, *vision* and *priorities*. These create a more general guidance and, if used effectively, will prevent an organisation becoming *measurement obsessed*. In our vignettes, time and time again, our leaders talked about the vision and the priorities and their role in taking the organisation forwards. However, direction setting on its own is not sufficient for assuring success; it needs to be supported by values and culture.

The values of the organisation are the beliefs – how we believe we should treat our people, customers and suppliers. They should be the bedrock of everything the organisation does and a point of reference to guide behaviour. In many organisations the values are very explicit, displayed on flagpoles in reception, on the notice board and intranet, but it is the directors, managers and staff who make them live day to day. Performance requires three beliefs: (i) about the way people should be treated, (ii) about external relationships and (iii) about openness and transparency.

Staff that are treated well, engage with the organisation and support the delivery of its purpose. External stakeholders who have a positive relationship with the organisation will have a similar effect, so a belief in the importance of these external relationships is critical for success. However, for effective performance, openness and transparency are also critical so that information flows both up and down the organisation quickly and effectively, enabling the organisation to develop and survive.

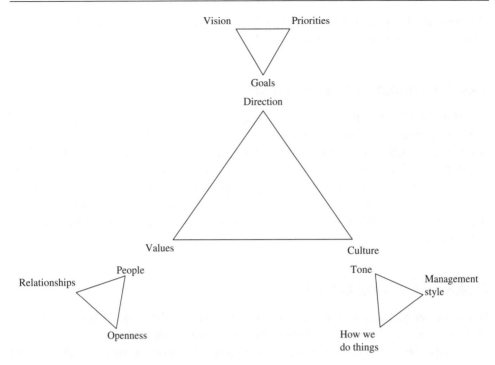

Figure 20.4   The elements of performance leadership

The culture is concerned with 'how things are done round here'. How things are done needs to reflect both the organisation's direction and its values, with the result being a distinct tone to the organisation and management style. Many organisations have the same values, but how they are put into practice can be very different. Figure 20.4 captures these elements.

The direction, values and culture bind people to the organisation. In practical terms, this is important, as we know from research and experience that the more people engage with the organisation the better the organisation performs. However, the leadership of the organisation is also important for the performance measurement and management. Direction, values and culture either support the performance system or undermine it.

20.4.1 Establishing position

To establish position accurately there needs to be openness and honesty. The culture of the organisation needs to make it acceptable to provide bad news and leaders need to be able to listen, so they can hear both good and bad news. Organisations that conducted flawed external comparisons or hide bad news will find themselves at a considerable disadvantage. They will be constantly surprised and caught out by information that was not readily available.

20.4.2 Communicating direction

Creating the vision, setting priorities and communicating the goals of the organisation are all leadership tasks. A culture of openness will enable a frank discussion of where the organisation is going and constructive feedback. If the organisation values its people it will cascade the vision so that everyone knows where the organisation is going and what their role is in delivering the goals that have been set. Organisations that do not have a culture of openness or a culture of engagement will find that people are not motivated to support their aims. These organisations usually do not perform well.

20.4.3 Influencing behaviour

Behaviour plays such an important part in performance delivery. Management style plays a critical role. We have shown throughout this book that it is so much easier to improve the results of a measure rather than the performance itself. Further, most improvements come from improving the coordination between departments and within teams. Measures do not always support this activity as they have a tendency to be focused on what is measurable. Creating a supportive culture, where measures are important but are not an end in themselves, can make the difference. Such measurement systems are so much more human and engaging, creating real performance.

20.4.4 Stimulating action

Taking action is always a dangerous thing to do because it disrupts the organisation. Because it is best to deal with a problem at the time it occurs, it is important to empower people at all levels in the organisation to take action required to put it right. However, such an approach will inevitably lead to some mistakes. How the leadership deals with these mistakes is important as in many organisations people are too afraid to act.

20.4.5 Facilitating learning

Creating a learning culture is not an easy task, but learning is one of the fundamental uses of a performance system. Organisations have to value the information their measurement system provides and use it as the basis for their decision making. This has to become part of management practice, helping develop a transparent and open culture. Organisations have to learn from their mistakes too. Leadership therefore has to create the openness and trust for mistakes to be recognised quickly so learning can begin. Leaders also need to value the implementation of ideas as much as their creation in order to engender a culture where good practice is rapidly disseminated. Organisations that learn slowly because they cannot identify mistakes quickly are more likely to fail. A 'not invented here' syndrome is equally damaging.

FURTHER READING

Deming, W. E. (1986) *Out of the Crisis: Quality, Productivity and Competitive Position*, Cambridge University Press, Cambridge, UK.

Index